399 Log	DATE DUE		20
JAN 25	OCT 24	MAR 16 '81	
MAY 2	NOV 20	APR 27 '81	
OCT 24	DEC 16	NOV 23 '81	
NOV 30	MAR 9		
DEC 14	MAR 26	SEP 28 '82	
JAN 5	APR 14	NOV 8 '82	
FEB 15	APR 23	9 '83	
APR 5	NOV 11	OCT 14 '83	
FEB 19	DEC 21	FEB 27	
APR 3	JAN 18	Faculty	
APR 18	NOV 18	JUN 4	
JAN 8	NOV 28	APR 16	
JAN 22	DEC 20	OCT 12	
JAN 22	JAN 17	OCT 8	
MAR 20	MAR 6	MAR 15 1999	
APR 17	NOV 3 '80	FE 26 '01	
MAY 15	NOV 5 '80 MA 5 '81		
OCT 17	JAN 21 '81		
GAYLORD	JAN 29 '81		PRINTED IN U.S.A.

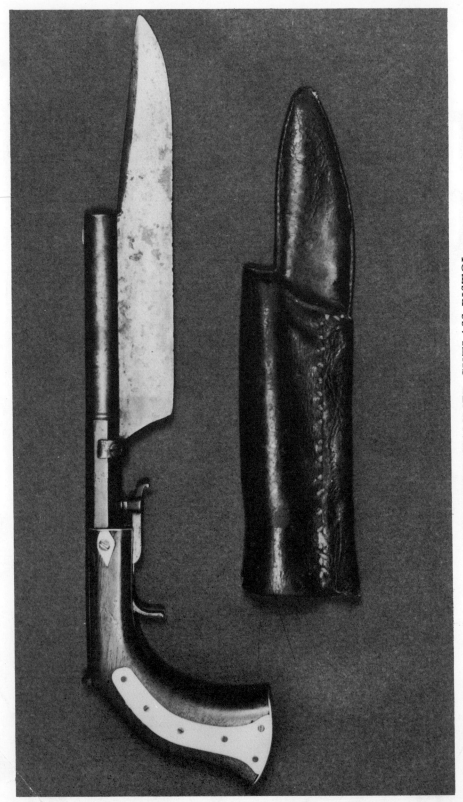

OAK UNDERHAMMER CUTLASS PISTOL

A most interesting and unique pistol of American origin

UNDERHAMMER Guns

399
Log
20

Herschel C. Logan

ARTIST, AUTHOR, COLLECTOR

With a Foreword by
MAJOR HUGH SMILEY

THE STACKPOLE COMPANY
HARRISBURG, PENNSYLVANIA

20

Printed and bound in the United States of America
by THE TELEGRAPH PRESS, *established 1831*
Harrisburg, Pennsylvania

DEDICATION

*To my friends everywhere who have
helped on this and previous research
. . . and, to those men and women who,
through the collecting and study of old
arms, are helping to preserve the history
of the past.*

CONTENTS

Foreword

THE AUTHOR of this volume is well known to Arms Collectors through his previous works, both in the way of books and magazine articles. His two important volumes, *Hand Cannon to Automatic,* now out of print, and *Cartridges,* now in its fourth printing are too well known to review here.

In *Underhammer Guns* the author has turned his attention to a field of arms long neglected, guns with the hammer on the under side. Few men are better qualified by background, skill and experience for such an undertaking than my good friend Herschel C. Logan. Artist, author and collector, he approaches his task with a sincerity and thoroughness of purpose too seldom found today.

The esteem in which he is held by collectors, dealers and arms authorities is ample testimony of his ability and standing as a researcher. His nationwide contacts, plus his own fine collection of arms, make him eminently qualified to do a study of this nature.

In over fifty years of firearms collecting, and research, the Underhammer pistols were the first love of the writer of this Foreword. I have sought them on the highways and byways of nearly every state in the Union. These typically American weapons seem to have an endless fascination unequalled by any other form of pistol. This book then is, to me, the fulfillment of a long awaited and cherished dream, and I am proud, and happy, to have had a part in it.

Major Hugh Smiley

Henniker, N. H.

UNDERHAMMER · The gun with the hammer under the barrel ·

INTRODUCTION
and *Acknowledgments*

SOME MONTHS prior to the start of this research, a few gun collector friends and myself were holding a "gab-fest" in my den and gun room. The conversation drifted around to that unique class of arms with the hammer on the under side of the barrel . . . Underhammers, in collectors' parlance.

When the possibility was advanced of my doing a book on the subject, a chuckle went around the group. The idea at first seemed a bit preposterous, for after all I had done an article on such guns for the *American Rifleman* at one time which, they felt, covered the field rather thoroughly. Some twenty-five guns had been illustrated by photographs and a few others by pen sketches. Surely they reasoned this just about exhausted the field.

But as the evening wore on and the discussion continued, it was agreed that perhaps the idea might be worth exploring further. One suggested that maybe an additional twenty-five could be found to supplement the illustrations already on hand. Another felt that, by diligent research, a total of seventy-five might be turned up. And, one hardy soul ventured the seemingly ridiculous assertion that a hundred guns should be sought out . . . and he even suggested that the title of the book might well be . . . "The Story of One-Hundred Underhammers."

How wrong all of us were, and how little we knew of the Underhammer story will be evident throughout the pages of this book. For indeed research over the past many months following that little "gab-fest" has opened a vast Pandora box of Underhammers the like of which has been little short of amazing. Passed were the fifty, the seventy-five and, even the hundred specimens. And the end is not yet in sight. In all probability it never will be, for long after this study is in print other specimens, marked and unmarked, will continue to make their appearance.

Yet today's attendance at guns shows, scanning of advertisements and dealers' lists brings the startling realization that these unique guns of other years are fast disappearing from the American scene.

The research, and study, of Underhammer guns has been a thoroughly fascinating experience. Mainly, it is though, because so little has previously been written about these ingenious arms. The long months of tireless effort in digging out data, following leads which might throw further light on the period, operation and use of the guns, the continual search for specimens to personally examine, photograph or sketch has been a most rewarding one. It is an experience which has been enriched and made easier by the simply wonderful assistance given by fellow collectors, friends and organizations without whose kindly help and suggestions the compiling of such material would have been a most arduous, if not impossible, task. To each of them my humble and sincere thanks. It is hoped that the results of the research contained here will, in a measure, serve to reward them for their cooperation.

Special recognition and appreciation go to the following who unselfishly and unstintingly gave of their time, talents and knowledge to assist in the gathering and presenting of this story on Underhammer Guns:

CAPT. RICHARD E. CAMPBELL and E. D. CAMPBELL for the rare privilege of personally examining the unique Cutlass pistol, and through whose graciousness this arm now holds an honored place in the author's collection.

PAUL N. CROCKETT whose kindness and unselfishness permitted the study, and acquisition, of the full-stocked Chase.

SAMUEL E. DYKE for the splendid example of the unusual "pill-lock" Underhammer, and for his help in the study of this ignition system as applied to the Underhammers.

THOMAS E. HALL, Curator of Arms, Winchester Museum, Winchester Repeating Arms Co., who made possible the inclusion of photographs of guns from the company's noted collection.

DALE HOAG, TOM WESTMAN, ED C. GUNNERSON and HOWARD D. SCOTT for their patience and proficiency in the photographing of arms, and other material, in the author's collection.

WALTER J. HOWE, Editor, *The American Rifleman,* for his kind permission to use excerpts from the author's article "Single-Shot Underhammers" published in the March, 1956 issue of the magazine.

ALTON J. JONES, master craftsman, whose interest in this study resulted in his making the beautiful, working miniature, Underhammer illustrated.

SAM LOGAN, my son, for his kindly counsel and unselfish assistance in double-checking the manuscript.

MAXWELL L. McCORMACK, collector, who so graciously supplied photographs, and data, of specimens from his own collections.

RAY MITCHELL, skilled gunsmith, who through the fabricating of modern target Underhammer is helping to keep alive the tradition of these fine old arms, and for the tiny Underhammer illustrated.

W. KEITH NEAL, noted English collector, who furnished valuable photographs, and data, from his outstanding collection and, whose kindly counsel has been of real help.

RAY RILING, for his assistance on this and other studies by the author.

JAMES E. SERVEN, whose friendship and valued suggestions for nearly a quarter of a century have been a source of much inspiration.

MAJOR HUGH SMILEY, dean and grand old man of the arms fraternity, who made possible the inclusion of many specimens, and whose encouragement to the author over the years has been a joy and inspiration.

MILES W. STANDISH, for photographs of arms from his own collection and for his valued assistance on this, and former, research by the author.

ELDON G. WOLFF, Curator of Arms, Milwaukee Public Museum, who provided photographs of interesting types from the famous Nunnemacher Collection.

RAY C. YOUNG, collector, and student of New England types whose assistance has been of real value, both in this and previous works by the author.

And a big bouquet of public thanks to the following whose help and encouragement have been so genuinely appreciated:

Robert Abels	Jacksonville Public Library	Joseph Race
John Amber	Paul C. Janke	Glode M. Requa
Mark Aziz	Chester H. Johnson	H. Lloyd Resor
Mrs. M. J. Barlow	W. G. C. Kimball	Mrs. John C. Riddell
Harry Berry	Joe Kindig, Jr.	Jack Ross
J. & I. Boffin	Osborne Klavestad	Frank N. Russell
C. A. Brown	Harry C. Knode	A. F. Roddy
Graham Burnside	Lt. Col. R. C. Kuhn	Avelyn W. Rowe
Carl C. Cowles	Harry E. Lewis	H. H. Schoen
Herman P. Dean	Kenneth W. Liggett	Norman E. Sharp
F. Theodore Dexter	Art Livingston, Jr.	Jack A. Smith
Joseph W. Desserich	William M. Locke	Samuel E. Smith
Edward Ellis	John K. Lounsbury	Wayne and Peggy Sondergard
Joseph E. Evans	Dr. Joseph R. Mayer	David C. Squier
Norm Flayderman	Frank McCoy	L. E. Statler
Herbert E. Green	Philip J. McFarland	Henry M. Stewart, Jr.
Walter Grote	Robert G. McReynolds	Howard J. Swinney
Paul Gruenberg	Dr. Frank A. Mitchell	Albert M. Sullivan
Gun Report, The	William Moslander	Frank G. Traeger
Blanchard M. Guthrie	Burton D. Munhall	Jack Turner
Thomas Haas	Museum of Historical Arms	Philip F. Van Cleave
Robin C. Hale	Vincent W. Nolf	Charles T. Waller
John D. Hammer	Eddie J. Null	S. A. Warner
G. Charter Harrison, Jr.	Waldo E. Nutter	Paul J. Westergard
John Hintlian	Eldon J. Owens	Frank Wheeler
Thomas E. Holt	John E. Parsons	F. Wilkinson
Dr. Thomas T. Hoopes	C. G. Peterson	Herman W. Williams, Jr.
Frank R. Horner	Roger C. Peterson	Frank E. Williams
Col. Leon C. Jackson	Pony Express Sport Shop	Charles G. Worman

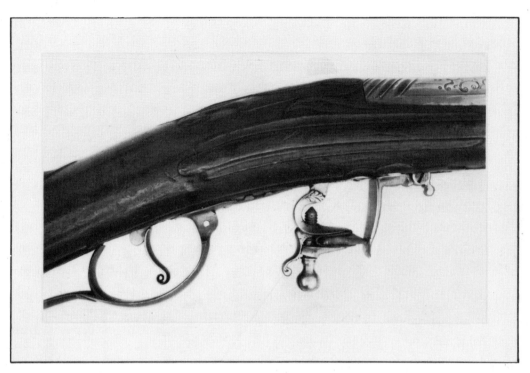

FIGURE 1. The earliest known use of the Underhammer principle is
to be found on this German flintlock rifle.

Background . . .

ONE OF THE MOST interesting of American arms is a
type, which until comparatively recently, has been more or less neglected
by collectors generally. True, many collections include a specimen or two
merely to show the type, but there has been no definite effort to study and
collect them as is the case with many other arms peculiar to this country.

Today this unique class of arms, with the hammer on the under side
of the barrel, is rapidly taking its place alongside those cherished arms
which are considered so thoroughly American. "Underhammers," in collectors' parlance, are perhaps more distinctly American than either the
Deringer, Kentucky pistol or the Kentucky rifle. For while these guns
followed a more or less general pattern, or style of arms then in current use,

both here and abroad, the Underhammers were truly a totally different and distinct type of arm.

In classifying them as "typical American" we are, of course, referring to the ingenuity and variety displayed in their design and construction by those who made them rather than designating the principle of the Underhammer as wholly of American origin, which of course it is not. For centuries the continent of Europe was the cradle of arms development. Her gunsmiths, steeped in the heritage of fine craftsmanship, let few gun innovations escape their attention. Against such a background of skill and inventiveness it should be easily understandable that the principle of the Underhammer should have had its beginning in the old world. Such was the case, for guns with the firing mechanism on the under side of the barrel were produced in Central Europe nearly a hundred years before the practice became prevalent in America.

But where they first came into being in Europe it remained for the new world to accord them their rightful place among arms types. Thus the spotlight of attention in this study is focused, for the most part, on the arms fabricated in this county. Understandably so, since it was here that this novel principle of mechanism found its greatest fruition. Here the Underhammers achieved their ultimate in distinctive design, mechanical simplicity and shooting proficiency.

Having recognized, with appreciation, the origin of this class of arms, attention is now returned and directed to its history and development both here and abroad.

Why the Underhammers have escaped the notice of serious writers on the subject of arms for so long is a bit difficult to understand. In interest and variety they far exceed many of the better known, and more common, types of arms of their era. Even a cursory examination of the illustrations contained in this study will indicate, that in addition to placing the hammer on the under side of the barrel, the general design of the guns themselves is more varied and individualistic than can be found on most any other class of arms. It is well that they are, at last, on their way to becoming choice Americana.

One reason for their growing appeal is that being handmade they reflect the individuality of their makers. This is why it is rather difficult to find two pieces agreeing in minute detail, even though made by the same gunsmith. Many, no doubt, were made as a sideline, others as an occasional extra arm for some specific purpose. Small wonder that there is an awakening appreciation of these splendid examples of Yankee ingenuity. From

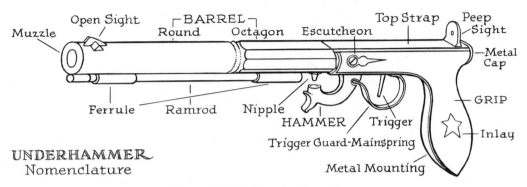

UNDERHAMMER
Nomenclature

FIGURE 2. Underhammer Nomenclature.

their relative scarcity it is doubtful if a sizeable quantity was produced by one maker. Indeed it seems highly probable that some gunsmiths made only a single, or very few specimens, during their entire gunmaking activity. Truly they were never the mass product of assembly lines which are typical of today's arms manufacture.

While a considerable number of these interesting arms are marked with their maker's, or agent's, name, there are some to be found with only the gunsmith's initials, or totally unmarked. These unmarked arms range from the rugged primitives to specimens of splendid design and workmanship. Occasionally a fully marked arm turns up by which a like, though unmarked, piece may be identified. Regardless for the preference of collectors generally for marked arms, there is a lot of pleasure in the finding, and study, of a gun by an unknown maker. Often such a gun was made for the personal use of the gunsmith himself. The extent to which he lavished work upon it depended upon its intended use. Usually if it was to merely serve as a side arm for plinking or defense, it did not receive the attention, or the nicer finish, accorded the one for target shooting. Many times it was the only one of its kind produced. Had some of those early gunsmiths but realized the worry their unmarked guns would cause collectors at a later date they would, I'm sure, have placed their name upon the gun.

What the unmarked Underhammers lack in identity they often make up in individuality. Therein lies much of their charm, for they reflect the whims, desires and idiosyncrasies of their makers a feature not usually found on arms produced for sale in quantity.

It is believed that the readers of this monograph will enjoy seeing the variety of design to be found among the goodly number of unmarked specimens illustrated fully as much as those stamped with their maker's name, intriguing as they are.

In addition to those carrying the name and address of the maker,

[3]

specimens will be encountered which also include the name of the agent or jobber stamped on them. Three such agents were:

E. HUTCHINGS & CO., BALT. MD.
ROGERS BROS. & CO., 52 MARKET ST., PHILAD.
A. W. SPIES

... the latter was one of the better known agents, being an agent for Ethan Allen arms from around 1835 until 1848.

A sizeable number of the New England pieces, particularly in the Massachusetts area, are stamped with an American eagle on the top strap. Why? No one seems to know. While appearing nearly identical to the naked eye, when examined under a magnifying glass the eagle will be found to have points of difference. Obviously the stampings were from separate and individual dies, though following a single pattern or design. One arm has turned up with two eagles, one of the regular style and the second one totally in outline. It was the only one of its kind noted. Both types are illustrated in Figure 3. It could well be that it was some sort of "guild" mark of the men working in that certain area. We can but speculate at this distant date.

Concerning the similarity in design of many of the New England Underhammers, it would seem that there should be a reasonable explana-

FIGURE 3. Two types of American eagle stamping to be found on some of the New England Underhammer pistols.

tion. At first it was thought that perhaps the guns were made by only a few shops, and that many times the name on them was little more than that of an agent. However there is another reason not generally considered. If one studies the period of operation of these early companies, the shortness of their arms activity at once becomes apparent. This would result in the shifting around of the skilled gunsmiths employed by them. Thus in the space of twenty years these men could well have been connected with several different companies for short periods of duration. What would be

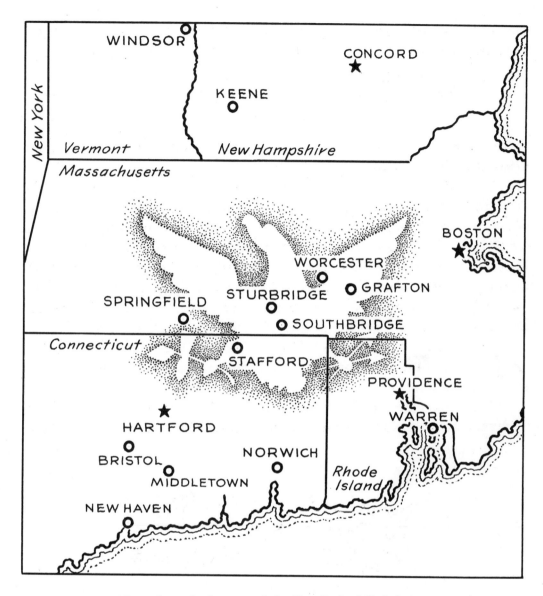

FIGURE 4. The main production area of the New England Underhammers carrying the American eagle stamping.

more natural than for them to continue to fabricate Underhammers in each place of employment. And, since the arms were handmade, it would be understandable that certain changes would be made, even though the design remained similar. It is also conceivable that these same workmen fabricated a few guns bearing their own names, even while serving an apprenticeship in, or being employed by some large company.

This interesting and significant note appeared in *Barber's Historical Collections*, by John Warner Barber, and published by Dorr, Howland

& Company in Worcester, Mass., in 1839. On page 608 under Sturbridge he wrote:

"In 1837 . . . value of pocket rifles manufactured $20,275, hands employed, 36."

Judging from this bit of information, it would appear that the production of Underhammers was a thriving little business at that early date. That many of the New England pieces were manufactured for a comparatively few years is evidenced by the fact that no reference is made to such pistol making after the late 1840's. By this time they were gradually being superceded by the mass produced single-shot pistols, and by the multi-shot pepperboxes and revolvers.

Data on the majority of makers is very meager indeed. In many, many cases the maker is known only by the virtue of a specimen being found bearing his name, or name and address. On the other hand, enough is known regarding a few of the early makers to give a fairly accurate idea as to the actual period during which the Underhammers were in the heyday of their popularity. ,

While some of the early makers are known, it may never be possible to ascribe to any one gunsmith the honor of having produced the first American Underhammer.

The true origin of the unique principle of the Underhammer appears shrouded by the mists of antiquity. While it is commonly thought that the guns were of the percussion era, it may come as a surprise to learn that the principle dates back at least into the flintlock period.

A friend, Chester H. Johnson, has brought to our attention a pair of American flintlock Underhammer pistols fabricated by Calderwood of Philadelphia. These exceptional pistols which Mr. Johnson had examined in detail in an English shop are best described by his splendid sketch, and in his own words.

"The Under-hammer flint pair was perhaps the most unusual pair of pistols I have ever seen. They were very much the same size as the enclosed drawing (11½-inches) which I made then and there.

"The barrel was composed of twist iron and has two straps, top and bottom, into which the grip fitted. The box-lock was square sided and was enclosed on each side by the panels which were held in place by the hammer screw . . . having a small toe

[6]

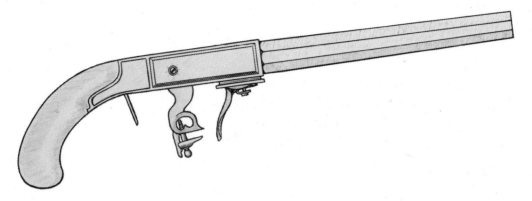

FIGURE 5. Early American Underhammer flintlock pistol by Calderwood of Philadelphia. (From a drawing by Chester H. Johnson.)

on each which in turn projected into a slot cut into the shoulder of the barrel ending just under the frizzen and pan. The odd raised rim around the pan and frizzen was a fence, oval in outline, and about one-eighth inch in height was supposed to keep rain from dripping into the powder pan from the upper surfaces of the pistol.

"The snap open trigger was connected by a longitudinal bolt with the actual sear which engaged the rear interior curve of the hammer. The hammer, when at full release, bore directly by its forward edge against the end of the slot cut for it in the bottom strap. The trigger opened when the hammer was pulled to full cock and could be snapped in again when the hammer was let down to half cock. The pan was circular; the frizzen spring was held in tension by a screw in the pan cover. The whole was very much like the usual pocket, box-lock flint pistol, but inverted.

"Engraved in small block letters was, CALDERWOOD—PHILADELPHIA on the top strap or upper plate of the box-lock. The pistols were in a case which seemed to fit but no name plate or card within. Included was an old letter, undated or signed, listing a lot of household things, room by room, and mentioning in the library, '. . . *a brace of upside down pistols marked Philadelphia.*'

"The pistols were of very severe workmanship, no engraving other than the name and a slight inner margination on the upper parts of the box-lock. The grip was flat in cross section and the upper and lower strap came down only an inch or two."

[7]

Illustrated on page 175, Fig. 232, is a German Underhammer Flintlock rifle of around 1740 from the noted W. Keith Neal collection of England. Of it Mr. Neal writes:

"This gun is of German make, period circa 1740. It is not signed though of excellent quality. The barrel is approximately 42-inches in length and has straight rifle grooves for firing shot. It is handsomely inlaid with silver. The gun was from the personal armoury of the Grand Duke of Saxe Weimar, at Etterburg Castle, Saxony. The pan is very deep and holds a lot of priming. The sparks would catch the stream of priming as it fell out of firing, and as gunpowder burns up it would presumably fire the gun. The piece is not unique, there was at least one other like it in the same collection. The idea was to make it rain proof, and give less flash in the eye."

In a subsequent letter Mr. Neal writes:

"First of all I must tell you about shooting my underhammer flintlock!!! I have always contended that it would shoot, but everyone who has looked at it says, 'Oh No . . . it is crazy!!!' But I have contended that the sparks would catch the priming as it started to fall, and that as powder burns UP, it would fire the gun immediately through the vertical touch hole. So, I made a test and fired my underhammer flintlock, and it *never* misfired once!!! Also it went off quickly. I was delighted."

Let us hope that some day a fully marked and dated specimen may come to light which will help to more accurately pinpoint the place, and period, of the first gun to utilize the unique method of placing the hammer on the under side of the barrel.

It appears highly probable, due to their simplicity, that the first American "under-strikers" or "undercocks," as they were more commonly referred to at the time, were the products of individual gunsmiths working in a small way and that they were patterned after the occasional Underhammer rifle then being fabricated by some "gunsmith-shooters." These early primitives, marked or unmarked, add color to any collection of Underhammers. Many times their barrels were made from rifle barrels cut down to the desired length. All metal parts were forged entirely by hand, and even the wood was fashioned by the use of crude tools. No finely appointed pieces these, they were built for service on the frontier.

Of the states in which the Underhammers were produced, Connecticut, Massachusetts, New Hampshire and New York were, by long odds, the leaders in listed makers. Fabricated mainly in the East, some few were later produced as far west as Michigan, Wisconsin, Indiana, Iowa and California . . . and as far south as Florida, Georgia, and Texas.

From a few dated specimens, patent dates where known, and the active period of their makers, it is possible to place the era of Underhammer production from around 1835 to 1860, give or take a few years either way. That they were actually in use at a later date is borne out by the fact that such arms were picked up on some battlefields of the Civil War. This would indicate that they were used occasionally at least as personal side arms by soldiers on both sides of that conflict. But with the rise in popularity of percussion revolvers and early cartridge arms, the life of the Underhammers soon drew to a close. Though specimens of later date are known, it is highly improbable that more than a few were made. And, these were, for the most part, fine target pieces by such makers as Billinghurst and Hilliard.

One of the first questions asked by the layman whenever an Underhammer pistol is displayed is, *"Why did they put the hammer on the under side of the barrel?"* Admittedly it is a fair question, to which there would appear to be three logical answers—which may, or may not be, given in their relative importance.

First, if one accepts the theory that many of the earlier Underhammer pistols were made for target shooting, following the pattern of the Underhammer target rifles of the day, then we should subscribe to the belief advanced at the time, namely, that the hammer was placed on the under side of the barrel to lessen the danger of flying bits of the metallic percussion caps striking the shooter's eye, and also for better aiming as there was nothing on top to interfere with the line of sight. Then, too, as strange as it may seem, there were relatively few gunsmiths who advanced the belief that, with the nipple and hammer underneath, quicker fire could be achieved. Or, could such belief have been merely sales talk? It is to be admitted, however, that the unobstructed barrel top did have its advantages.

Second, and if anything a more important consideration, was their utter simplicity. Even to anyone not especially mechanically minded, it is quite obvious that the average Underhammer is the personification of simplicity when compared to most arms.

[9]

A. W. SPIES & CO.

IMPORTERS OF AND DEALERS IN

GUNS, RIFLES, PISTOLS, GUN MATERIAL,

ADAM W. SPIES.

PATENT

SIX BARREL SELF-REVOL-VING AND REPEATING PISTOLS.

JOHN J. SPIES.

SPORTING APPARATUS & FINE CUTLERY,

91 MAIDEN LANE, N. Y.

Offer for sale on the most accommodating terms, to Gunsmiths, and the CITY and Country Trade generally, a large and full assortment of every article in their line of business.

GUNS.

Single Barrel Boy's and Mens' Guns,—common.
" " " " imitation of twist and (patent breech.
" " Guns, imitation of wire twist,
" " Guns, real twist and patent breach—sizes for fowling, ducking and deer.
Double Guns, imitation of twist and patent breach—very (low prices.
of wire and Damascus twist,
" real twist and Damascus,
" real Wire and Damascus,
" real Swedes stub & twist & chain Damascus.
A very large stock of GUNS, common and fine qualities, single and double, of every variety of length, calibre, style of mounting, and finish, of our own importation and manufacture, always in our Show Cases, and offered at prices as cheap as any house in New York.
English and American double-barrel Rifles and Shot Guns, assorted length and calibre.

RIFLES.

Flint and Percussion Rifles, full and half stocked, brass, German silver, and blue steel mountings, of every variety of length and calibre.
U. S. Muskets at lowest market prices

PISTOLS, in great variety.

Common brass and blued iron barrel Pistols,
Screw off barrel and secret trigger, do.
Cast steel barrel Pistols, with side and undercock, 4 to 8 in.
Belt, Holster and Duelling Pistols, 10 inch.

REVOLVING PISTOLS.

" Colts" Patent Revolving Chamber Pistols $16, $17, $18, $19, each.
Stockings' Revolving Lever Pistols, $6, each.
Bacon's $6, Allens' and others'.
Single Cast Steel Barrel Rifle Pistols, 2 to 10 inches
Rose wood, mahogany and leather cases for the above Pistols.

POWDER FLASKS

Powder Flasks, with Rifle and Pistol Chargers, 1 to 6 oz.
Do. 8 to 16 oz, with and without cords. plain and patent tops.
Dixon & Son's Powder Flasks, in great variety, of every size and pattern, with and without cords.
Dixon & Son's Glass, Britannia, and leather covered Dram Bottles.
" Shot Pouches, 2 to 6 lbs.
" with lever and knuckle joint charger.
" Game Bags,
" Powder Magazines from 2 to 6 lbs.
Shot Belts, single and double, with Irish, Patent & Lever Chargers.

FIGURE 6. Early advertising sheet of the A. W. Spies & Co. Note the reference, under the heading of Pistols, to "Cast steel barrel Pistols, with side and undercock."
Courtesy of John E. Parsons

This simplicity of lock construction was a most important one to the early gunsmith in the fashioning of Underhammers. Whether the mainspring was of the flat type attached to the under side of the straight frame extending back from the breech of the barrel or whether it was of the unusual type in which the trigger guard served as the mainspring, both were simple enough to be made by himself. Often working in remote places away from sources of supply for locks, such a simple construction readily appealed to these craftsmen. No longer was it necessary to depend upon a regular locksmith for this important part. These pioneer makers could, and did, fashion the entire gun in their own shop, easily and inexpensively. This fact alone accounts for the great variety of lock construction to be found on these unusual arms. It was as Milton Warren, an apprentice to John M. Whitesides of Abington, Virginia, wrote, that in addition to their rifles they made a great many Underhammer bootleg pistols . . . "these," he said, "were simple things and one could be made in a day."

FIGURE 7. It was this convenient carrying place which gave the name "bootleg" to many of the Underhammer pistols.

It has been said, and truthfully, that the simplest locks ever devised, the ones having the fewest and strongest parts, were those where the trigger guard also served as a mainspring. Such construction was often applied to the Underhammer target rifles of the time.

Third reason, and one not to be overlooked in establishing the reason for the Underhammer pistols is their streamlined design. No cumbersome top or side hammer to bother. They could be, and were, carried with equal

[11]

FIGURE 8. Pen sketch of the top strap with the scarce "Mississippi Pocket Rifle" stamping.

ease in the belt, pocket, holster or boot. In fact it was the latter place that gave to them the nickname of "bootleg" pistol. Or, was such an appellation given to them due to the similarity between their general shape and that of a boot? Be that as it may, it seems quite probable that many of them were carried in the top of their owners' boots. It should be understood, however, that the name "bootleg" alone does not necessarily denote an Underhammer pistol. Other single-shot pistols of the time with conventional type hammers, and no wooden forestocks were sometimes referred to as "bootleg" pistols. Likewise the name "buggy rifle" while referring to a handy gun which was often carried by early day Doctors, and others in a buggy for protection, or for the shooting of small game, does not always denote an Underhammer. Buggy rifles usually denote pistols with barrels of 12- to 22-inches in length. So, while an Underhammer may be designated as a bootleg, or buggy rifle . . . neither of the latter titles can refer solely to a gun with the hammer under the barrel.

Another unusual name attached to some of the single-shot pistols, Underhammer as well as regular types, was that of "Pocket Rifle." From all available data it appears that Ethan Allen was the first to assign this term not only to his Underhammer pistols, but also to some of the first side hammer and bar hammer pistols produced by Allen & Thurber. In searching around for some explanation for the term "Pocket Rifle" the following note from an 1875 J. Stevens catalog may be of interest, even though of a later period, and on a regular type of arm rather than an Underhammer. It will be recalled that Stevens used the name in connection with some of their small single-shot arms of early manufacture.

"A remarkable little fire-arm, a 'Breech-loading Pocket Rifle,' weighs only eleven ounces yet shoots with great accuracy and power, from 30 to 100 yards or more. Can be loaded and fired five times a minute. Can be carried in a side pocket while working in the fields, ready to bring down game at short notice. Exceedingly convenient in new countries as a defense weapon, or for picking off game, and useful generally upon the farm where wild animals, large or small are common."

[12]

Even though the term Pocket Rifle was applied by Stevens primarily to pistols having extension stocks, it had been used to describe other pistols without such stocks. In the main the name appears to have been used to describe a handy gun capable of being carried in the pocket and yet efficient enough to take the place of a larger cumbersome rifle, when the occasion called for it in traveling or at work.

So much for the background of the Underhammers, let us now take a look at the guns themselves.

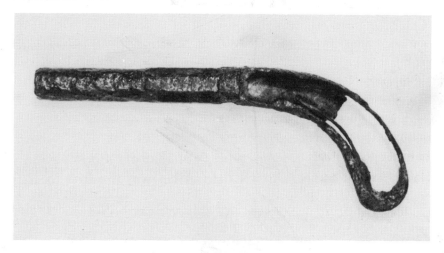

A relic of the old Warwick Stage Route, an early trail which ran from Paterson, N. J. through Ringwood, to Warwick, N. Y.

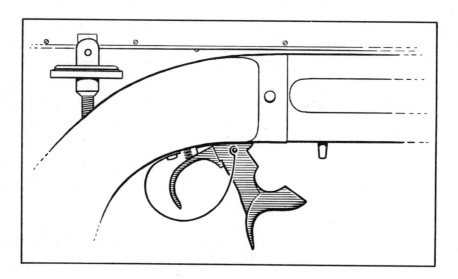

FIGURE 9. Simplest of the Underhammer locks was the one on which
the trigger guard also served as a mainspring.

Simplicity of Operation ...

PROVING THE WELL-KNOWN SAYING, attributed to
the Chinese, "One picture is worth ten thousand words," pen and ink
sketches are utilized here to graphically illustrate several of the many
types of simple locks to be found on these intriguing Underhammers of
yesteryear.

The old adage which says that there are exceptions to every rule is
again proven in this research. Amidst all the single-action Underhammers
there crops up occasionally a double-action. Now double-actions are not
unknown or rare in percussion arms, as witness the early pepperboxes,
some single-shots and a few revolvers, but they are infrequently met with
among the single-shot Underhammers. Here the hammer is ordinarily
pulled down by hand, into cocking position. Several exceptions to this
will be noted throughout this book. A few such are deserving of special
attention.

Two specimens, one marked only J.E.W., (Fig. 162), and the other by A. J. Jones, (Fig. 124), employ the usual double-action, that of actuating the hammer by the pull of the regular-type of trigger. On the Jones gun however, the mainspring also functions as the trigger guard, a rather unusual feature to be found on a double-action underhammer.

Arms representing three different countries, America (Fig. 99), Spain (Fig. 289) and Belgium (Figs. 275, 276) are mentioned here because they utilize a similar double-action mechanism, and a ring trigger. On each of the pistols the hammer is in the nature of a long spring on the under side of the barrel, and attached at the end nearest the muzzle. The "spring-hammer" is turned to the side to permit capping, then returned to its position with the projection on the ring trigger between it and the barrel. When the trigger is pulled rearward, it raises the spring-hammer until it falls free of the projection, and springs back to detonate the cap. A very simple and effective mechanism.

One of the truly outstanding exceptions, insofar as the trigger mechanism is concerned is to be found on the pair of *Side Button Trigger* Underhammer pistols illustrated in Fig. 165. The maker of these guns employed the unique principle of placing the trigger, in the shape of a button, on the right side of the frame. When pulled to the rear, the trigger released the hammer for firing.

The Carleton pistols are another departure from the usual. It will be noted that whereas on all other Underhammers illustrated the hammer

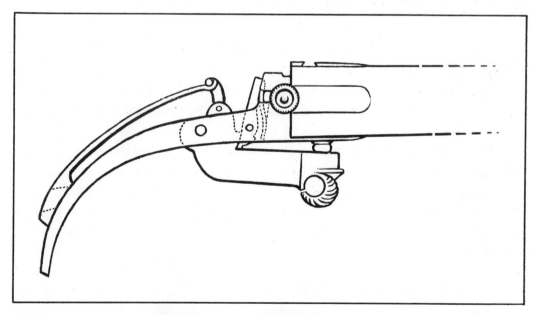

FIGURE 10. The mechanism of the unique, and rare, Side Button Trigger Underhammer Pistol is well illustrated by this simple pen and ink drawing.

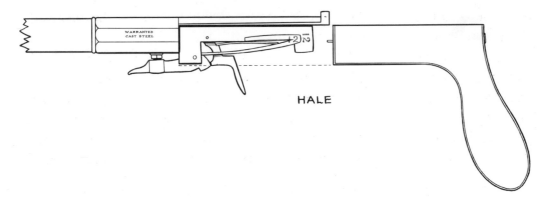

WARRANTED
CAST STEEL

HALE

FIGURE 11. Cross-section drawing illustrating the simple construction of a typical Underhammer pistol.

strikes directly upward to detonate the cap, the hammer on these early guns operates in a horizontal line. The mainspring also serves as a trigger guard on these early American Underhammers.

Serving also as a trigger guard, the hammer on the Demeritt is operated from a mainspring under the grip. The gun has a most ingenious mechanism for holding the hammer in cocked position, which is described in a later chapter. It is mentioned here due to the fact that it departs from the usual in its mechanism. Fig. 103 gives a good idea of the gun with the guard-hammer in cocked position.

Three most unusual pistols have been encountered in the course of this study. All three are illustrated, either by photographs or line drawings. While the Underhammers are primarily considered as percussion arms, utilizing a percussion cap, it has remained for the three illustrated to pose a question. Are they actually "Pill-lock Underhammers" as has been thought for many years, or are they something else? Due to the fact that a spur on the hammer strikes directly up into the touch hole, on the under side of the barrel, they have generally been regarded as pill-locks. One cannot help but wonder though just how the tiny pellets were held in place on the under side. Unlike the powder in the Underhammer flintlock arms which was ignited from sparks, the tiny pellets of the pill-lock arms have to be crushed by the hammer. Much study has been given to the type of ignition employed by these guns, the result of which has been to give a background of the ignition from which the reader can draw his own conclusions as to which method the guns employed.

In 1823 an American physician by the name of Dr. Samuel Guthrie hit upon the solution for making fulminate of such composition that it could be rolled into tiny pills, or pellets. The Doctor was, without question, the originator of the pill-lock in America even though the principle was not unknown in England at the time.

Early in the evolution of the percussion cap there was introduced a class of lock known as the Pill-lock, or pellet-lock. In these locks the charge was fired by means of a small pellet of detonating compound, which was often enclosed in a paper cap, not unlike those used in present day cap pistols. The following description, from J. N. George's book *English Pistols and Revolvers,* gives the method employed in making such caps.

". . . cases of pill-lock arms were occasionally fitted with the complete apparatus for mixing the detonating compound, and for working it up into pellets, consisting of a small pestle and mortar of lignum vitae, a pair of chemist's scales, and a flat copper plate about one-sixteenth of an inch thick, and pierced with a number of round holes one-eighth of an inch in diameter.

"In making the pellets, the composition, consisting of one part each of charcoal and sulphur mixed with five parts of potassium chlorate, was first weighed out, and was mixed in the mortar, being worked up into a paste with water and a small quantity of gum-arabic to give it cohesion. The copper plate was then laid upon a sheet of glass, or any other flat, smooth surface, the past was spread upon it, being pressed well down into the holes, and the residue was scraped off level with the surface of the plate. Upon the plate being dried the minute portions of the mixture contained in the holes formed small, hard pellets of detonating compound, each of which was afterwards enclosed between two discs of gummed paper, forming a simple type of percussion cap."

Experiments have proven that an ordinary cap pistol cap, when held in place over the vent hole by a smear of beeswax, or other suitable adhesive, will work quite effectively. This, and another method, has been suggested by some present day authorities, and by explosive engineers. They report that fulminate produced in the early nineteenth century could readily have been made into a paste or pill, with the known chemical binders existing at the time. In other words a bit of fulminate paste could have been applied by hand to the wall of the vent hole, where it would be ignited by the blow of the hammer, or the fulminate could have been preformed into a cone shaped unit, which, when allowed to dry could have been pressed or wedged into the vent for firing.

One writer of many years ago offered the following explanation:

"In operation, the pill, (made of either fulminate of mercury or a mixture of charcoal, sulphur and potassium chlorate) a little smaller than a BB-shot, was pressed into the opening on the under side of the barrel and a thick paste of beeswax and mutton tallow was smeared over it to hold it in place. The opening is similar to the vent on a flintlock except that it is reamed out to form a funnel-shaped hold having its smallest diameter on the inside of the barrel. The hammer, on contact, explodes the pill, which in turn ignites the charge in the barrel."

There is yet another answer to the question.

In 1833 Charles Jones of England secured a patent for a unique double-barrel sporting gun. Even though the gun itself had a novel arrangement of having the hammers enclosed with only the cocking levers on the outside, it is not so much the gun that intrigues us as it is the cap Jones originated to go with the gun. As is correctly assumed, all percussion caps, large or small, have the fulminate placed on the inside of the crown. Not so with the Jones cap. It had the fulminate on the outside top of the cap!

 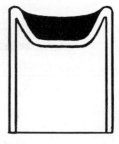

FIGURE 12. An enlarged sketch of the Jones, outside primed, percussion cap. This, or a similar cap, is believed to have been used on some Underhammer guns.

It is believed that this, or some similar cap, may have been used on some of these unusual Underhammer pistols, heretofore labeled pill-lock. In this belief we are joined by no less an authority than W. Keith Neal of England, an internationally-known collector of arms. After personally examining both specimens, Fig. 166 and Fig. 167 he gave as his considered opinion that both pieces, in all probability, used an outside primed cap. Such caps, while on the scarce side, are still to be found in England. There is little doubt but that they, or a close facsimile thereof, were also used, perhaps to a lesser degree, on some guns of this type made in this country.

In fact, our good friend James E. Serven, for many years a leading dealer in antique arms, wrote that he had found such caps in the cap boxes of some Billinghurst-type pill-lock arms. All of which would lend credence that such externally primed caps were in use in this country.

One of the earliest explanations of how the pill-lock was charged is to be found among the writings of Edward C. Barber in 1868. Taken from the article, "William Billinghurst" by James E. Serven in the Feb., 1945, issue of *Muzzle Blasts* it reads as follows:

"I have had occasion to speak with the great shot and veteran sportsman, Seth Green of Mumford, N. Y., and it may be well to mention in this connection that, at the past sportsmen's meet at Leroy, N. Y., he proved the best shot in New York State. He fired with a rifle made by William Billinghurst of Rochester, who besides being a thorough sportsman and good shot, is one of the best, if not THE VERY BEST, riflemaker in the United States. He is quite a Solon among the sports of that section, and his shop is the headquarters for all shooters. * * * The rifle that Green shot was a regular American target rifle; barrel 31" long, exclusive of the patent muzzle, and weighing 28 lbs.; caliber .60 and carrying 28 conical balls to the pound; the charge of powder in the barrel was 3" in the barrel. * * * Billinghurst had practiced with the rifle a good deal previous to the match, and in a letter to me, speaking of the performances, he says, 'In reasonably fair weather we have been in the habit of making strings of from 10" to 15", 10 shots at 220 yards or 40 rods, measuring from the center of the bullet holes to the center of the mark. Sometimes they would measure a little more and sometimes a little less, according to the weather.' I forgot to mention that the rifle was eight grooved, with a gaining twist commencing with one in 6' and ending with one in 3'."

Barber further states: "Seth Green, the best shot in New York State, prefers a rifle made by Billinghurst of Rochester, on Miller's patent. It is a seven-shooter, having a cylinder similar to Colt's patch ball, round or long, and pill-lock. In loading, the powder is put in the cylinder and the ball patched and pushed down the barrel to the cylinder, turning the cylinder every time a ball is put down, until the cylinder is loaded. Then drop a pill in the prime hole *and tallow it over,* and you are all right for

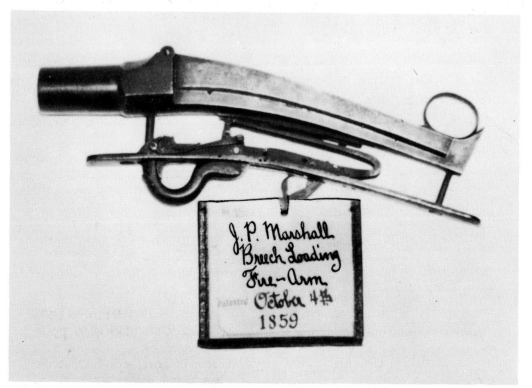

FIGURE 13. Patent model of the J. P. Marshall Underhammer. The operation is described by its owner as follows: "Fire was transmitted through a hollow bolt between the barrel and trigger guard frame. Quite ingenious in that it also has a feed, cutoff, etc., for a roll of caps . . . (a la Maynard) that is inserted above the loop of hammer and fed by a rachet on cocking. Hammer has a cutoff knife for roll on rear edge. It is one of my favorite patent models as it jams so much in such a "small space." Whether or not any guns were actually produced under the patent is not known.

Henry M. Stewart, Jr. Collection

seven shots. With this type of rifle, Green has shot for many years and always found it answered well. In his own words: 'When you are in the woods with one of these guns, you feel you are monarch of all you survey and do not fear anything that wears hair.'"

It is believed that this interesting explanation, written at the time the pill-locks were in use offers the most plausible solution as to how the guns were actually made ready for firing.

Several cross-sections of various mechanisms to be found on Underhammer pistols are illustrated on the following pages. All are drawn from guns included in this study and illustrated by photographs in the Pictorial Section. It is believed that these sketches will prove of interest to those who like to know "what's on the inside."

THREE PATENTS INVOLVING GUNS WITH UNDERHAMMERS

(taken from "Digest of Patents Relating to Breech Loading and Magazine Small Arms. By V. D. Stockbridge. 1874)

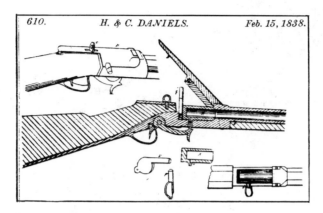

FIGURE 14.

Henry and Charles Daniels
No. 610   February 15, 1838

CLAIM—We do not claim to be the inventors of a moveable chamber to receive and contain the charge. Such chambers having been used by others, but we do claim the manner in which we have applied such a chamber by fitting it into a recess in the breech, and confining it there by means of the hinged strap, constructed and operated in the manner described, adapting the same either to precussion of flint guns and confining the chamber as herein set forth.

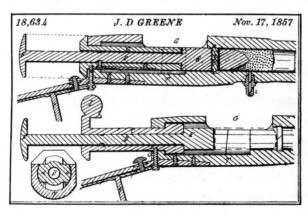

FIGURE 15.

J. D. Greene
No. 18634   November 17, 1857

In this improvement, the barrel A, is extended back to form a loading chamber T, into which there is an opening G, for the insertion of the cartridge. Through the rear of the chamber passes a revolving sliding plunger C, and through the center of this plunger a rod D, which carries at its forward end a breech-plug E, and at its rear end a button F. The plunger is also furnished with a ball or button I, by which it is manipulated, and carries two projecting ears *d,* which, when the plunger is in the position seen in the engravings, enter recess *e,* in the walls of the chamber and rest against the shoulder *r,* by which the plunger is revolved 90°, the ears *d,* clear the shoulders *r,* and the plunger may be drawn back.

CLAIM—First. The groove *i,* or its equivalent, operating in connection with the wad at the rear of the cartridge, in the manner substantially as set forth. I do not claim a sliding breech-plug, secured to the barrel by ears and shoulders, as such device does not constitute my present invention.

Second. The sliding breech-plug E, in combination with the revolving plunger *i,* operating in the manner set forth.

Third. The bolt C, and stop Y, operating in the manner set forth, to interrupt the movement of the trigger, as described.

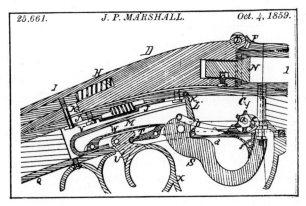

FIGURE 16.

J. P. Marshall
No. 25,661   October 4, 1859

CLAIM—First. The combination of the lockbolt (of the movable breech) or its equivalent, and the discharging lock of the arm, with intermediate parts, for the purpose above set forth.

Second. Arranging the lock for the tape primers, in the manner above described, and for the purpose specified.

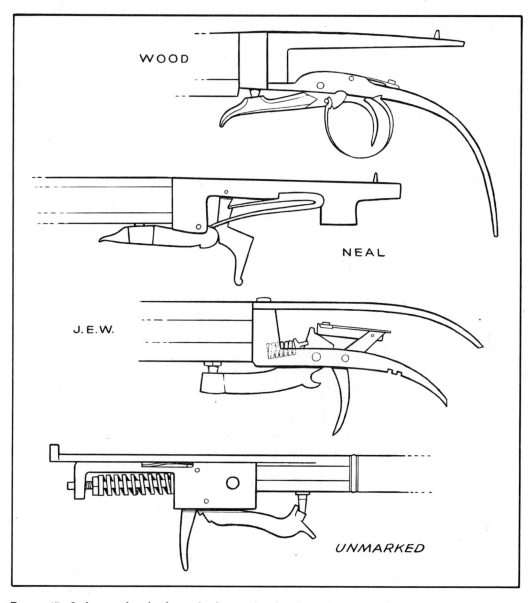

WOOD

NEAL

J.E.W.

UNMARKED

FIGURE 17. Owing to the simple mechanism to be found on the vast majority of Underhammers, it is felt that the cross-sections to be seen in this figure and in figures 18, 19, and 20 require no further explanation.

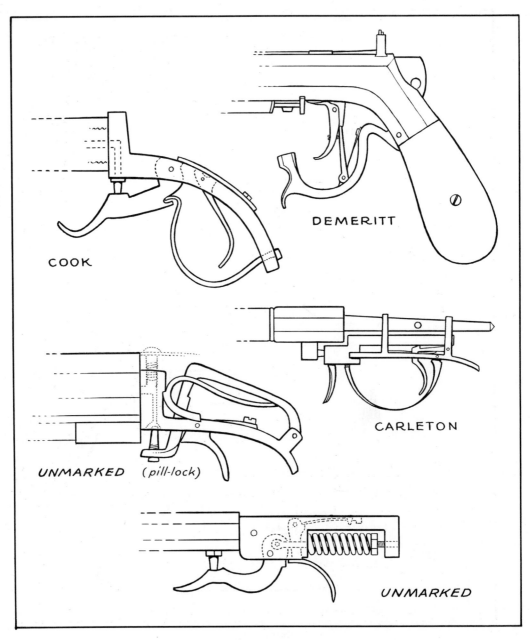

COOK

DEMERITT

CARLETON

UNMARKED *(pill-lock)*

UNMARKED

FIGURE 18.

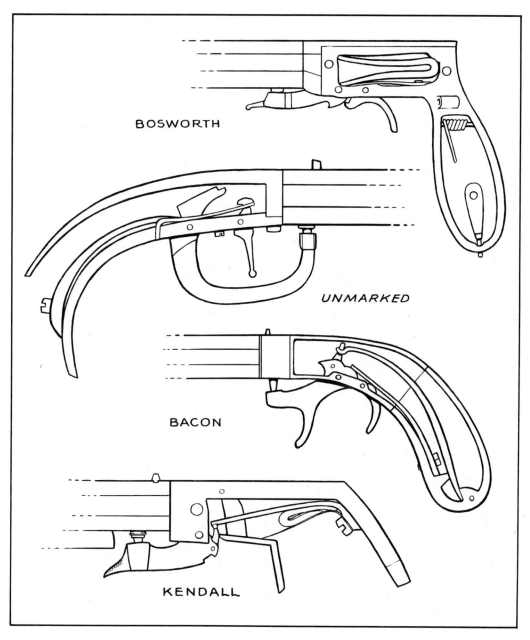

FIGURE 19.

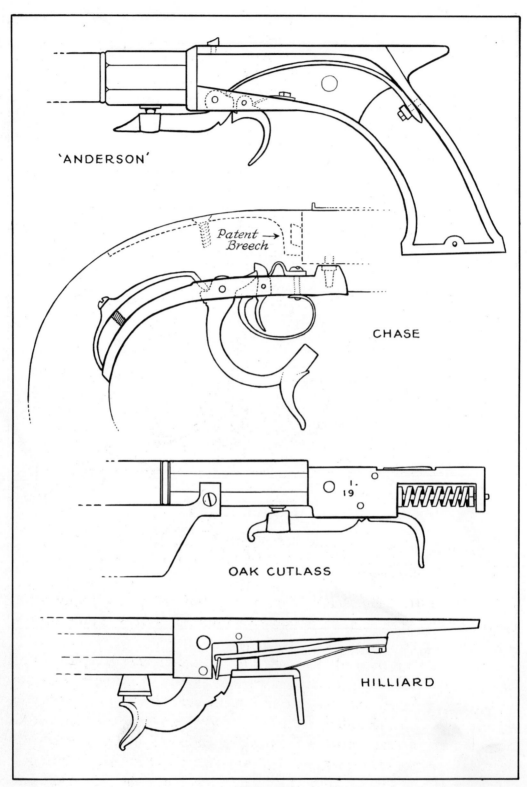

'ANDERSON'

Patent Breech →

CHASE

OAK CUTLASS

HILLIARD

Figure 20.

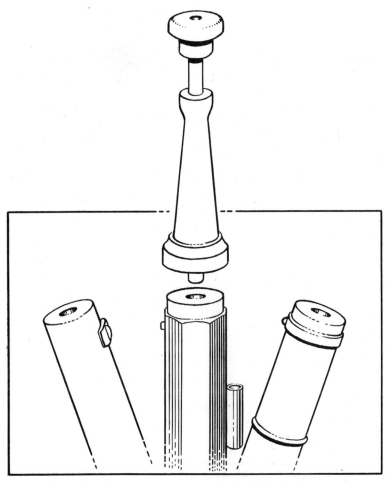

FIGURE 21. Quite varied are the barrel styles found on the Under-hammer guns.

Barrels and Calibers ...

TO ACHIEVE a more or less uniformity in arriving at the caliber of the various arms personally examined, a very simple method was followed, the use of a Caliber Gauge.

The accompanying illustration, Fig. 22, shows such a typical gauge and how it was used to give an indication of the size of the bore. This simplified, yet granted not too accurate, method of designating calibers is widely known among collectors; hence its use here. Due to the fact that the muzzle may become worn, or rounded, at the point of measurement, the exact caliber may be in question. However, such a method will at least give a general idea as to the size of the bore, in relation to the size of the gun.

Measurements were taken across the bore, from land to land, as shown in Fig. 22.

Barrels on the Underhammers ranged from full octagon to all round, from half-octagon and half-round, to cannon shaped. In length they are to be found from three or four inches on pocket models, up to 18-inches or more for target or buggy types. These long-barreled models, carried in buggy or wagon were used principally for target shooting, or for the shooting of small game. In either use they were often rested across the shooter's arm or against some stationary object.

The barrels were not always made by the one who fabricated the gun. Sometimes they were purchased from professional barrel makers. In the

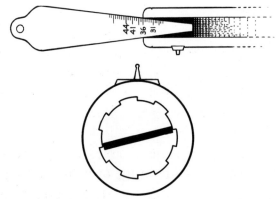

FIGURE 22. Method employed in this study to designate calibers.

1850's E. Remington & Sons of Ilion, N. Y., advertised barrels for the trade. Among purchasers of their barrels were N. Kendall and D. H. Hilliard, specimens of whose work are to be found in the illustrated section. On the barrel of the Hilliard appears the name of REMINGTON . . . while on the rifle by Kendall the barrel is stamped: S & P REMINGTON (Samuel and Philo Remington were sons of E. Remington). Hitchcock & Muzzy of Low Moor, New England were also barrel makers. Examples of their barrels are to be found on rifles made by Durkee and Hamilton.

In these instances the barrels were stamped with the maker's name, and, it may well be that the gunsmiths felt that the marked barrels by such makers as Remington carried an added advertising value as well as giving them a better gun. However, marked barrels are definitely the exception. Most of them, where marked, carry only the gun maker's name

[28]

and, in some instances the words: CAST STEEL, or WARRANTED CAST STEEL.

In his excellent book *The Muzzle-Loading Cap Lock Rifle* the late Ned Roberts writes: "Cast steel for rifle barrels was not highly carbonized, gave a steel that was tough and durable and not brittle, and really was a very excellent barrel steel for muzzle-loaders." By 1840 many of the arms makers in the United States were using the new cast steel in the making of their barrels. As time went by, this identifying mark gradually disappeared as a selling feature.

Without doubt there were other barrel makers whose names, and work, were not as well known but who also supplied barrels to some of the early gunsmiths.

Definitely on the scarce side, insofar as pistols are concerned, are the target models equipped with a bullet starter. A few such are illustrated, one unmarked but identified as a STORY due to its similar features to a marked pistol by STORY. The others are by Wm. Billinghurst, one of the really fine gun makers of his time. Of course there may have been others, but they are indeed few and far between. It has been suggested that many of these fine old target models were used in the turkey shoots of the olden days, and of that we have no doubt.

Whether designed for protection, game or target shooting, the Underhammers were produced in a wide range of calibers ranging from the tiny small bore indoor target arms to the large .50 caliber, or larger, outdoor weapons, and even shot pistols. Some were rifled very nicely while others are to be found with only a smoothbore barrel. Collectors have long been puzzled by the numbers stamped on the barrels of some of these guns.

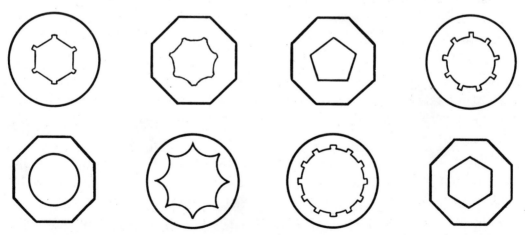

FIGURE 23. Bores of Underhammer barrels range from the plain smoothbore to the variety of rifling illustrated here.

For instance the number 140 appears on many of the guns made by H. J. Hale. This in addition to a serial number. Around the muzzle of the two Hilliard specimens are to be found the number, 130 on one and 132 on the other. The following paragraph, we believe, offers a clue in part, at least, as to the meaning of these numbers.

One of the oldest types of bullets is the round ball, which in various sizes has been used in firearms from their invention down to the present time. In fact for centuries it was the only type of bullet. In the old days the size of a round ball was not given in calibers, as they are today. Instead they were referred to as so many to the pound. For instance if a gun used a size of ball of which it took 140 to weigh a pound it was designated as a "140." Even though the gun gauged "140" the ball it used could be of varying smaller diameter depending upon the thickness of the patch used. In other words a "140" pistol could conceivably use balls weighing 141, 143 or 144 to the pound. This simple method, while admittedly not very accurate, was nevertheless the only way of gauging the size of the round ball, or bore of a pistol or rifle for some two hundred years.

For the benefit of collectors, a few comparative calibers, together with the old designations are given in the following table.

Approximate Caliber Designation	Number of Balls To the Pound	Inches and Decimals of Inches
26	280	.269
28	240	.280
30	170	.305
31	160	.310
32	140	.324
33	130	.332
36	100	.364
38	90	.383
41	64	.416
45	52	.453
50	36	.506

The following paragraphs are taken from *The Muzzle-Loading Cap Lock Rifle,* and even though they apply in the main to rifles, they will throw further light on shooting in the days of the Underhammers.

"The pioneer rule for ascertaining the correct charge of powder for a round ball rifle was: place a ball in the palm of the hand and pour out from the powder horn enough powder to completely cover the ball. Then make from a piece of bone hollowed out, or the tip of a small horn, or from a brass tube with a cork in one end, a charger which this quantity of powder exactly fills even with the top, 'stricken measure.' This method is still best for ascertaining the correct charge for different gauges of round ball rifles, and gives charges that average in weight about as follows:

Balls Per Pound	Caliber	Grains Weight of Powder
150	31	25
100	36	40
56	44	60
18	60	80

"Another old-time rule for this purpose was: use 3-grains weight of powder for each 7-grains weight of balls, which when applied to the above caliber round balls works out very nearly the same charges as above. Thus .31 caliber round balls weight 60-grains, divided by 7 equals 8 4/7 x 3 equals .25 5/7-grains of powder. .36 caliber round ball; weight 90-grains divided by 7 equals 12 6/7 x 3 equals 38 4/7-grains of powder. .44 caliber round ball, weight 118-grains divided by 7 equals 16 6/7 x 3 equals 50 2/7 grains of powder, or nearly 10 grains less than the other rule."

A few standard size balls for use in percussion arms are also given here for those who might wish to fire the old guns of other days.

.28 caliber uses a .285 diameter ball
.31 caliber uses a .319 diameter ball
.32 caliber uses a .323 diameter ball
.34 caliber uses a .345 diameter ball
.36 caliber uses a .375 diameter ball
.38 caliber uses a .389 diameter ball
.44 caliber uses a .451 diameter ball
.45 caliber uses a .457 diameter ball

In between, and other calibers take proportionate sizes. Hand guns, of course, would use a lesser powder charge than that indicated for rifles. For instance a recommended powder charge for a .31 caliber single-shot pistol would be 12-15 grains of FFg or FFFg black powder.

Breech-loading Underhammers are not too frequently encountered. Only 8 or 10 specimens are pictured in this study. This is not saying that

FIGURE 24. In addition to caps, patches, powder and balls other necessary items for shooting the Under-hammers included bullet mould, powder measurer, loading block and bullet starter.

there are not many more, only that they were not encountered during the months of this research. One of those illustrated, Fig. 273, is of foreign manufacture. Made for indoor shooting, its small bore required but a speck of powder, if indeed the cap alone was not sufficient to do the job. The lever in front of the hammer turns the drum which permits the powder and ball to be loaded through the small hole on the right side. It was a simple and convenient arrangement and one wonders why more of them were not made. It is highly probable that they were only made near the end of the percussion era, and against the new cartridge arms they could hardly have been expected to hold their place for any great length of time.

The Demeritt target pistol has an easily removable breech-plug. This permits loading from the breech, if desired, and also makes for a more convenient cleaning of the finely rifled barrel.

Sights on the Underhammers were, for the most part, of the open type. Exceptions were where the arm was designed primarily for target shooting, such as the Billinghurst, Hilliard and others. These guns were often equipped with special sights—adjustable, hooded and even tele-scopic. Rear sights were adjustable, folding, buckhorn, elevating or peep. On the smaller pocket models, made principally as defense arms, or for casual shooting, it is not uncommon to find them without sights of any kind.

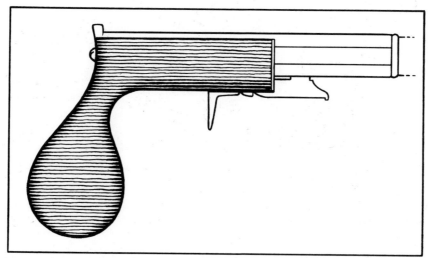

FIGURE 25. As individualistic as their makers are the grips used on the Under-hammers.

Grip Styles and Triggers ...

GRIPS, INSOFAR AS shape and style are concerned, are as individualistic as the men who made them. The great majority are quite plain, but occasionally specimens will be found with wire, metal, ivory or bone inlays which lift them out of the ordinary. Fluted grips are to be found almost entirely on foreign arms, particularly on those of French or Belgian origin. On many of the New England pieces the grips are trimmed, or mounted, with brass or German silver. Walnut and curly maple seem to have been the choice of woods selected by the gunsmiths who fashioned the Underhammers. Infrequently grips of all-metal, brass or pewter, and even ivory or stag, may be found.

Shapes range from the rather stiff right angle, the oblique, curved, saw-handled and so on to the extreme birdshead design. Each style differed slightly, depending upon who produced it.

Mention has been made of the New England types. These pieces are

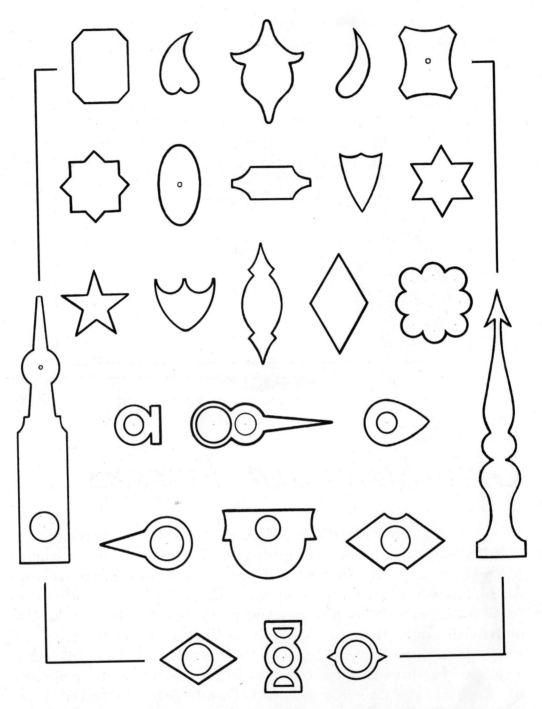

FIGURE 26. Brass or silver inlays and escutcheons of simple design add beauty and interest to the Underhammers.

easily identified by the individualistic style and shape of their grip, a design which has come to be so closely associated with the Underhammer guns. Their rather oblique, pointed shape is best illustrated in Fig. 27. Just why so many of the gunsmiths of that area adopted this style of grip is not known, but the fact that they did has left its mark in the publics general conception of these unique weapons.

Pistols equipped with an extension stock, of metal or wood, are not unknown, but they are at best uncommon. Definitely unusual, if not unique, is the specimen illustrated with the integral shoulder stock. It is the only one observed in many, many months of searching for unusual specimens.

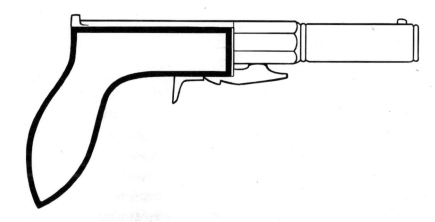

FIGURE 27. The familiar and distinctive shape of the New England Underhammer grip.

By far the greater number of Underhammers were produced without trigger guards. In the majority of cases where a guard was employed, it also served a dual purpose: that of a mainspring, or hammer. The specimens by Wm. Billinghurst, H. Pratt, A. J. Jones, B. C. Wood and A. Cook are typical examples of this simple but effective lock mechanism.

Notable exceptions to the guard serving as a mainspring are to be observed in two specimens: one, the scarce Demeritt, Fig. 103, in which the trigger guard is also the hammer; the other is an unmarked piece, Fig. 177. In both instances the "guard-hammer" is actuated by a spring in the grip. The somewhat complicated mechanism of the Demeritt is worthy of note. When the hammer is pushed downward, into cocked position, a spring fastened to it pushes an anchored pin into locked position against the back of the trigger, thus holding the hammer at cocked position. A tiny screw through the trigger makes it possible to adjust it for a feather touch in target shooting.

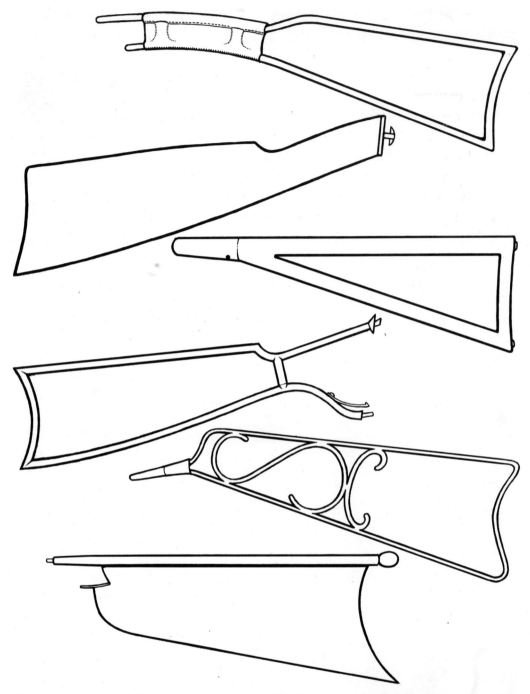

FIGURE 28. Extension stocks used on some of the Underhammer pistols. They ranged from the simple, all-metal, skeleton type to those of full wood construction.

Trigger design followed more or less a standard pattern. Now and then ring triggers will be found, as will be evidenced by the few specimens included in the pictorial section. Much more scarce are the Underhammers with folding triggers. These are principally the products of foreign makers.

Special mention should be made of one kind of trigger, which, while scarce on regular types of arms, is virtually unknown on Underhammer guns. This is the "button trigger" which, up to now, has been found on only one pair of Underhammer pistols, (Fig. 165).

Illustrated in Figures 29, 30, and 31 are pen and ink outline sketches of a sizeable group of Underhammer pistols. Though not all-inclusive it is hoped that they will give a fair idea of the wide variety of grip styles to be encountered on these interesting guns.

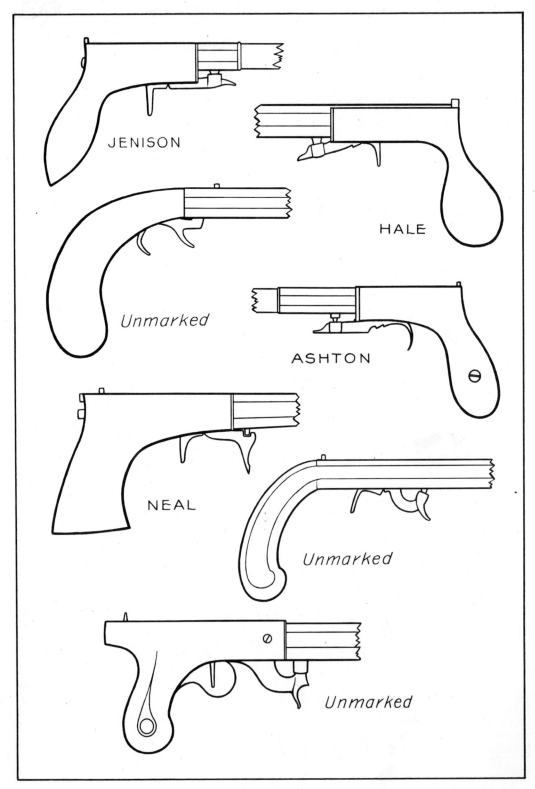

FIGURE 29.

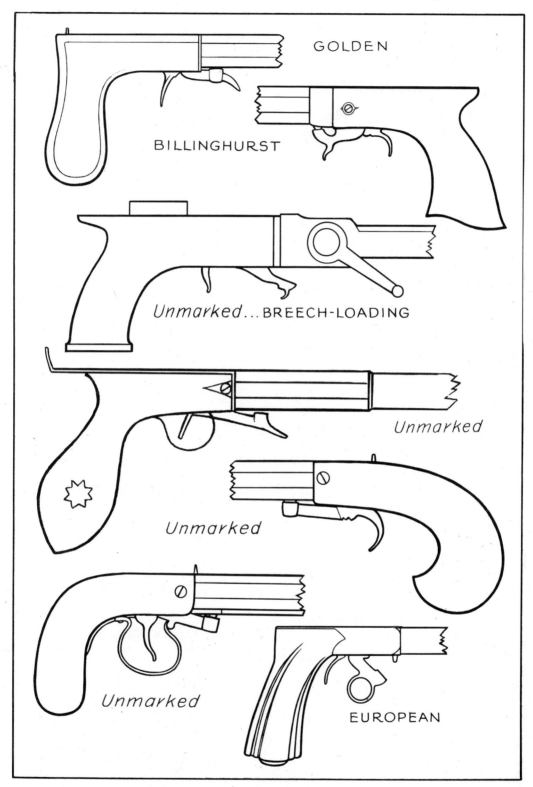

GOLDEN

BILLINGHURST

Unmarked...BREECH-LOADING

Unmarked

Unmarked

Unmarked

EUROPEAN

FIGURE 30.

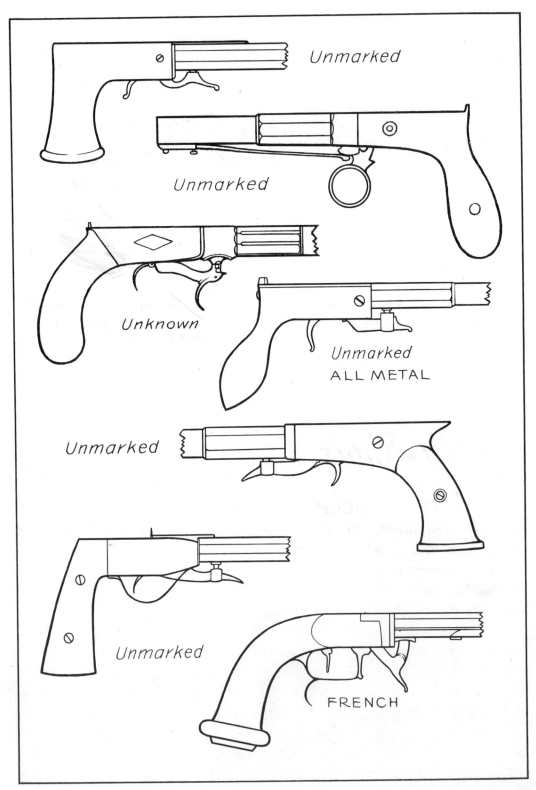

Unmarked

Unmarked

Unknown

Unmarked
ALL METAL

Unmarked

Unmarked

FRENCH

FIGURE 31.

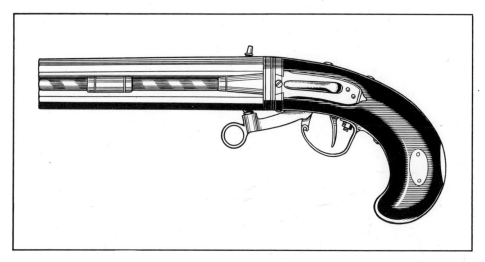

FIGURE 32. A splendid example of an American Multi-shot Underhammer pistol. The over-and-under barrels are revolved by hand for firing.

Multi-Shots ...

THE UNDERHAMMER PRINCIPLE was not confined to single-shot pistols. Multi-shots in double-barrel, over-and-under and pepperbox models while definitely in the minority, are interesting and unusual enough to include in the Underhammer story. The few specimens illustrated will, it is felt, give a general idea of how the principle was adapted to arms of more than one shot.

First to deserve attention are three over-and-under pistols. Each employs the manually rotated type of barrels, released by a catch on the left side of the frame. On the top specimen, Fig. 212 it will be observed that the hammer moves in a slot in the trigger guard, while on the lower guns, (a pen and ink drawing of one which is illustrated in this chapter heading) the trigger guard also serves as a mainspring. The second gun, Fig. 213, is a true "Forty-niner." Taken to Colorado in 1847 by its owner, it went on to California in 1848 to take part in the colorful Gold Rush of 1849. The third specimen, Fig. 214, was a presentation piece to President William H. Harrison. Truly these two unusual Underhammers were a vital part of the history of this great nation.

Lewis Winant in his definitive book, *Pepperbox Firearms,* describes a pepperbox as, *"any hand firearm with three or more barrels encircling a central axis, firing shots successively with only one striker."*

The Pepperbox, instead of having one directing barrel as on a revolver, was made up of a single cylinder composed of separate "chamber barrels." It was really the first type of multi-shot arm to appeal to the public's fancy. Such guns were made in both single and double action.

It was only logical that those who produced arms, with the hammer on the underside, should likewise look with inquiring eyes at this multi-shot principle as something which they might incorporate in their guns. While definitely in the minority, insofar as their number is concerned, Underhammer pepperboxes are of real interest in the study of understriker arms.

By far the greater number of Pepperboxes with the hammer on the under side of the barrel were the product of European manufacturers, principally Belgian. These Pepperboxes were of the Mariette system, in which each barrel was a separate unit and was screwed into a standing breech, which contained the nipples and powder charges for each barrel. The guns employed a ring trigger to activate their double-action feature, in which the breech-block, made up of various number of barrels, rotated and the underhammer was released by merely pulling the trigger for each shot. For the most part the barrels on the Mariette-type pepperboxes were of the Damascus design, and guns with up to 24 barrels fastened to a single breech-block are known.

European pepperboxes of the Mariette system were produced with an eye to two distinct markets: the very wealthy and the citizens of average circumstances. Highly ornamented and elaborate guns, often with gold inlay, are not uncommon. Along with these fine ornate arms there will be found very plain and simple specimens to sell for a low price. For the collector who desires an attractive and desirable example of an Underhammer Pepperbox, the European Mariettes offer a splendid solution. Specimens at reasonable prices appear frequently on dealer lists.

Most common, if the word may be used so loosely, of the American Pepperboxes of Underhammer pattern are the Blunt & Syms and the Bacon. It has long been a question as to whether or not Blunt & Syms actually manufactured the Pepperboxes attributed to them, or if they merely served in the capacity of an importing agent. If one can judge by their sales sheet, Fig. 50, they must have, at least, produced some of the guns themselves. Be that as it may, the guns, of which there are various styles, are desirable examples of the Underhammer principle as applied to the pepperbox type of arms.

The Bacon Pepperbox is, of course, strictly American and is very similar in general outline to their single-shot Underhammer pistol. It is a six-shot, single-action type and was the only multi-shot Underhammer model manufactured by Bacon.

Four other Pepperboxes are worthy of particular note. One is marked E. B. WHITE and the other three pieces, of nearly identical design, are totally unmarked as to maker's name. On the three unmarked pieces the solid cylinder, in which the chambers are bored, revolves mechanically as the hammer is cocked. On the White gun the cylinder must be rotated by hand.

The location, and activity, of E.B. White is not known. But if one must judge only by this single specimen of his work, he was a gunsmith of considerable merit.

After personally examining the three unmarked pieces, Figures 216, 219, and 220, it is the opinion of the author that they are undeniably American in origin. This premise is based upon their design, style, construction and workmanship. No similar Pepperboxes of foreign manufacture were encountered during the course of this study with the distinctly New England type of grip.

Rumors still persist that an individual named Goddard secured permission from Darling to essemble a few pistols of his own Underhammer design from some left-over parts of the very rare Darling first model Pepperbox, when Darling turned to their later and more generally known models. If such be true, it might well provide the reason for the guns being unmarked as to name.

Comparison of the cylinder and of the rotating mechanism with those of the Darling reveals a striking similarity. The cylinder fluting is identical, and, both cylinders are bored for the same size cylinder pin. The cylinder on the Underhammer has been shortened to 3½-inches from the 4¼-inches of the Darling. On two of the specimens, which are serially numbered #2 and #6, the chambers are numbered from one to six on the muzzle end. A study of the patent drawing for the first model Darling discloses that the revolving mechanism is virtually identical to that actually in use on the three Underhammers.

Noted collectors who have examined the three guns are in agreement that the guns are undeniably at the top in rarity and desirability among American Underhammer Pepperboxes.

Attention is called to the foreign made CERWENKA Pepperbox, Fig. 224. This 16-shot mongul has a weight of 4 lbs. 6 ozs., truly a handful by any standard.

From the foregoing it will be observed that in the Pepperbox field, as in other types, the Underhammers are not wanting in variety, design or rarity.

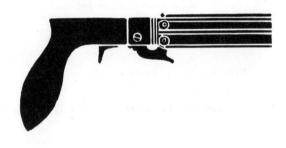

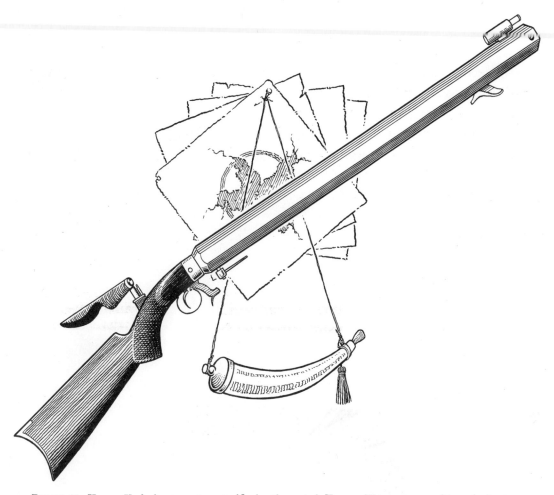

FIGURE 33. Heavy Underhammer target rifle by the noted Horace Warner, gunsmith and shooter.

Long Arms . . .

WHILE THE ORIGIN of placing the hammer on the under side of the barrel remains unknown, it is generally conceded that the principle was first popularized on sporting, rather than military arms. This being true, no writing on the subject of Underhammers, even though concerning itself in the main with handguns, would be complete if mention of the long arms were omitted.

That the Underhammer-type of rifles had ardent supporters is quite evident, not only from past writers on the early makers and their guns, but also from the examples of these fine old arms which have survived the years. A few of the gunsmiths, and shooters, felt that the Underhammers offered greater advantages than were to be found in the regular side hammer, top nipple, or mule-eared type of rifles.

The early adaption of the Underhammer principle to a flintlock musket has been previously described and will not be repeated here. Suffice to say, it is believed that it represents the earliest use of the principle.

Following nearly a hundred years later was a percussion adaption, the patent of Henry Wilkinson of London (June 22, 1839) He described the operation of his gun in his patent as follows:

"The cock and mainspring of the lock in one piece and so are the trigger sear and tumbler. The mainspring is shown underneath the barrel. The mainspring is screwed at one end to the stock, the other end forms the cock and is pulled back by the thumb of the left hand, and is engaged in the notch of a plate attached to the trigger. On pulling the trigger the spring is released and strikes upwards discharging the piece. Percussion caps may be used, or priming pellets formed of detonating powder, fastened upon or between paper or cardboard discs; these may be contained in a tube, and are advanced successively and placed over the nipple, as required by self acting apparatus."

Another of the early and genuinely interesting Underhammer guns is the one known as the Koptipter Lock. It is described in *The Gun Collector,* (issue of September, 1950, #33). It is copied here by the kind permission of G. Charter Harrison, Editor and Publisher.

"Perhaps the strangest of all percussion locks was that invented by Charles Louis Stanislas, Baron Heurteloup. Fulminate has long been respected as tricky stuff, but Baron Heurteloup's lock takes astonishing liberties with it. As he puts it, in his United States Patent, No. 2,203, granted July 29, 1841; 'Several years have elapsed since I discovered that a tube of soft metal . . . as for instance, of lead or pewter . . . when filled with detonating powder —that a small portion might be cut off or separated from the remainder of such tube by a sharp instrument without exploding the other parts of the tube.' Taking advantage of this peculiarity, Baron Heurteloup's lock was fed the priming encased in a continuous tube of lead or pewter. The hammer nose was in the shape of a blade which sheared off a portion of the tube, without detonating the remainder, while an instant later the flat of the hammer exploded the cut off segment against the nipple.

"Henry Wilkinson, in *Engines of War* published in 1841 says regarding this lock: 'Baron Heurteloup . . . has named it the Koptipter from its peculiar action of cutting and striking . . . .'

"The patent drawing provides for the fulminate strip to be fed out by hand turning a small feed roller . . . but the Milwaukee Public Museum specimen has a rachet device which moves 3/16 of an inch of fulminate strip under the hammer each time it is cocked. The channel for the tape extends about 10-inches past the feed roller, thus providing ignition for some 50 shots.

"Baron Heurteloup, who describes himself as a 'subject of the

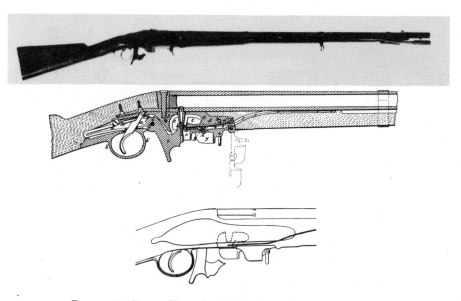

FIGURE 34. Baron Heurteloup's Koptipter Lock Underhammer.

King of the French, and now residing at Albany Street, Regent's Park . . .' was given a British patent on February 23, 1839, his American patent being antedated to correspond."

Not generally known, except to students of arms, is that the United States Government at one time used an Underhammer rifle, the Greene Oval-Bore, patented, November 17, 1857, (No. 18634) by Lt. Col. J. Durrell Greene. The gun was manufactured at the A. Waters Armoury at Millsbury, Mass. The oval type bore used in the gun was the invention of Capt. Birnes of England, in 1835.

The bolt-action Greene rifle used a cylindrical Minie bullet with an expanding base. The bullet was placed at the rear of a special paper cartridge to serve as a gas check. In loading, a single bullet was inserted, and seated by the bolt; then the special cartridge was placed in the chamber. Upon firing, the rear bullet remained in the chamber, to become the advance bullet for the second shot. The 2¼-inch long paper, combustible cartridge contained 68 grains of powder.

Ordnance reports indicate that 900 of the Greene rifles were purchased by the government for use in the Civil War. However it is believed that many more hundreds were actually produced.

The United States government was not alone in experimenting with the Underhammers. Included here are two foreign pieces, one French

FIGURE 35. Cross-section view of the odd cartridge used by the Green Underhammer rifle.

and the other Norwegian, both of which utilized the underhammer principle.

From the earliest times, gunmakers had sought to carry over into long arms the principles used in repeating pistols. The adaptation, in most cases, did not prove too satisfactory—for very good reasons. The main defect was the gap between the cylinder, or block, holding the charge and the bore of the barrel. Holding a handgun at arm's length was quite different from firing the heavier charged rifle close to the face. Higher pressure of the escaping gas, and fire, made it risky to say the least. And, too, there was always the possibility that the flash might set off the charges in the adjoining chambers, a most disconcerting thing in a long arm where the shooter's hand was on the forestock ahead of the charges!

Taking these facts into account it is understandable why multi-shot long arms are relatively scarce, and therefore have a definite appeal to

Norwegian Carbine, 1842 Model.

FIGURE 36. This illustration showing the operation of the Norwegian Underhammer is taken from W. W. Greener's book, The Gun and Its Development, second edition, 1884.

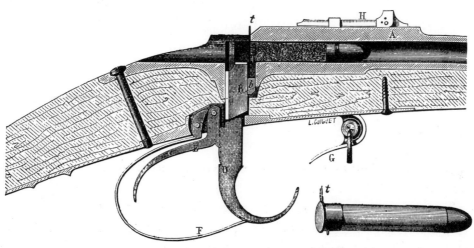

Early French Military Breech-loader.

FIGURE 37. Since Underhammer cartridge guns are not common, it is believed that the description of this early gun, taken from the book, The Gun, by W. W. Greener (1884), will be of more than passing interest.

"The Mousquetoon des Cent Gardes was invented in France . . . the cartridge used is similar in construction to the Lefaucheux. The pin, A, for the cap is placed under the base of the cartridge, and projects barely 1/8 of an inch. The long pin, F, on the top of the case is to withdraw it from the chamber after discharge. The stock is hollowed behind the breech to readmit of the cartridge being pushed into barrel, A. The breech-block, B, carries a small stud, b, which strikes the cap of the cartridge, C, when the gun is fired. Affixed to the block, B, is a sear, D, forming part of the trigger-guard, the other part being composed of the sear and trigger-spring, F, one end acting upon the trigger, E, and the other causing the breech-block, D, to fly upwards with sufficient velocity to close the breech of the barrel and detonate the cartridge cap. G is a swivel and. guard to prevent the finger coming under the sear tail."

many collectors. Makers of the Underhammers also endeavored to incorporate the multi-shot, or repeating, principle to long arms—with varying degrees of success. Existing specimens of their work are eagerly sought by present day collectors.

Three methods seemed to have been employed in the design of these unusual repeating arms: a flat bar with parallel chambers, a flat round radial cylinder, in which the chambers radiate out like the spokes of a wheel, and the regular type of percussion cylinder with the chambers parallel.

One of the earliest Americans, if not the first, to apply the repeating idea to an Underhammer long arm was Nicanor Kendall of Windsor, Vt. His rifle utilized a sliding-bar breech-block containing five chambers. Bringing the underhammer to half cock, and depressing the spring catch on top of the frame permitted the breech-block to be moved over for each succeeding shot. It was this novel feature that gave to the gun the nickname of "harmonica rifle." (See Addenda for the Browning Repeating Rifle.)

Another Underhammer employing a sliding-bar breech-block was the Chamberlain's Patent Rifle made by C.·B. Allen of Springfield, Mass. Three chambers were contained in the breech-block of this little-known arm, which was patented on April 17, 1837, (No. 168) by Elijah Fisher and Dexter H. Chamberlain of Springfield and Boston. A stud on top the frame holds the bar in firing position, and, when released the bar can be moved in either direction. This rifle had an added safety measure. Pressing a catch on the small of the stock raised a shield around the nipple to prevent the flash from setting off adjacent chambers, a most ingenious idea.

Illustrated here in a line drawing is perhaps the most unusual placing of a cylinder on a rifle to be found. Instead of the usual position of the cylinder below the barrel this arm has the axis of the cylinder above the barrel. A patent for this feature was secured by Elijah Jacquith on July 12, 1838, (No. 832). His request for a patent was worded as follows:

> ". . . this arrangement, in the case of any accidental discharge
> of the neighboring charges, renders the forward hand of the
> person using the gun more safe."

Sighting on this unique arm was done through the axis of the cylinder, which was left hollow to serve as the rear sight. The back of the cylinder was slotted in a zig-zag fashion to permit it to revolve to the right when the underhammer was cocked.

Several minor variations, as well as in the number of shots, are to be found in the Cochran horizontal radial cylinder Underhammer rifle. Produced by C. B. Allen of Springfield, Mass., it is certainly one of the most unusual repeating Underhammer long arms to be encountered. The guns were made with a ring trigger, hammer forming the trigger guard, and hammer ahead of a regular trigger guard, as is found on the Chamberlain gun, also produced by Allen. Release of a catch on top of the frame permitted the cylinder to be revolved to the next position for firing.

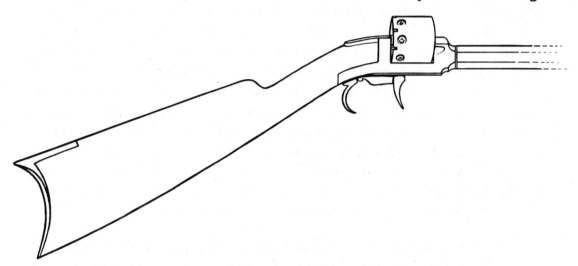

FIGURE 38. This simple line drawing illustrates the unusual position of the cylinder on the Jacquith Underhammer Revolving Rifle.

The cylinder could be removed for cleaning and loading by lifting the hinged top strap. The latch for this strap was notched and served also as the rear sight.

Very much on the scarce side, and yet not to be overlooked, are the double-barrel Underhammer rifles. A pen sketch of one such (Fig. 58) will be seen in the chapter entitled "Gleanings." It was the only one noted in this research. Each barrel had its own hammer and trigger, differing from one pistol encountered which fired both barrels at the same time with a single hammer.

No specimen of an over-and-under rifle in which the barrels revolve was encountered during this study. But such does not mean that they were not made, or that one will not turn up at a later date, for the story of Underhammers is one of surprises and thrills at finding a "new one."

Fortunate indeed is the collector who can show one or more of the multi-shot, or repeating, rifles which are so definitely an integral part of the whole Underhammer story.

No chapter on Underhammer long arms would be complete without a mention of the three-barrel guns produced by Charles and Henry Slotterbek. These unusual arms employed a combination of the regular side hammer and an under hammer. The two upper, side by side, shotgun barrels used typical shotgun type of hammers while a third barrel (rifle) centered under the upper two utilized an under striker.

Charles Slotterbek, the older of the brothers, was born in Germany and started as an apprentice in the gunsmith's trade when but 12 years of age. This was understandable, since both his father and grandfather had followed the same trade. For some years after coming to this country the brothers worked at their trade in Philadelphia. At one time or another they were both employed by the noted Henry Deringer.

In 1858 Charles left for San Francisco, where he continued in the business of making guns. Henry in company with a younger brother, Frederick, and two other partners, formed the well-known firm of Slotter & Co., in 1860. This firm was the maker of Slotter derringers and rifles.

On Nov. 17, 1868, a patent (No. 84,224) was granted to Charles Slotterbek for an "Improvement in Firearms." This invention is best described in his own words, as taken from the patent application:

"The nature of my invention consists in a certain construction and arrangement of two triggers, to operate three cocks, or hammers, whereby three barrels can be 'fired' by means of the same two triggers or 'locks' . . ."

> In the drawing . . .
> "A"   represents a partial side view of a fire-arm having three barrels;
> "B"   is an elevation of the guard, and its plate, triggers, attachments, and extra hammer or cock, etc.;
> "C"   represents a transverse section of the barrels and stock, showing a recess for a ramrod.

The application then goes on to describe, in detail, the functioning of every piece in the mechanism. The rear trigger actuates only the left-hand hammer. The front trigger (k) operates the right hand lock, firing the right hand barrel. The under hammer (f) is also operated the same as the right hand hammer by means of trigger (k). To make it more sensitive, or to work as a hair trigger, either before cocking or after cocking the under hammer, the trigger (k) is moved slightly forward.

Guns produced under this system were manufactured by both brothers, operating in their own respective plants, in different cities. Later the

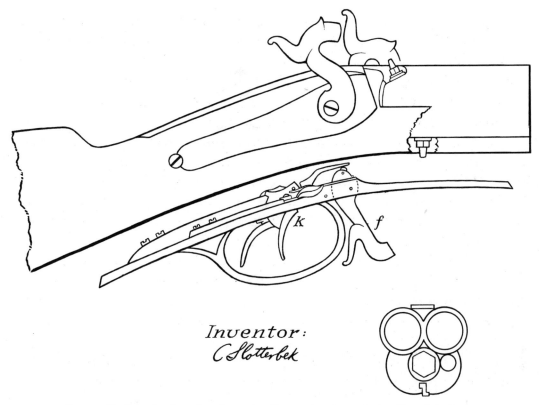

Inventor:
C Slotterbek

FIGURE 39. Pen sketch, taken from the Patent drawing, of the Slotterbek Lock.

firm of Villegia & Slotterbek, in which Charles was a partner, also produced guns of the same patent.

An unusual arm produced by William Billinghurst of Rochester, N. Y., while utilizing the top and under hammer, principle was different enough to warrant mention here. In the August 10, 1852, issue of the *Rochester Daily Democrat* there appeared an interesting account of this arm.

The gun, a revolving pill-lock rifle of .40 caliber had a 4-inch cylinder of seven chambers. The charges were loaded through the muzzle end of the barrel, the cylinder being revolved by hand, as a charge was seated in each chamber. Attached to the gun below the rifle barrel, and running through the axis of the cylinder, was a barrel of 14-gauge for shot. Operating separately by means of an under hammer it could be fired before or after the rifle, or simultaneously. Though made by Billinghurst, the gun was patented by J. Miller. Originally made for pill-lock ignition, the gun was later produced for percussion caps.

Highly prized among collectors are underhammer rifles by Wm. Billinghurst of Rochester, N. Y., N. Kendall of Windsor, Vt., D. H. Hilliard, Cornish, N. H., N. S. Brockway of Bellow Falls, Vt., and others of the fine makers. From the heavy fourteen pound bench target rifles to the light and graceful sporting rifles these guns are beautiful examples of the gunsmith's art.

As late as July 6, 1940, the late A. O. "Pop" Niedner shot in a match at Canal Fulton, Ohio, using an Underhammer rifle for which he had made the barrel. "Pop" was then 77 years of age, but he shot the remarkable score of a five-shot possible 50, string measure of $4\frac{1}{8}$ inches at 100

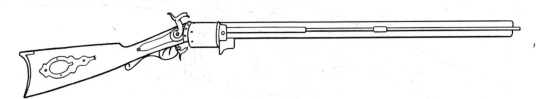

FIGURE 40. Billinghurst Revolving Pill-lock Rifle with an Underhammer for the lower shotgun barrel.

yards, using a rest and telescopic sights. The underhammer lock and stocking for the rifle was done by Wm. W. McQuerry of Jeffersonville, Indiana, himself a noted shot. The first match in which the rifle was used (Mariette, Ohio, 1940) netted Mr. McQuerry the gold medal first prize. With it he shot a possible 50 with 2 x's, having a string measure of 2-11/16 inches for the five shots. Later in California he won first place in two out of four matches.

One of the last rifles "Pop" Neidner made was the splendidly designed Underhammer illustrated here by means of a simple line drawing.

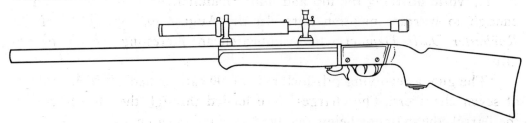

FIGURE 41. Outline sketch of the A. O. Nieder Underhammer Target Rifle.

Raymond P. Gorning, M.D. of Detroit, Mich., was another staunch supporter of the Underhammer rifle as a target arm. His rifle was built along the lines of the old Kentucky long rifle: full stock, patch-box and all. It too is illustrated with an outline pen sketch.

With the present day interest in shooting the old muzzle-loading guns it should not be too surprising to again see examples of the Underhammer rifles on the "firing line."

[54]

FIGURE 42. Gorning Underhammer Target Rifle.

Since writing the above it has come to our attention that Underhammer Target Rifles are indeed being produced once again, and, within the very shadow of the noted Hilliard's gunshop. Located at West Lebanon, N. H., along the Connecticut River is the shop of Ray Mitchell. Here are being produced some splendid rifles based on the D. H. Hilliard style and tradition. Mr. Mitchell also makes, on order, Underhammer "Bootleg" Pistols. Thus it is that once again in the quiet of the New Hampshire countryside, the old spirit of gun making still lives to bring pride of ownership to those lucky enough to possess one of these modern day Underhammer Target Rifles, or Pistols. (For other modern gunsmiths see Addenda.)

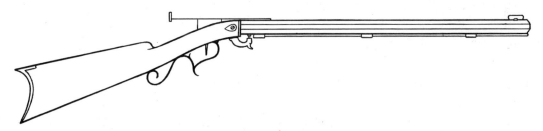

FIGURE 43. Pen sketch of the type of Underhammer rifle being produced by Ray Mitchell.

Another of the present day shooters who also finds enjoyment in building, as well as shooting the Underhammer guns is Al H. Woody of Cheyenne, Wyoming. A machinist by trade he has designed and built, "from scratch," both pistols and rifles on the under-cock principle, because as he says, "I like it best of all." Two of his fine guns are illustrated in the Pictorial Section.

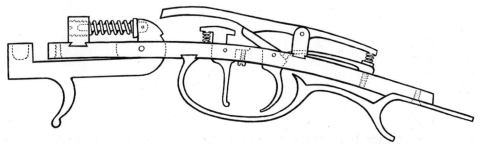

FIGURE 44. Cross section view of the unusual set-trigger Underhammer lock mechanism used on the fine target rifle made by Al H. Woody, illustrated in the pictorial section.

CANE GUNS

One type of arm which never fails to attract attention of both collector and layman is the dual purpose cane gun. Designed primarily as a walking stick it concealed, in varying degrees, a firearm for protection of its owner, or for game poaching if perchance its owner happened to be a bit on the shady side.

One of the earliest of the percussion cane guns, and incidentally the most popular and widely sold were those made by John Day of England. Two specimens are to be found illustrated in the Photographic Section of long arms. One is of special interest in that it is quite different from the usual Day Cane Gun. Designed and finished to resemble a gnarled piece of wood, it has, when thrown to the shoulder, the swing and feel of a well-designed rifle. This is different from the usual type of cane gun, which it would appear are sometimes rather awkward to hold and fire.

John Day of Barnstaple, Devon, England, secured the patent for his interesting Underhammer Cane Gun in 1823 (English Patent No. 4861) and appears to have been producing the guns some thirty years later. An unusual length of life for a dual-purpose arm, which frequently is popular for only a relatively short space of time.

Another of the very desirable cane guns is the specimen marked only BROWN'S PATENT, Fig. 268. This piece is a combination arm in every sense of the word. Without the long barrel or detachable stock it offers a most excellent example of a small pocket pistol. A long wooden ramrod with a walking ferrule is inserted in the muzzle of the barrel, which is painted to resemble a modern walking stick. Held in place by a polished knob at the breech end of the barrel, the combination affords a first class cane. Replacing the short pistol barrel with the long barrel and adding the accompanying rifle stock provides the owner with a splendid single-shot fowling piece. The original mould, which has a key on one of the handles with which to unscrew the pistol barrel, completes the ensemble of this remarkable gun.

Truly the cane guns were but another example of the ingenuity of those who have fabricated arms through the centuries.

Even though not a "firearm" in the strict sense of the word, the unique air rifle is included here for the very simple reason that it is an Under-hammer. Our good friend G. Charter Harrison, who sent the photo of the gun in his collection, gives this description.

"The under hammer is upon an unmarked compressed air gun, which is peculiar in that it has over and under barrels. What is

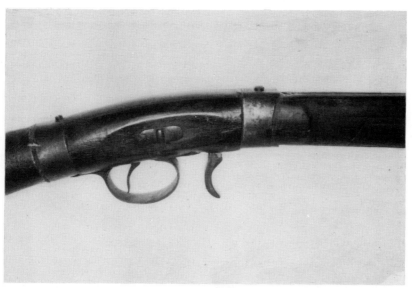

FIGURE 45. Unusual adaptation of the Underhammer principle to an Air Rifle.

most strange about it is that a peculiar spring loaded ramrod screws into either the upper, or lower, barrel. Should the gun be discharged when the ramrod is in position, the ball in that barrel is caught by the spring and allowed to go only part way up the barrel after which the spring returns it to the breech end for subsequent discharge. If the ramrod is taken out of the barrels, then the upper and lower discharge simultaneously, in other words a double shooter."

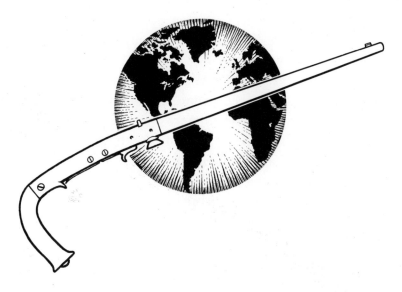

FIGURE 46. The Underhammers were not the product of any one nation or period of time. Their unique principle spanned both centuries and continents.

Foreign . . .

NO ONE COUNTRY held a monoply on the fabrication of Underhammer guns. Arms employing this unique principle, in various types and styles, were made in England and on the Continent before and during the period of their production in America. In spite of their fine workmanship they did not achieve the height of popularity, nor the varied individuality, to be found in American pieces.

Specimens have been found bearing the names of such noted makers as: Durs Egg, Samuel Nock, John Day, Redferry, Bentley, and Henfield of England; Gosset and Cessier of France; H. Anschutz & Sohne in Suhl; John Muller in Switzerland; C. A. Rubans in Spain, and N. S. Jesson of Kiobeule (perhaps Kobenhaven for Copenhagen) to say nothing of J. Hermand of Belgium and others of undetermined location.

Mention has been made in a previous chapter of the unusualness of the all-metal Underhammer pistols. For the most part these uncommon arms are of American origin. It is therefore of real interest to encounter not one foreign Underhammer of all metal construction, but a cased pair—complete with accessories. Such a set is the pair by H. Anschutz & Sohne. This striking pair of odd, yet somewhat dainty design and excellent workmanship was made early in the percussion period by one of the noted German makers. Not only is it unusual in all-metal but all the more so with folding triggers, which are not ordinarily found on the all-metal Underhammers. First sold in 1924 by the Walpole Galleries, this splendid pair has, at one time or another, graced prominent arms collections in America.

Most of the foreign Underhammers have a bit more professional, or refined, appearance than do those made in this country. This may be due in part to the fact that many of them were made by men long experienced in the art of gunmaking. Then too, the Continental gunsmiths were noted for their fine craftsmanship. It was something in which they were trained from early childhood, after which they were required to serve an extended apprenticeship to a master craftsman in their respective field. Thus, in addition to the principle of the Underhammer, they add the fine engraving, attention to detail and excellent finish so typical of their arms. All of which add up to some mighty nice Underhammer specimens. Let it be hoped that someone over there may undertake a serious study of the European arms with the hammer on the under side for the benefit of all collectors, and students of arms.

European makers of Underhammers had at least one thing in common with their American contemporaries; they did not produce the guns in quantity. Uncommon as they are, it is most unusual to encounter more than one (or a very limited number at best) from any one maker. In fact it is seldom that two unmarked pieces of identical design show up. Certainly the Underhammers were never the product of mass production, either in Europe or America.

From the specimens observed it appears that breech-loading Underhammers received more attention from gunsmiths abroad than was accorded the system in this country. Outside of the Greene rifle, it is rarely that guns employing breech-loading are encountered in this country.

Representative specimens of the well designed, and produced, Foreign Underhammers add a touch of color and sparkle to any collection of this intriguing class of arms—with the hammer on the underside of the barrel.

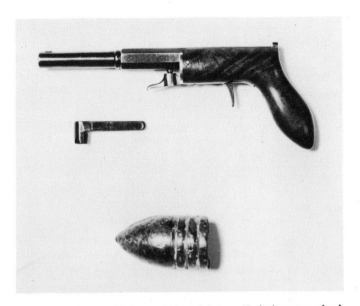

FIGURE 47. A completely working miniature Underhammer pistol of the New England type, fabricated by the skilled, and eminently noted Alton J. Jones. The tiny guns made by this master craftsman have for years held the admiration of all who appreciate beautiful craftsmanship. Stamped on the top strap A. JONES Serial No. 1. Reproduced actual size, with a .58 caliber minie ball for comparison. *Author's Collection.*

"*Pieces De Resistance*"...

AS IN EVERY OTHER PHASE of gun collecting, so it is with the Underhammers, there are to be found specimens which by their very nature, design, ornamentation, mechanical ingenuity or uniqueness are lifted out of the ordinary and set apart from the otherwise common types. Sometimes they may be the product of some noted maker—as for instance the fine Billinghurst target arms, which are prized in any collection or the unusual and desirable all-metal pistols by such makers as Bosworth, Anschutz and others.

More often, however, they are the only ones of their types or makes known to collectors. This fact, plus some outstanding feature or char-

[61]

acteristic, serves to place them in a class by themselves. A few such pieces will be described in this chapter.

Appealing to both collector and layman alike are the two miniature Underhammers illustrated in the book, Fig. 47 and Fig. 52. Even though of contemporary fabrication they are the special pets in the author's collection. Made by two fine craftsmen they are exquisite examples of the gunsmiths' art, and are the only ones known.

Marked or unmarked, the all-metal Underhammers fall into this group of prized pieces, for they are seldom encountered. Less than half a dozen were noted among all the guns studied. Of this number only the Bosworth, and Anschutz, pairs carry the name of the maker. The fabricators of the others are unknown. In design and shape, these guns of all-metal, follow the general pattern set by the rest of the Underhammers—that of individuality.

As out of the ordinary as the all-metal Underhammers are, it is a rare treat, and rewarding experience, to find a pair of them together with accessories. Such sets are the Bosworth and Anschutz pairs illustrated in the Pictorial Section. Not shown is the metal case, which may not have been original with the Bosworths, but is of the same period as the guns, and there seems to be no doubt but what it has encased the guns and accessories from that time to the present. On the other hand the Anschutz pair, with all accessories are to be found in their original case.

Cased pairs of Underhammer pistols, particularly of American make, are seldom encountered. This may be attributed to the fact that each maker followed his own inclination in making the guns and rarely made two with the same identical features as is usually associated with a pair. Then, too, the majority of Underhammers, whether pistols or rifles, which have been examined have seen considerable use, an indication that they, like their cousins the Kentucky pistols, were designed primarily for service. One pair of pistols, with consecutive serial numbers is to be found in the illustrated section. It is the only such pair to put in an appearance in this survey, and is believed to be most unusual. Needless to say they are the special pets of their owner.

Unquestionably each collector has pieces, which for one reason or another he considers as notably outstanding, and therefore as particular pets, or to put it more definitely, his "pieces de resistance."

Without detracting from any other fine Underhammers, and there are many, two "ultra" pieces are presented here for the first time, in a setting amidst their kind. They are the full stocked Chase and the Oak Cutlass Pistol.

As if the unusual method of having the hammer operate around the trigger guard were not enough to set it apart from the ordinary, its maker, J. Chase, gave it an added feature, a full stock! Even though the Under-hammers were produced during the era of the percussion Kentucky pistols it remained for this maker to fabricate one of the few known specimens of a true Kentucky type Underhammer.

Although the stock had been roughed up a bit from usage, the metal parts, some of which are beautifully engraved, are in splendid condition; and the gun itself is in fine shooting condition. Illustrated with the gun is a target recently shot by Paul N. Crockett, former owner, with this fine old "prize" of the Underhammers.

It is regrettable that nothing seems to be known of the maker, J. Chase, for certainly the work displayed on this gun sets him apart as a master gunsmith. The underside of the barrel retains much of its original brown finish. The patent breech and tooling on the metal parts is of the finest workmanship, and the balance of the gun is excellent. Truly it is a splendid example of a most unusual Underhammer of other years.

Without doubt one of the "pieces de resistance" among Underham-mers is the Cutlass Pistol bearing the name C. OAK & SON, JACKSON-VILLE. So far as is known it is the only one of its kind, and the story of its finding is proof that even in this day and age anything can happen in gun collecting.

Some years ago George W. Campbell, father of Capt. Richard E. Campbell, U.S.M.C., former owner of the gun, purchased a house in Owosso, near Flint, Michigan. Upon close examination, the attic of the old house of pre-Civil War construction, yielded three old guns of other years. Hidden away under the eaves were found an Allen & Thurber pistol; a Colt Model 1860, .44 caliber revolver; and this Cutlass Pistol. The latter two were in excellently preserved condition, so well in fact that Mr. E. D. Campbell, father-in-law of Capt. Campbell, won the first prize in the Greenfield Village Revolver match of 1957 with the old Colt six-gun.

What a story the old Underhammer could tell if it but had the means to talk. That it was carried for quite a spell by its original owner is attested to by the well-worn leather holster in which the gun was found. Was it carried by a member of the Anti-Slavery Underground movement, did it see service in the War between the states, could it have been a trophy

[63]

of War from some particular engagement, did it once belong to a sea captain, when and by whom was it hidden away in the attic? These and many other questions will in all probability, plague us for years to come. Because it seems that any answers to all such questions will at best be but conjecture, for the past of the old gun is destined to remain in obscurity.

Even though the gun bears the name of C. OAK & SON there may be a question that it was actually produced by them. It may be that it was made up on special order for them by some unknown gunsmith. In 1852 Calvin Oak, his family including two sons, C. D., age 17, and B. E., age 7, moved from Vermont to Jacksonville, Florida. In 1856 he opened an Undertaking Establishment and a Marble Works at 71 West Forsythe Street, under the name of C. Oak & Son. In the 1870 City Directory of Jacksonville he is listed as having been a maker of metallic burial cases at Oak's Marble Works. His son, C. C. was listed as a watchmaker. The younger son, who took over the business in 1881 at the death of his father, was in the business with the elder Oak.

It seems reasonable to assume then that the Cutlass Pistol was made sometime during the first four years of Calvin Oak's residence in Jacksonville. Perhaps he carried it with him on the long journey from Vermont to Jacksonville; who knows. It is hoped that further research will throw more light on this unique Underhammer Cutlass Pistol.

Even though there are no identifying marks to be found on it, the beautiful specimen illustrated from the Dr. Norborne Clarke's collection most certainly falls into the category of prized pieces. For sheer beauty of design and workmanship it is in a class by itself. Undoubtedly the one who fashioned this arm was a master decorator, both in wood and metal. The amount of care, patience and time lavished upon the gun must have been amazing, if we are to judge by the finished product. It is most unfortunate that the photo of it cannot be reproduced in color so that those who have not had the privilege of personally examining this work of art could also enjoy its beauty. It is said that the gun was once one of a pair, the mate to it having lost in a fire when a southern plantation home belonging to Mr. R. C. Peebles in Aliceville, Alabama, was enveloped by flames. What a pity that it should have come to such a tragic end.

Just because an Underhammer is unmarked does not necessarily mean that it is less desirable. The fact is that some unmarked specimens are more to be desired than many marked pieces. Take for example the unmarked pair included here and shown in Fig. 165. Without doubt this unique pair of side button trigger Underhammers serves to prove the fact that most guns stand on their own insofar as desirability is concerned, and that value is based on the condition, uniqueness and scarcity of the individual arm. Judged by these standards this pair, by long odds, are assured of a prominent place in this category of prized arms. They are unique in mechanism, nearly in original condition, and, the only ones known. What more can be said? Then too, consider the case of the full stocked pill-lock pistol (Fig. 306). Neither a pill-lock or Underhammer are scarce in themselves—but the combination of the two makes for a highly desirable addition to any collection—even though the gun is totally unmarked.

On the other hand value alone may not set this or that piece apart in its owner's eyes. Small guns, such as the Carleton pair may, by the very fact of having been brought together after several years separation, reserve for them a special place in the inner sanctum of a collector's favorites. Or perhaps the beauty of workmanship of the Barlow pair, the novelty of the Day Cane gun, the sentimentality which may be attached to the first Underhammer in your collection—these and other idiosyncrasies of the individual collector will offer reasons enough for the including certain arms in his favorite "pieces de resistance."

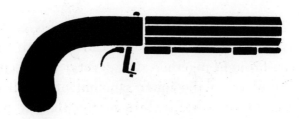

FIGURE 48.

ETHAN ALLEN

Born September 2, 1808
Died January 7, 1871

Noted American gunsmith, and one of the earliest
producers of Underhammer pistols in this country.

Pen sketch from a photo supplied by Philip F. Van Cleave

Some Noted American Makers . . .

IT IS TO BE REGRETTED that little or nothing is known
of the majority of gunsmiths who made Underhammers. Working quietly
and unobtrusively in village, hamlet or city they were often more concerned with making a good gun than with publicizing themselves. In the
thinking of that day, to do the best possible job on whatever they were
doing was the finest kind of advertising for their product. Thus it is that

many of the fine old guns have come down to us through the years with nothing known of their makers, even though names do appear on the arms.

Take for instance the case of WILLIAM BILLINGHURST, one of the most noted and skilled of the early gunsmiths. Guns by him are well known and prized. It is known that he received several orders from Royalty abroad, so fine was his work. His target rifles and Underhammer pistols are outstanding examples of the gunsmith's art, and noted for their accuracy. But even in Rochester, N. Y., where he lived and worked for more than forty years, very little is known of the man himself. So it is that often a man's work lives after him.

The following paragraphs then can, at best, be but a brief, flitting sketch of a few of the makers of Underhammers. No effort will be made to place them in proper sequence, either as to period or prominence.

ASA STORY, West Windsor, Vt., emerges today as one of the earliest makers of Underhammers, both rifles and pistols. He was active before and after 1830. Though specimens of his arms are rarely encountered, and little is known of him, he did pass on to gun lovers a legacy in the form of a well-known pupil.

NICANOR KENDALL, Windsor, Vt., one of the truly great names among gunmakers, was, according to old family records, an apprentice to Asa Story. That he learned his trade well is evidenced by the examples of his splendid Underhammer pistols and rifles which are to be found in many collections today. Kendall opened under his own name in 1835. Many of his guns were made at the Windsor prison, using prison labor. Finer work was done by more skilled mechanics. At least some of the barrels used on his arms were made by Remington. In 1838 the name of the firm was changed to Kendall & Co. Kendall gave up the gun business in 1842, but a year later he formed a partnership with Richard S. Lawrence, a man destined to go far in arms manufacturing. In 1844 S. E. Robbins joined the firm and the name became Robbins, Kendall & Lawrence. Kendall died on December 24, 1861.

DAVID H. HILLIARD, Cornish, N. H., is reported to have purchased the rights to produce the Kendall Underhammers around 1842, at the time Kendall ceased to be active in gun making. Some of the finest Underhammer target pistols bear the name of Hilliard. In addition he also made rifles, both of the Underhammer and regular types. Hilliard on occasions used barrels made by Remington. D. H. Hilliard continued in business until his death in 1877, when he was succeeded by his son, George C. Hilliard.

H. J. HALE, Worcester, Mass., was active from around 1840 to 1852. His guns which show up more frequently than do many others are well made both as to workmanship and finish. All of his pistols examined bear the caliber designations mentioned earlier in the book. Some of his pistols bear the US stamping, which affords a puzzle to many collectors.

ETHAN ALLEN, Grafton, Mass., started the manufacture of "under-cock" pistols in 1834 and continued making them for several years after his merger with Thurber, his brother-in-law, in 1838. In 1842 Allen & Thurber moved to Norwich, Conn., and in 1847 to Worcester, Mass. The late Harley J. Van Cleave, who did a prodigious amount of research on the Allen arms (and which work is being carried on by his son, Philip F. Van Cleave) had access to some of Allen's day books and wrote that the Allen pocket rifles sold for from $4. to $4.50 per pair in 1847. Those with long barrels brought $5. It will be a notable day when the Van Cleave research is made available to collectors in the form of a book.

GIBBS, TIFFANY & CO., Sturbridge, Mass., largest of the manufacturers in the Sturbridge area, was a partnership formed in 1833 between Enoch Gibbs and Lucian Tiffany. They began the manufacturing of pistols in a small building in Westville, a part of Southbridge, Mass. Later they moved into a better structure built by David K. Porter near a dam across Hobb's Creek in Sturbridge. The place was known at the time by the name of Pistol Shop and Pond. Due to the number of pistols carrying their name which have come down to us today they must have been more productive than many of the others. In 1838 Mr. Tiffany moved from Sturbridge to Hartford and apparently the firm ceased operation soon thereafter.

NATHANIEL RIDER & CO., Southbridge, Mass., was located in "Shuttleville," a part of Southbridge; and their active period seems to have been from 1840 to 1857. Early historical accounts mention "the Riders were engaged at one time or another in the manufacturing of pistols." This would indicate that there must have been more than one, perhaps father and son, or brothers. This same account continues: "The term 'Rider's Pistol Factory' has often been applied to the plant of the Litchfield Shuttle Company, and it is probably true that pistols were made there, perhaps in the building which occupied the spot of the one burned down."

QUINNEBAUGH RIFLE MFG CO., Southbridge, Mass., was, according to old reports, but another name for the Rider Company. Active date appears to have been around 1850.

ASHTONS—P. H. ASHTON, W. ASHTON, or W. A., Middletown, Conn. These noted gunsmiths were no relation to Henry Aston (note name spelling), well-known maker of martial arms, even though Peter Ashton was at one time a partner of his. Peter H. and his brother William were gunsmiths in their own right. Sons of Peter Ashton of England, they came to this country at the same time. Their main period of activity seems to have been around 1850, possibly before and afterwards for some years. Peter H. continued through the time of the Civil War and had a war contract for making Springfield rifled musket barrels. He is reported to have used the building formerly occupied by the famous Simeon North, previous to his death in 1852.

BACON & CO., Norwich, Conn., was one of the few makers of Underhammer pistols who also made a full line of other guns: single-shot, pepperboxes, revolvers—both in percussion and cartridge types. Established in 1852 by Thomas K. Bacon, the firm, under three name changes, continued in operation until 1888.

NORMAN S. BROCKWAY, Bellows Falls, Vt. Many users of muzzle-loading rifles regard this Vermont gunsmith as one of the most remarkable gun makers of his time. He was born in South Charlestown, N. H., on March 13, 1841. Three years later his family moved to Bellows Falls, Vt., where he grew to manhood. During the Civil War he worked as a filer in the Springfield Armory; and in 1864 he went to work for the Norwich Arms Company of Norwich, Conn. This firm at the time was engaged in fulfilling a government contract for making rifles. In March, 1865, Brockway became associated with Smith & Wesson as a turret lathe operator. After a year in their employ he returned to Bellows Falls to assist his father in building

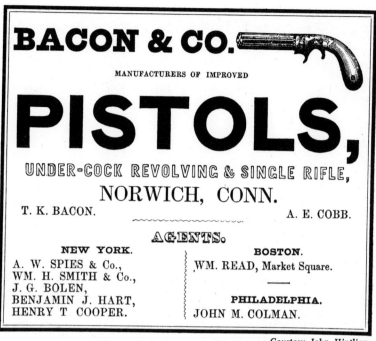

Courtesy John Hintlian

FIGURE 49. Around 1847 Bacon & Co. used this advertisement to feature their new 6-shot Underhammer Pepperbox. It appeared in the *Connecticut Business Directory*.

a house. Upon its completion he set to work to build a shop of his own, even to fabricating his own tools.

His rifle barrels were made from "the best English Cast Steel," or cast steel from E. Remington & Sons when he couldn't get the former. While the majority of his rifles were based on the regular side-hammer style, he did, on occasions, produce the finest of Underhammer target rifles. "Uncle Norman" Brockway lived to the ripe old age of 95 years, a lifetime which saw the greatest development in gun making of any like period in recorded history.

THE LATEST IMPROVEMENT IN
FIRE ARMS!

THE SIX BARREL SELF-REVOLVING & SELF COCKING
PISTOL,
MANUFACTURED BY
BLUNT & SYMS, 44 Chatham-st.
NEW YORK.

This Pistol is decidedly the best constructed self-cocking Pistol in use, for the following reasons:—1st. The simplicity of the Lock, there being but six working parts, being much less than in an ordinary Gun Lock.—2. The Barrel being made of one solid piece of cast steel, cannot be bursted or blown apart.—3d. It has no Lock or Hammer on the top to obstruct the sight, and the nipples or cones being placed in a horizontal direction in the barrel, prevents the Caps from being lost off, or struck so as to cause them to explode in any accidental manner.

This Pistol can be discharged six times in a very few seconds by merely pulling the Trigger. These Pistols are warranted not to get out of repair, all the working parts being made of steel; and they can be furnished by the manufacturers lower than any other in the market, at wholesale and retail.

N. B.—We have constantly on hand for sale the largest quantity and the best assortment of *FOWLING PIECES, &c. &c.* to be found in the city, viz:

Single Barrel Guns, from - - $2 to 25 00	*Rifles of our own make, from* - $5 to 40 00
do American made, our own manufacture at $2 75	*Muskets for Military, Prize do. and a large quantity*
Double Barrel, from - - - $6 to 75 00	*Low priced for Shipping.*
Dueling Guns of every size and quality,	*Pistols of all the various qualities.*

Ships, Cutlasses, Blunderbusses, Percussion Caps, Powder Flasks, Shot Bags, Powder, Shot, and every other article in the line, which they offer on good terms, at Wholesale and Retail.

BLUNT & SYMS,
44 CHATHAM ST.

FIGURE 50. Early Blunt & Syms broadside featring their 6-shot Underhammer pepperbox. This advertising sheet would indicate that the firm did manfacture some of the Underhammers themselves, even though they were generally regarded as importers.

Courtesy New York Historical Society, Belle C. Landauer Collection

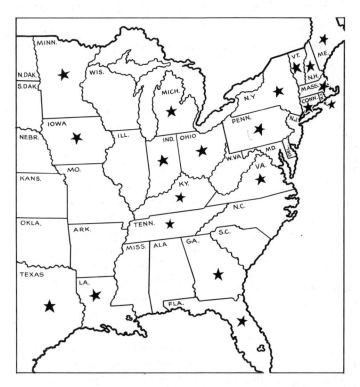

FIGURE 51. Map showing states in which Underhammer guns are known to have been fabricated. Not shown is California, in which Underhammer rifles were also produced.

Listing of Makers or Agents . . .

SINCE MANY of the makers of rifles also made an occasional pistol, or perhaps vice versa, the following list will include all known makers of Underhammer arms, principally American. Mention should be made here that sometimes the name to be found on a gun does not indicate the actual maker. It may well be that it is that of the dealer, agent, or even the owner. However, for the sake of identity, and convenient reference, the names are listed as they have appeared on various specimens.

This list is compiled from names taken from actual arms, standard reference books, listings in early catalogs, and from meager writings of the past. Such a list cannot, at best, be final or complete. As the years go by additional arms may be encountered stamped with names not included here. This does not make the arm any more rare or desirable; it only means that through the years it has remained in more or less the same hands and has not therefore become generally known through published lists.

It is hoped though that this listing will serve as a start in the right direction for a more complete unveiling of the real story of the Underhammer guns.

AMERICAN MAKERS, OR AGENTS

Name	Address	Date
C. B. ALLEN	Springfield, Massachusetts	1836-1841
ETHAN ALLEN	Grafton, Massachusetts	1832-1838
ALLEN & THURBER	Grafton, Massachusetts	1838-1842
	Norwich, Connecticut	1842-1847
	Worcester, Massachusetts	1847-1849
ANDREWS FERRY & CO.	Stafford, Connecticut	
ANDRUS & OSBORN	Canton, Connecticut	1847-1850
	Southbridge, Massachusetts	1850-1851
	Middletown, Connecticut	circa 1852
PETER H. ASHTON	Middletown, Connecticut	circa 1854
WM. ASHTON	Middletown, Connecticut	circa 1854
ASHTON'S		
J. BABCOCK		
MOSES BABCOCK	Charlestown, Massachusetts	1838-1874
BACON & CO.	Norwich, Connecticut	1852-1888
GEORGE A. BADGER	Concord, New Hampshire	1865-1868
B. A. BAILEY		
S. S. BAIRD	Chittenden, Vermont	
J. BARLOW	Moscow, Indiana	1840-1859
J. BARNES		
A. C. BARRINGTON	Lebanon, New Hampshire	
S. BASSETT		
T. BENNETT		
WM. BILLINGHURST	Rochester, New York	1830-1880
C. BIRD & CO. (Bird Bros.)	Philadelphia, Pennsylvania	1790-1830
BLUNT & SYMS	New York, New York	1837-1865
B. M. BOSWORTH	Warren, Pennsylvania	circa 1849
JAMES BOWN	Pittsburgh, Pennsylvania	1848-1886
WM. BRIGGS (W. B.)	Norristown, Pennsylvania	1848-1850
NORMAN S. BROCKWAY	Bellows Falls, Vermont	1867-1900
JOHN BROWN	Fremont, New Hampshire	1857-1870
JONATHAN BROWNING	Kanesville, Iowa	circa 1849
WILLIAM CALDERWOOD	Philadelphia, Pennsylvania	1807-1819
S. W. CARD		
MICHAEL CARLETON & CO.	Haverhill, New Hampshire	1830
CASE WILLARD & CO.	New Hartford, Connecticut	
JOHN M. CASWELL	Lansingburgh, Albany and Lewisburg, New York	1815-1836
E. CHAMBERLAIN	Southbridge, Massachusetts	circa 1850
P. F. CHARPIE	Mt. Vernon, Ohio	

Name	Address	Date
J. CHASE		
D. H. COLSON	Eaton, New York	
ASHABELL COOK	Clayton, New York	
J. R. COOPER	New York, New York	1844-1850
COX & SON	Atlanta, Georgia	1845-1847
MARION F. CRANDALL	Gowanda, New York	circa 1850
A, DAVIS, Jr.	Stafford, Connecticut	
NELSON DELANY	Reading, Pennsylvania	1845-1872
J. DEMERITT	Montpelier, Vermont	
A. C. DUNHAM		
H. E. DUNHAM		
J. H. DURKEE	Lebanon, New Hampshire	
J. I. EASTMAN	Jaffrey, New Hampshire	
J. EATON	Concord, New Hampshire	
D. S. EBERSOL		
H. S. EDGERTON	German, New York	circa 1855
	Chenango, New York	
H. E. ESTES	Columbia, Tennessee	
WILLIAM B. FARRINGTON	Lebanon, New Hampshire	1855-1864
GILMAN E. FOGG	Manchester, New Hampshire	1845-1870
B. FOWLER, Jr.	Hartford, Connecticut	1835-1850
J. A. FRANCE	Cobbleskill, New York	circa 1860
WARREN GILL (W. G.)	Whitneyville, Connecticut	circa 1846
GIBBS & FOSTER	Sturbridge, Massachusetts	1840-1845
GIBBS TIFFANY & CO.	Sturbridge, Massachusetts	1833-1837
R. GOLDEN		
RAYMOND P. GORNING	Detroit, Michigan	
E. GRAY		
J. GRAVES	Bangor, Maine	circa 1860
H. J. HALE	Bristol, Connecticut	1840-1852
HALE & TULLER	Hartford, Connecticut	
HALL (Hall's Patent)		
H. B. HAMILTON	Lebanon, New Hampshire	
J. HARDING	Covington, Ky.	
H. B. HARRINGTON	Lebanon, New Hampshire	
T. HEATON		
DAVID H. HILLIARD	Cornish, New Hampshire	1860-1880
HITCHCOCK & MUZZY	Low Moor, New England	
N. JARVIS	Heidelberg, Township, Pennsylvania	1840
J. JENISON & CO.	Southbridge, Massachusetts	
WM. JOHNSON	Haverhill, Massachusetts	
A. J. JONES		
N. JONES		
DAVE KEMMERER, Jr.	Lehighton, Pennsylvania	circa 1850
NICANOR KENDALL	Windsor, Vermont	1835-1842
KENDALL & LAWRENCE	Windsor, Vermont	1842-1844
W. K. NEW YORK		
L. & S. NEW YORK		

Name	Address	Date
A. D. LAWS		
HENRY E. LEMAN	Lancaster, Pennsylvania	1834-
HIRAM LEWIS LEONARD		circa 1850
JAMES LITTLE	Bellefonte, Pennsylvania	
WILLIAM LONG	Augusta, Maine	
M. D. & A. G. LULL	Woodstock, Vermont	
TURNER LULL & CO.	Woodstock, Vermont	
W. W. M.		
M. MARBLE		
WM. W. McQUERRY	Jeffersonville, Indiana	
MEAD & ADRIANCE		
H. C. MILLIKEN	St. Louis, Missouri	circa 1835
MORGAN		
WM. NEAL	Bangor, Maine	1845-1878
A. O. NIEDNER	Dowagiac, Michigan	
NORCROSS & ALLEN	Evansville, Iowa	
C. OAK & SON	Jacksonville, Florida	circa 1854
S. OSBORN	Canton, Ohio	circa 1860
J. P.		
A. PARKER	Ludlow, Vermont	
	DeSota, Iowa	
SAMUEL PIKE	Troy, New York	circa 1834
J. D. PILLSBURY		
HENRY PRATT	Roxbury, Massachusetts	1832-1861
	Boston, Massachusetts	1861-1875
E. PUTNEY	Southbridge, Massachusetts	
QUINABAUG RIFLE MFG. CO	Southbridge, Massachusetts	circa 1850
CHARLES RAMSDELL	Bangor, Maine	
WM. RAYMOND	Winona, Minneapolis	1864-1865
P. A. REINHARD	Loudonville, Ohio	1853-1896
J. B. REVOL	New Orleans, Louisiana	1842-1885
NATHANIEL RIDER & CO.	Southbridge, Massachusetts	1840-1857
ROBBINS, KENDALL & LAWRENCE	Windsort, Vermont	1844-1846
A. RUGGLES	Stafford, Connecticut	circa 1855
D. D. SACKETT	Westfield, Massachusetts	circa 1860
M. S. SANDERSON ⎱	Vergennes, Vermont	1855-1860
GEORGE V. SEAVER ⎰		
J. SEABURY & CO.	Southbridge, Massachusetts	1861
SHAW & LEDOYT	Stafford, Connecticut	
H. SHEETS		
J. SIMPSON	New Britain, Connecticut	circa 1835
CHARLES SLOTTERBEK	San Francisco, California	circa 1858
	Lakeport, California	
HENRY SLOTTERBEK	Los Angeles, California	circa 1868
A. SMITH	Philadelphia, Pennsylvania	
M. SMITH	Greenfield, Massachusetts	circa 1835
ANTON SPELLERBERG	Philadelphia, Pennsylvania	circa 1861
A. W. SPIES	New York, New York	1832-1860

Name	Address	Date
T. J. STAFFORD	New Haven, Connecticut	1860-1861
ASA STORY	West Windsor, Vermont	1835-1843
CHARLES P. STUART	Binghamton, New York	1850-1883
SAMUEL SUTHERLAND	Richmond, Virginia	1852-1869
A. THRESHER	Stafford, Connecticut	1855
TILDEN & THURBER		
GEORGE W. TRYON	Philadelphia, Pennsylvania	1836-1866
VILLEGIA & SLOTTERBEK	San Francisco	1868
WALLACE & OSBORN	Canton, Connecticut	1850
HORACE WARNER	Ridgeway, Pennsylvania	1860-1890
J. E. W.		
WHEELOCK & STEWART		
T. H. WHIPPLE	Cambridge, Vermont	1855
E. B. WHITE		
J. D. WHITE	Williamstown, Vermont	
JOHN M. WHITESIDES	Abington, Virginia	
WILLARD & CO.	Boston, Massachusetts	1860
ABRAHAM WILLIAMS	Owego, New York	circa 1845
	Covington, Kentucky	
WILLIAM WINGERT	Detroit, Michigan	1845-1867
B. C. WOOD	Painted Post, New York	circa 1860
N. WOODBURY & CO.	Woodstock, Vermont	
A. C. WRIGHT	Fitchburg, Massachusetts	

FOREIGN

Name	Address	Date
H. ANSCHUTZ & SOHNE	Suhl	1793-1806
J. BARLOW	Lichfield, England	
JOHN BENTLEY	London	1852-1885
BROWN	England	
J. B. CESSIER	France	circa 1850
J. R. COOPER	England	1840-1853
JOHN DAY	England	circa 1832
DURS EGG	London	1785-1834
GOSSETT	Paris	circa 1840
COL. PETER HAWKER	London	
WARD HENFIELD	England	
J. HERMAND	Belgium	
N. S. JESSON	Kiobeule	
KENDALL	Windsor, Berkshire	1860
MONTAIGNY et FUSNOT	Brussels, Belgium	circa 1849-1851
JOHAN MULLER	Bern	circa 1840
SAMUEL NOCK	London	1806-1860
BARTHOLOMEW REDFERN	Birmingham	1790-1836
REDFERN & BOURNE	Birmingham	1836-1860
REDFERRY	London	
C. A. RUBANS	Spain	
J. TARATT (or TARRATT)	London	1850

MAKERS, OR AGENTS—alphabetical by States

CALIFORNIA
Slotterbek, Charles
Slotterbek, Henry
Villegia & Slotterbek

CONNECTICUT
Allen & Thurber
Andrews Ferry & Co.
Andrus & Osborn
Ashton, P. H.
Ashton, Wm.
Ashton's
Bacon & Co.
Case Willard & Co.
Davis, Jr., A.
Fowler, Jr., B.
Gill, Warren (WG)
Hale, H. J.
Hale & Tuller
Ruggles, A.
Shaw & Ledoyt
Simpson, J.
Stafford, T. J.
Thresher, A.
Wallace & Osborn

FLORIDA
Oak, C & Son

GEORGIA
Cox & Son

INDIANA
Barlow, J.
McQuerry, Wm. W.

IOWA
Browning, Johnathan
Norcross & Allen
Parker, A.

KENTUCKY
Harding, J.
William, Abraham

LOUISIANA
Revol, J. B.

MASSACHUSETTS
Allen, C. B.
Allen, Ethan
Allen & Thurber
Andrus & Osborn
Babcock, Mose
Chamberlain, E.

Gibbs & Foster
Gibbs Tiffany & Co.
Jenison, J. & Co.
Johnson, Wm.
Pratt, Henry
Putney, E.
Quinabaugh Rifle Mfg. Co.
Rider, Nathaniel, & Co.
Sackett, D. S.
Seabury, J., & Co.
Smith, M.
Williard & Co.
Wright, A. C.

MAINE
Graves, J.
Long, William
Neal, Wm.
Ramsdell, Charles

MICHIGAN
Gorning, Raymond P.
Niedner, A. O.
Wingert, William

MINNESOTA
Raymond, Wm.

NEW HAMPSHIRE
Badger, Geo. A.
Barrington, A. C.
Brown, John
Carleton, Michael, & Co.
Durkee, J. H.
Eastman, J. I.
Eaton, J.
Farrington, William B.
Fogg, Gilman E.
Hamilton, H. B.
Harrington, H. B.
Hilliard, David H.

NEW YORK
Billinghurst, Wm.
Blunt & Syms
Caswell, John M.
Colson, D. H.
Cook, Ashabel
Cooper, J. R.
Crandall, Marion F.
Edgerton, H. S.
France, J. A.

W. K.
L & S
Pike, Samuel
Spies, A. W.
Stuart, Charles P.
Williams, Abraham
Wood, B. C.

OHIO
Charpie, P. F.
Osborn, S.
Reinhard, P. A.

PENNSYLVANIA
Bird, C., & Co.
Briggs, Wm. (WB)
Calderwood, Wm.
Delany, Nelson
Jarvis, N.
Kemmerer, Dave
Lehman, Henry E.
Little, James
Smith, A.
Spellerberg, Anton
Tryon, Geo. W.
Warner, Horace

RHODE ISLAND
Bosworth, B. M.

TENNESSEE
Estes, H.

VIRGINIA
Sutherland, Samuel
Whitesides, John M.

VERMONT
Baird, S. S.
Brockway, Norman S.
Demeritt, J.
Kendall, Nicanor
Kendall & Lawrence
Lull, M. D. & A. G.
Lull, Turner & Co.
Parker, A.
Robbins, Kendall & Lawren
Sanderson, M. S.
Seaver, Geo. V.
Story, Asa
Whipple, T. H.
White, J. D.
Woodbury, N., & Co.

FIGURE 52. An engrossing and enjoyable hobby is the collecting and study
of the old guns of yesteryear.

Gleanings . . .

OVER THE YEARS illustrations of Underhammer guns have
occasionally appeared in magazines, books, catalogs and dealer lists. Often
the accompanying description, was inadequate, inaccurate or totally lacking; yet the picture of the gun was of more than passing interest. Rather
than discard such material which would, for the most part, prove disap-
pointing if reproduced direct from the source, pen and ink outline drawings have been called upon. In this manner it has been possible to include
many Underhammers, the whereabouts of which are unknown and where
actual photographs have not been available.

It is hoped that these simple illustrations of both marked and unmarked specimens, gleaned from many sources, will add to the interest
and presentation of the story of Underhammer Guns.

[79]

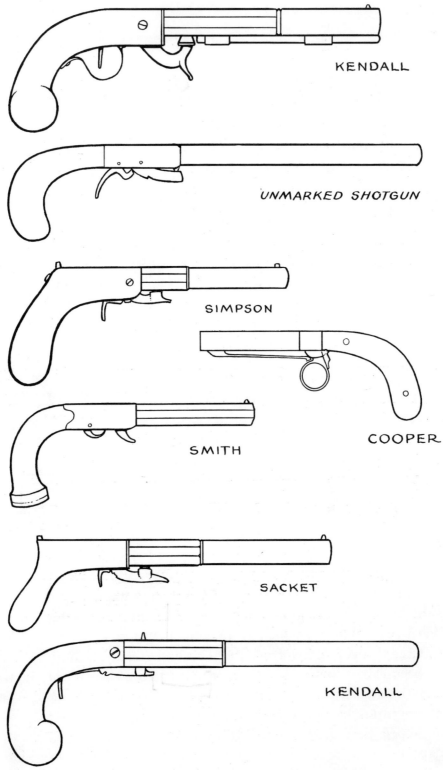

KENDALL

UNMARKED SHOTGUN

SIMPSON

COOPER

SMITH

SACKET

KENDALL

FIGURE 53.

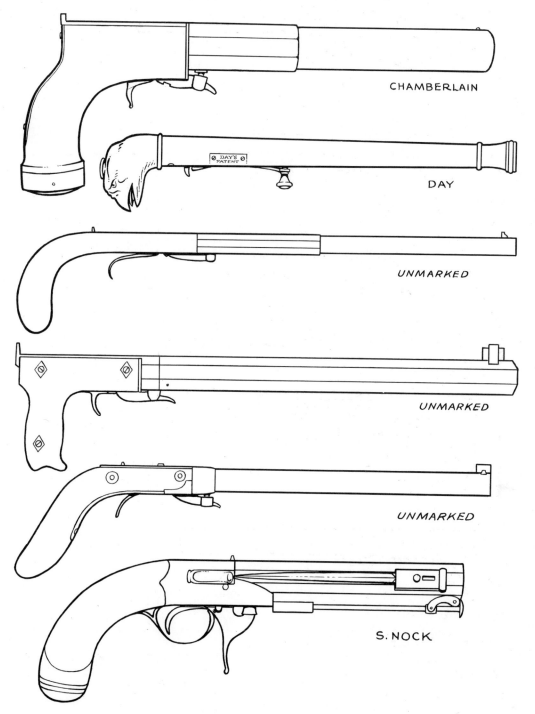

CHAMBERLAIN

DAY

UNMARKED

UNMARKED

UNMARKED

S. NOCK

FIGURE 54.

[81]

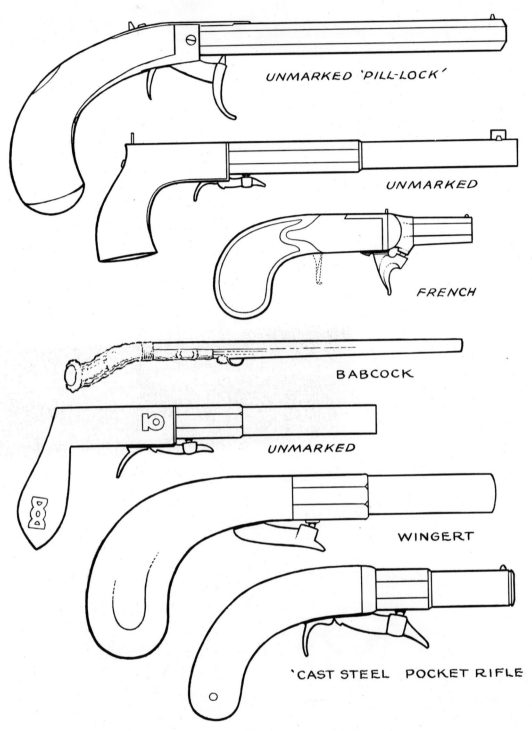

UNMARKED 'PILL-LOCK'

UNMARKED

FRENCH

BABCOCK

UNMARKED

WINGERT

'CAST STEEL POCKET RIFLE

FIGURE 55.

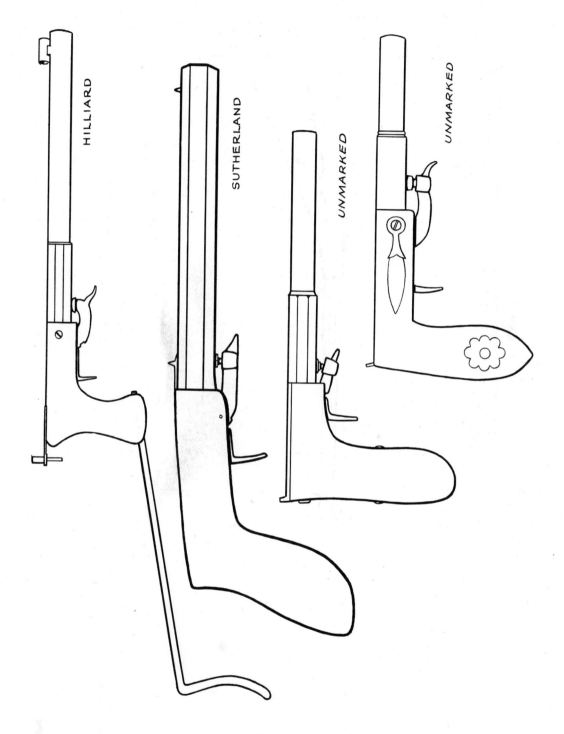

FIGURE 56.

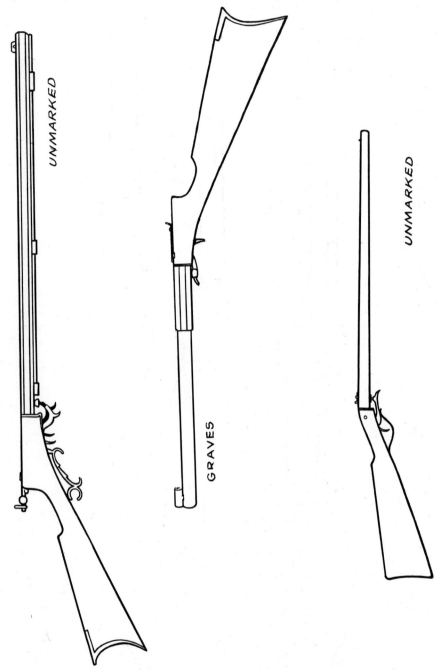

FIGURE 57

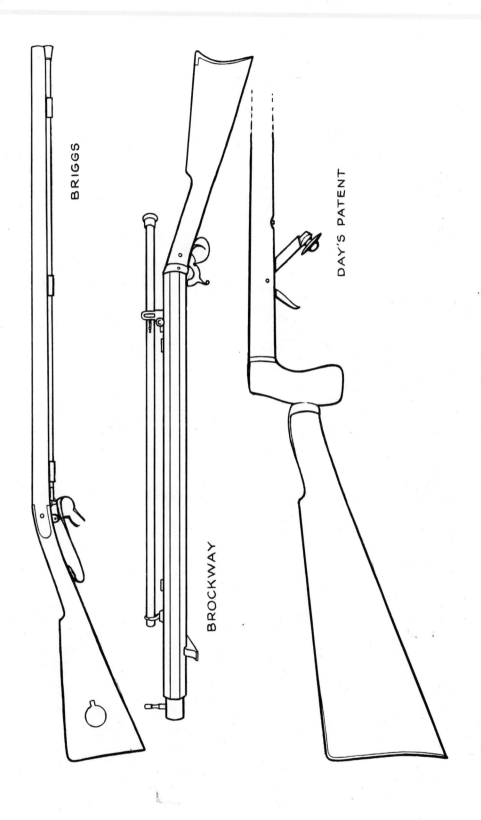

BRIGGS

BROCKWAY

DAY'S PATENT

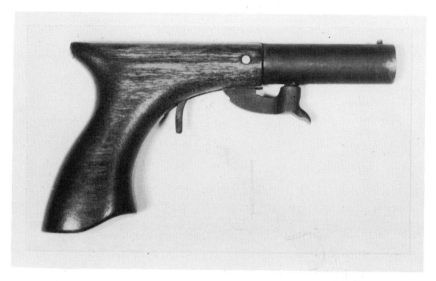

Figure 59.

R. W. MITCHELL   .20 caliber
1 3/8 inches round, rifled, barrel. Case hardened top strap stamped:
R. W. MITCHELL
W. LEBANON, N. H.
Curly maple grip. This tiny working model of an Underhammer pistol is
a beautiful example of the craftsmanship displayed by Ray W. Mitchell
in his fabrication of present day Underhammer guns.

Serial No. 1 on all parts
Reproduced actual size.

Author's Collection

Pictorial Section . . .

THE PHOTOGRAPHS here are not to scale. Gathered from
many sources they are reproduced with but one thought uppermost: to
illustrate a wide variety of arms, in the best possible manner. Additional
details, where known, are covered in the brief word descriptions of the
guns, on the opposite pages, or under the photographs, as the case may be.

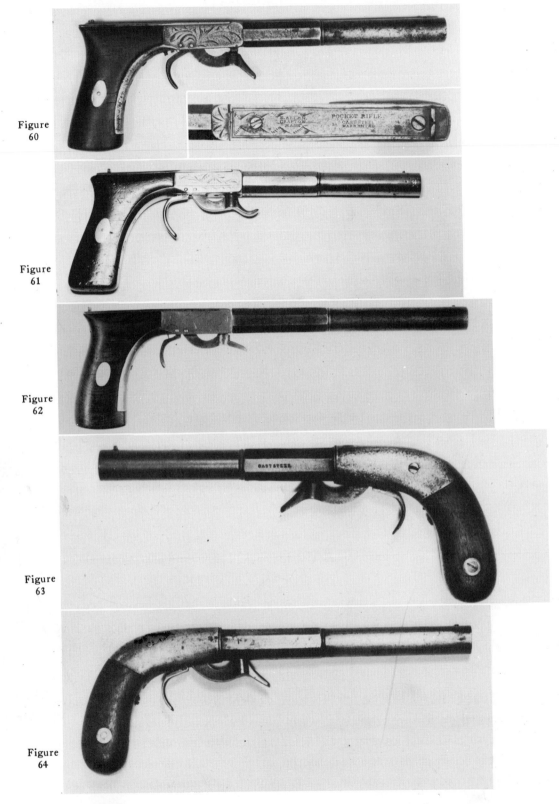

Figure
60

Figure
61

Figure
62

Figure
63

Figure
64

[88]

Section 1 — Marked Underhammer Pistols

E. ALLEN. Fig. 60   .31 caliber

5⅛ inch, round-octagon, rifled barrel, walnut grip with silver inlay on both sides. Top of frame stamped:

E. ALLEN   POCKET RIFLE
GRAFTON   CAST STEEL
MASS.   WARRANTED

Ethan Allen was one of the early makers of Underhammer pistols, having started in the middle 1830's. Many of his guns were sold through dealers, and their name will be found stamped on them, instead of Allen's. He is believed to have been one of, if not the first to use the term, "Pocket Rifle," for his handguns. It is most fitting that guns by this noted American gunsmith should lead this parade of Underhammer Guns.

Total length, 9¾ inches.   Serial No. 91
                                                              Author's Collection

E. ALLEN. Fig. 61   .32 caliber

5½ inch, round-octagon, rifled barrel. Engraved frame, the top of which is stamped:

E. ALLEN POCKET RIFLE CAST STEEL WARRANTED

Walnut grip with silver oval inlay on both sides.

Total length, 10 inches.

                                                    M. L. McCormack Collection

E. ALLEN. Fig. 62   .34 caliber

7 inch, round-octagon, rifled barrel. Engraved frame. Walnut grip with silver oval inlay on each side. Marked:

E. ALLEN   POCKET RIFLE
CAST STEEL   WARRANTED

Production ceased on this model late in 1847. During the last three months of its appearance on the market a total of 132 pairs were sold to dealers.

                                                  Winchester Museum Collection

ALLEN & THURBER. Fig. 63   .34 caliber

4¾ inch, round-octagon, rifled barrel, stamped on the top:

ALLEN & THURBER

and on the top left slant, WORCESTER. On the left side appears the familar stamping found on so many of the Underhammer guns:

CAST STEEL

Walnut 2-piece grip. Production on this model was started in 1848.

Total length, 8 inches.   Serial No. 197
                                                              Author's Collection

ALLEN & THURBER. Fig. 64   .36 caliber

5⅝ inch, round-octagon, rifled barrel. Walnut rounded grips. Top of barrel stamped:

ALLEN & THURBER

Total length, 9 inches.   Serial No. 85
                                                   Herbert E. Green Collection

[89]

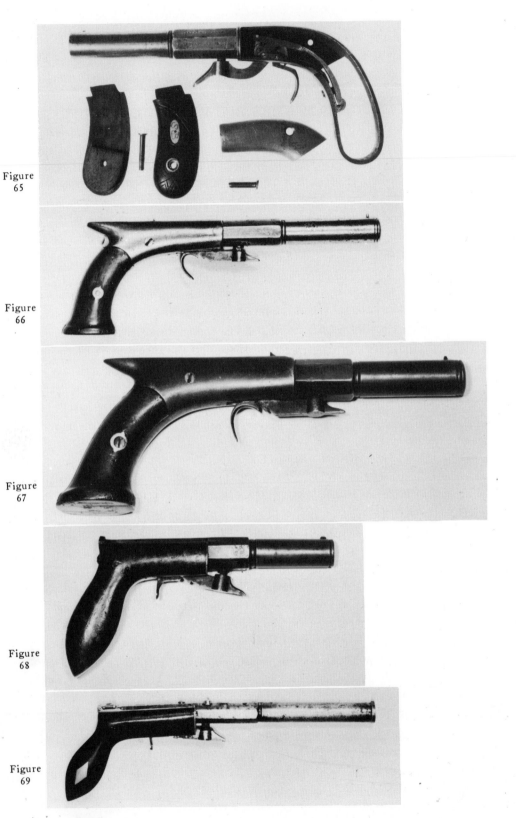

Figure
65

Figure
66

Figure
67

Figure
68

Figure
69

[90]

ALLEN & THURBER. FIG. 65   .36 caliber

4⅛ inch, round-octagon, rifled barrel. Stamped on the left top slant: ALLEN & THURBER and on the left flat: GRAFTON, MASS.
Walnut grips with oval silver inlay. This scarce arm bearing the early Grafton address is disassembled to show its simple construction.

Total length, 7¾ inches.   Serial No. 63
Philip F. Van Cleave Collection

"ANDERSON" (unmarked). FIG. 66   .48 caliber

5⅛ inch, round-octagon, rifled barrel. Steel frame with saw handle grip design. Walnut 2-piece grip. These guns of rather distinctive styling have been designated "Anderson" because diligent research by Paul C. Janke, noted collector of Houston, Texas, has indicated that they were produced in or around Anderson, Texas. Attention is called to two striking points of similarity between this piece and some of the Blunt & Syms pepperboxes. The shape and style of the saw handled grip, and the screw plates with projections to prevent turning in the wood are virtually identical in both guns. This raises the possibility that the Blunt & Syms pepperboxes may have been produced by the same maker who made these splendidly designed single-shot underhammer pistols. One point of difference between this and similar pieces is that the screw holding the side plate enters from the right side.

Total length, 10¾ inches.   Serial No. XXIII
Author's Collection

"ANDERSON" (unmarked). FIG. 67   .45 caliber

4 inch, round-octagon, rifled barrel. Rounded steel frame with saw handled grip. The unusual pocket size specimen of the commonly referred to Anderson underhammer pistol.

Total length, 10 inches.

M. L. McCormack Collection

ANDREWS FERRY & CO. FIG. 68   .36 caliber

3 inch, round-octagon, rifled barrel. Stamped on the top strap:

ANDREWS FERRY & CO.

Operating in Stafford, Conn. this company's pistols bear a striking resemblance to the guns of other makers in the immediate area. It may well be that they were agents rather than manufacturers.

Total length, 6½ inches.

M. L. McCormack Collection

ANDRUS & OSBORN. FIG. 69   .25 caliber

6 inch, round-octagon, rifled barrel. Walnut grips with silver mounting and inlays. Tiny silver stars inlaid on barrel. Top of barrel stamped with eagle and:

ANDRUS & OSBORN
CANTON, CONN.

Left side of barrel stamped CAST STEEL, under side of barrel stamped 320.

Total length, 10½ inches.

Herbert E. Green Collection

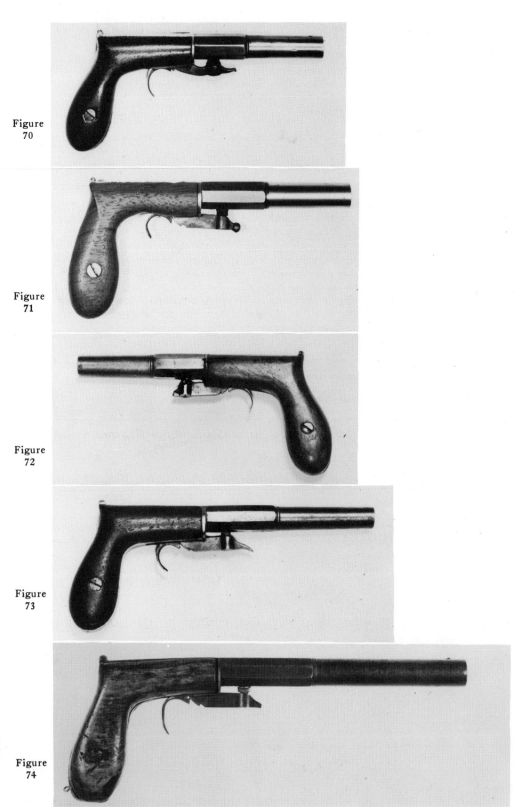

Figure
70

Figure
71

Figure
72

Figure
73

Figure
74

[92]

W. ASHTON. Fig. 70   .38 caliber

4 inch, round-octagon, rifled barrel stamped on top:

W. ASHTON

The letter N is stamped on the under side of the barrel to the rear of the nipple. Brass frame with walnut 2-piece grips.

Total length, 8 inches.

Author's Collection

W. ASHTON. Fig. 71   .28 caliber

4 inch, round-octagon, rifled barrel stamped on top:

W. ASHTON

The letter J is stamped on the left side of the brass frame, under the grip. A comparison of this Ashton with other specimens by the same maker will show that the grip has a decided right angle drop to it. William Ashton used the old Simeon North Pistol and Musket Mfg. shops around 1854. The Ashtons are often confused with Henry Aston, maker of U. S. Martial pistols. As will be noted, however, the names are spelled differently.

Total length, 7¼ inches.

Author's Collection

P. H. ASHTON. Fig. 72   .38 caliber

4 inch, round-octagon, rifled barrel. Walnut brass mounted grips. Stamped on the left side of the barrel:

P. H. ASHTON

Total length, 8 inches.

Serial No. 15
Herbert E. Green Collection

W. A. (William Ashton). Fig. 73   .38 caliber

5 inch, round-octagon, rifled barrel stamped on top:

W. A.
MIDDLN, CONN.

and, on the left slant WARRANTED CAST STEEL. Walnut 2-piece grip. This specimen has the rather unusual steel frame.

Total length, 9 inches.

Serial No. 8
Author's Collection

W. ASHTON. Fig. 74   .36 caliber

5½ inch, round-octagon barrel marked only:

W. ASHTON

Brass frame with 2-piece walnut grips.

Winchester Museum Collection

Figure
75

Figure
76

Figure
77

Figure
78

Figure
79

BACON & CO. FIG. 75   .34 caliber

3⅞ inch, round-octagon, rifled barrel, the left slant of which is stamped:

BACON & CO.
NORWICH, CONN.
CAST STEEL

Engraved steel frame. Walnut 2-piece grips.

Total length, 8 inches.   Serial No. 97

Author's Collection

BACON (unmarked). FIG. 76   .34 caliber

4⅞ inch, round-octagon, rifled barrel. Engraved steel frame. Rounded, 2-piece walnut grips.

Total length, 9 inches.   Serial No. 41

Herbert E. Green Collection

BACON. FIG. 77   .34 caliber

5⅞ inch, round-octagon, rifled barrel. Engraved steel frame. Rounded, 2-piece walnut grips. Barrel stamped:

W. A. MURRAY

AND, faintly BAC, indicating that Bacon produced the gun for W. A. Murray.

Total length, 10 inches.   Serial No. 34

Herbert E. Green Collection

BACON & CO. FIG. 78   .34 caliber

6 inch, round-octagon, smoothbore barrel. Stamped on the left top slant of the barrel:

BACON & CO.
NORWICH, CT.

and, CAST STEEL on the left flat of the barrel. Frame shows faint traces of engraving. Walnut 2-piece grips.

Total length, 10½ inches.   Serial No. 73

Author's Collection

BACON (unmarked). FIG. 79   .28 caliber

8¼ inch, round barrel. Two piece walnut grips. Though not marked, this piece has enough of the Bacon characteristics to warrant placing it in this section of the illustrated list.

Total length, 12½ inches.

Winchester Museum Collection

[95]

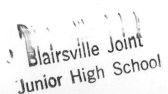

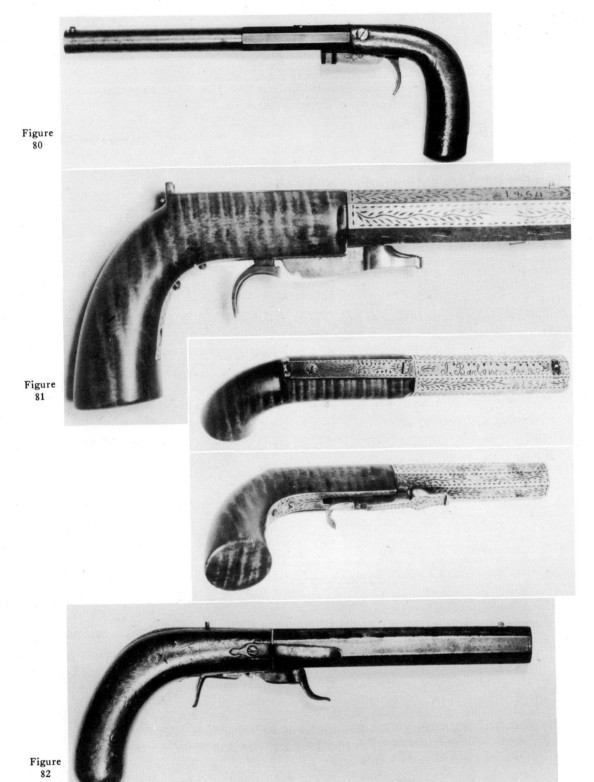

Figure
80

Figure
81

Figure
82

[96]

B. A. BAILEY. Fig. 80 .18 caliber

7¾ inch, round-octagon, smoothbore barrel. Stamped on the left top slant:

B. A. BAILEY

Walnut grip. A nice example of an indoor target pistol in which the percussion cap, plus a speck of powder, serves as the propelling agent.

Total length, 11¼ inches.

Author's Collection

J. BARLOW. Fig. 81 .34 caliber

4 inch, full-octagon, rifled barrel. Engraved on the top:

J. BARLOW   DEC 20

and on the top right slant   1854

Metal parts including, barrel, frame, hammer and screw heads are engraved with a distinctive broken line style of design. It was this makers custom to engrave his arms with the full date. Fine curly maple grip. A truly splendid example of a Mid-Western Underhammer Pistol, from the "Hoosier" State of Indiana.

Total length, 9 inches.

Author's Collection

T. BENNETT. Fig. 82 .36 caliber

6 inch, full-octagon, rifled barrel, stamped on the top side:

```
:  :  :  :  :  :  :
:   T. BENNETT    :
:  :  :  :  :  :  :
```

Engraved top strap. Walnut grip with belt hook on the right side. Underhammer pistols are rather infrequently encountered with belt hooks. A well made piece utilizing a barrel of rifle design.

Total length, 10⅝ inches.

Author's Collection

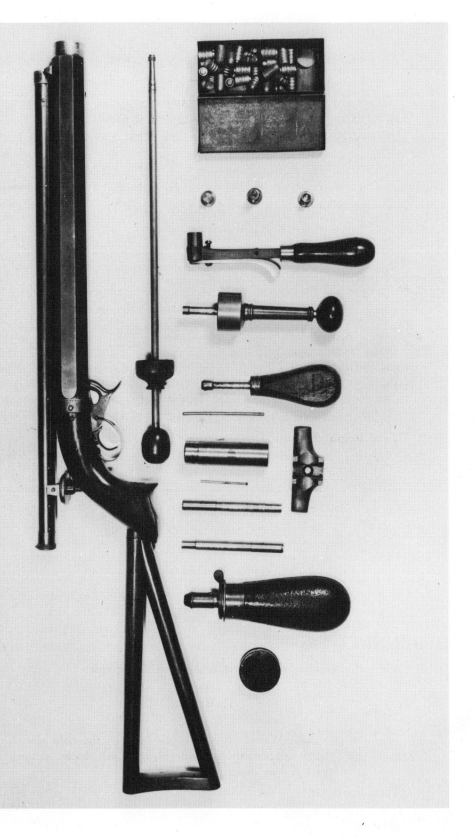

Figure
83

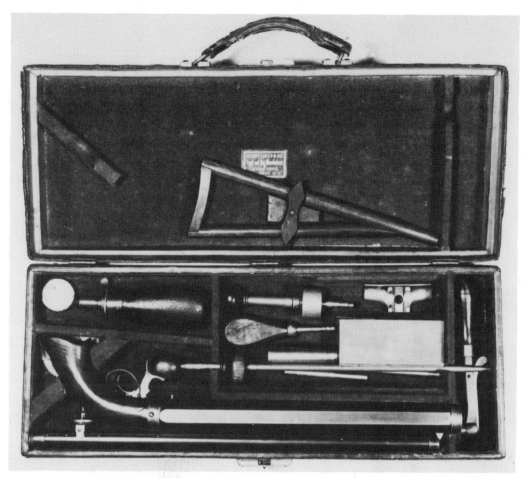

Figure
84

W. BILLINGHURST (cased set). Fig. 83-84   .38 caliber

13⅜ inch, full-octagon, rifled barrel, turned at the muzzle for a bullet starter. Top of barrel stamped:

W. BILLINGHURST   ROCHESTER, N. Y.

High finish walnut grip, with tapering hole for extension stock. The leather case includes such accessories as powder flask, bullet starter, bullet mould with three different inserts, nipple wrench, swadging tools, ramrod, bench rest, and extension stock. The entire piece is in very fine shooting condition. As will be noted, the gun is equipped with an adjustable telescope sight, and employs the usual Billinghurst type of trigger-guard mainspring.

Among those who know, Billinghurst "Buggy Rifles" are considered the finest. Few could match him for the workmanship on his arms. This cased set, made for George W. Crouch, Jr. of Rochester, N. Y., is eminently typical of Billinghurst at his best.

To have a fine Billinghurst Underhammer with all accessories is to have the acme of target Underhammer pistols.

Total length, 19 inches, not including stock.

Author's Collection

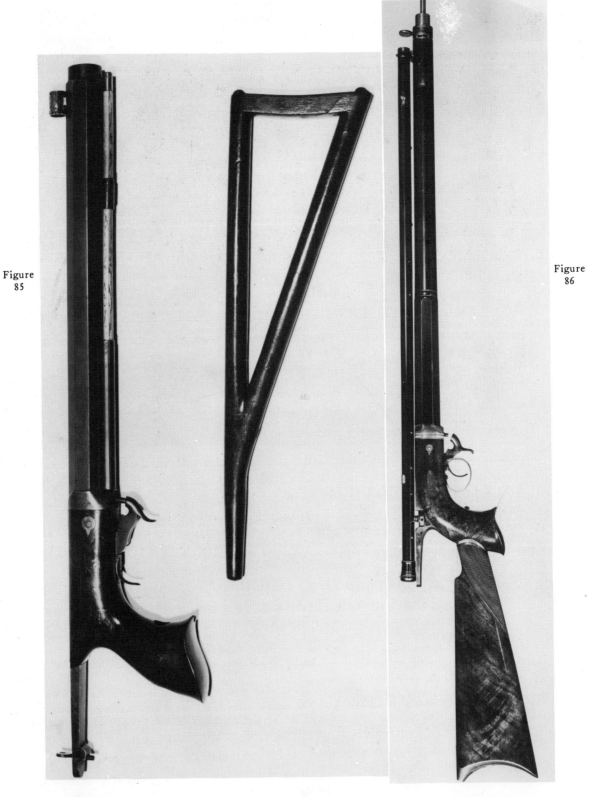

Figure
85

Figure
86

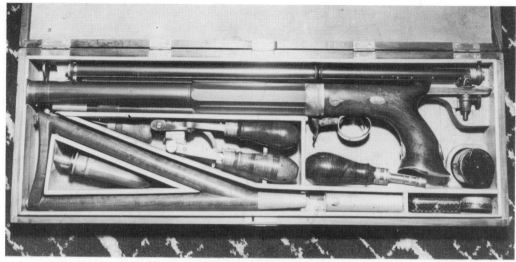

Figure
87

W. BILLINGHURST. FIG. 85 .32 caliber

12 inch, full-octagon, rifled barrel, turned at the muzzle for bullet starter. Hooded front sight and peep rear sight. Wooden extension stock.

Another of the fine Billinghurst Underhammer target pistols for which this maker was noted.

Total length without stock, 20 inches.

M. L. McCormack Collection

W. BILLINGHURST. FIG. 86 .30 caliber

18 inch, full-octagon, rifled barrel, turned at the muzzle for bullet starter. Stock of fancy American walnut. Nine gold inlays, including a layer of gold on the top of the false muzzle (designed to prevent rusting). Gold nameplate on the telescope, marked "W. Malcom, Syracuse, N.Y." Oval gold plate on butt with the name "N. Rawson," presumably the original owner.

A case of fancy walnut holds the rifle and its tools—mould, swedge, cleaning rod, etc.

Total length with extension stock, 33 inches.

John T. Amber Collection

W. BILLINGHURST. FIG. 87

Illustrating a cased, presentation, Billinghurst Underhammer Target Pistol. The gun is gold mounted and is of the saw handle variety. Both gun and accessories are in near mint condition. And the entire outfit, in a beautifully finished wooden case, is strictly fine—a real prize.

P. A. Keplinger Collection

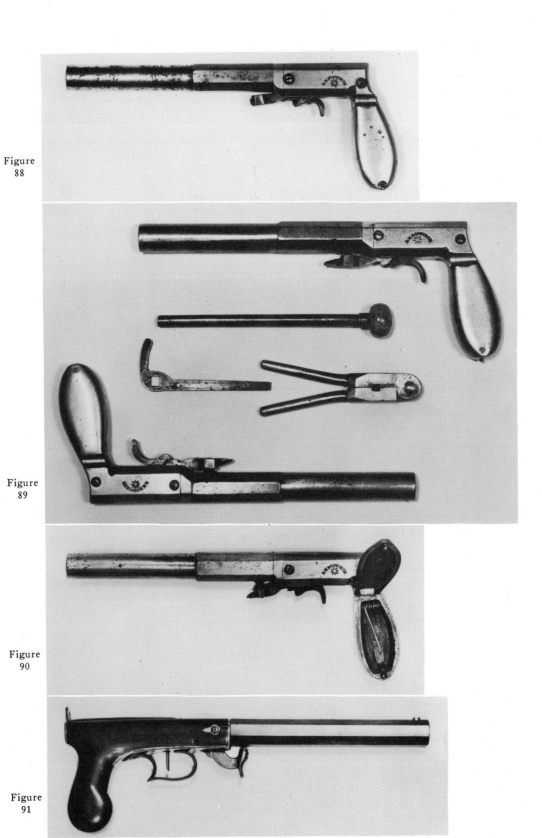

Figure
88

Figure
89

Figure
90

Figure
91

[102]

B. M. BOSWORTH. FIG. 88

.38 caliber

5⅞ inch, round-octagon, smoothbore barrel. All-metal with frame and grip of brass. Hollow grip serves as patch-box, with lid on the left side, hinged at the top. This early Bosworth does not have the catch to hold the lid down, nor the inside spring for raising the lid, as is found on the later pistols by this maker. The lid is held down by a screw in its lower edge. Stamped on the left side of the frame in a semi-circular style is the name: B. M. BOSWORTH over an asterisk.
Total length, 9½ inches.

Author's Collection

B. M. BOSWORTH. (a pair) FIG. 89

.38 caliber

5⅞ inch, round-octagon, smoothbore barrel. All-metal brass frame with patch-box in the grip. Cover, hinged at the top is on the left side. Stamped on the left side of the frame in a semi-circle:

B. M. BOSWORTH

Cased set, which includes brass bullet mould, nipple wrench screw driver and bone tipped ramrod. A highly desirable pair in fine condition.
Total length, 9½ inches.

Author's Collection

B. M. BOSWORTH. FIG. 90

.38 caliber

A view of the all-metal Bosworth with the hinged cover raised to show the hollow grip which served as a cap-box. The catch to hold the lid down, and the spring to raise the lid can be seen in the photo.

Author's Collection

W. B. (Wm. Briggs). FIG. 91

.36 caliber

7⅛ inch, full-octagon, rifled barrel, stamped on the under side:

W. B.

Adjustable rear peep sight. Walnut, brass mounted grip with iron trigger guard. The maker of this gun was undoubtedly influenced by the Hilliard style of design, which this pistol follows quite closely.
Total length, 13¼ inches.

Author's Collection

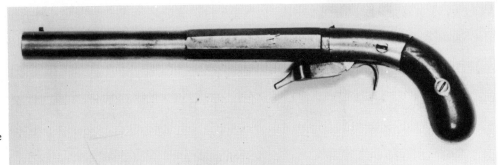

Figure
92

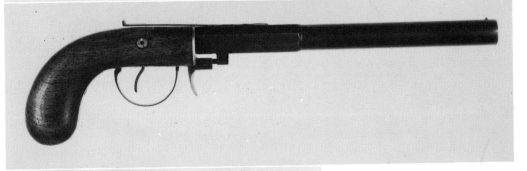

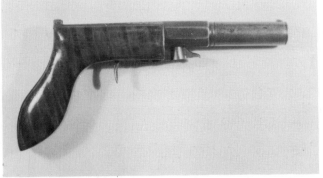

Figure
93

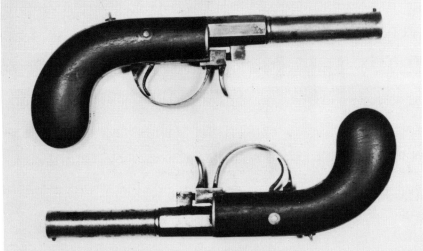

Figure
94

Figure
95

[104]

S. W. CARD. FIG. 92 .34 caliber

7¾ inch, round-octagon, smoothbore barrel. Stamped on top:

S. W. CARD   CAST STEEL

Walnut, 2-piece grip.
Another of the puzzling guns with features similar to the Blunt & Syms and Anderson pistols. This one also is stamped with the unusual Roman numerals.
Total length, 10¾ inches.

Serial No. XX
Author's Collection

M. CARLETON & CO. (a pair). FIG. 93 .34 caliber

3½ inch, round-octagon, rifled barrel. Walnut, brass mounted grip bears No. 20. Brass strap through which the trigger operates is stamped:

M. CARLETON & CO.
PATENT

Trigger guard is the mainspring, which actuates the hammer in a horizontal, rather than a vertical, manner. A patent for a "Percussion Lock" was issued to M. Carleton of Haverhill, N. H. on Dec. 23, 1830, but it is not known if it applied to the under-hammer pistols produced by him. The extension of the breech plug on one gun is marked thus, II II, and on the other II III. This is the only known pair of Carleton Underhammer Pocket Pistols.
Total length, 7½ inches.

Author's Collection

M. CARLETON & CO. FIG. 94 .30 caliber

7¾ inch, round-octagon barrel. Brass trigger plate stamped:

M. CARLETON & CO.
PATENT

Trigger guard forms mainspring, which pushes the hammer forward to hit the nipple, set parallel to the barrel. One of the early Underhammers.
Total length, 12 inches.

Winchester Museum Collection

CASE WILLARD & CO. FIG. 95 .31 caliber

2-15/16 inch, round-octagon, rifled barrel. Top strap marked:

CASE WILLARD & CO.
NEW HARTFORD, CONN.

Brass mounted, curly maple grip. A typical New England Underhammer pistol.
Total length, 6½ inches.

Ray C. Young Collection

Figure
96

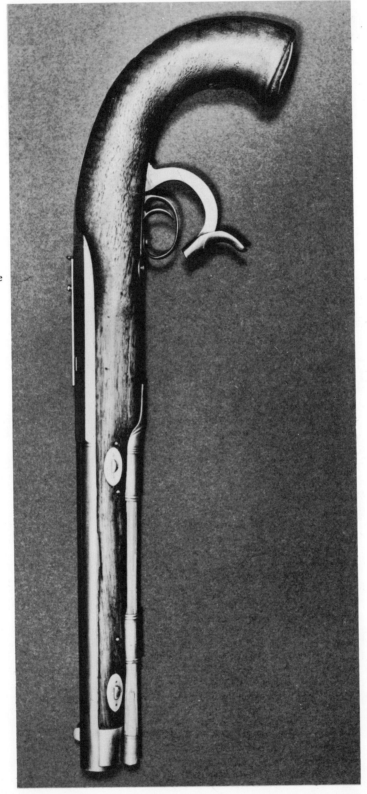

Figure
97

J. CHASE. FIG. 96-97   .34 caliber

11 inch, round-octagon, rifled barrel, the top of which is stamped: CAST STEEL.
Engraved in flowing script on the top left slant is the maker's name,

J. Chase

Barrel has patent breech, (Fig. 21). Adjustable rear sight. Engraved top strap.
FULL stock of walnut with birdshead grip. Silver shield set in rear side of grip,
and silver escutcheons for barrel pins. Brass ramrod ferrules.
This remarkable gun with its distinctive Kentucky-style full stock is still a fine
shooting old gun. Illustrated with it is a target shot by the gun's former owner,
Paul N. Crockett. The target was shot with .36 caliber Hensley & Gibbs conical
bullets, with a black powder charge of 15 grains. Shooting was done at the West
Paterson Pistol Club, Route 46, West Paterson, N. J., on Sunday March 21, 1958.
Weather clear, wind 20 mph., from East, shooter facing north, snow on the ground.
Range, standard 25 yards. Time 3 to 4 P.M. Mr. Crockett's comment: "This gun
sure handles nice. There is no heavy squeeze or side pull like when firing over hammer
guns."
Truly this is a most unique and beautifully designed Underhammer pistol.
Total length, 16 inches.

Author's Collection

[107]

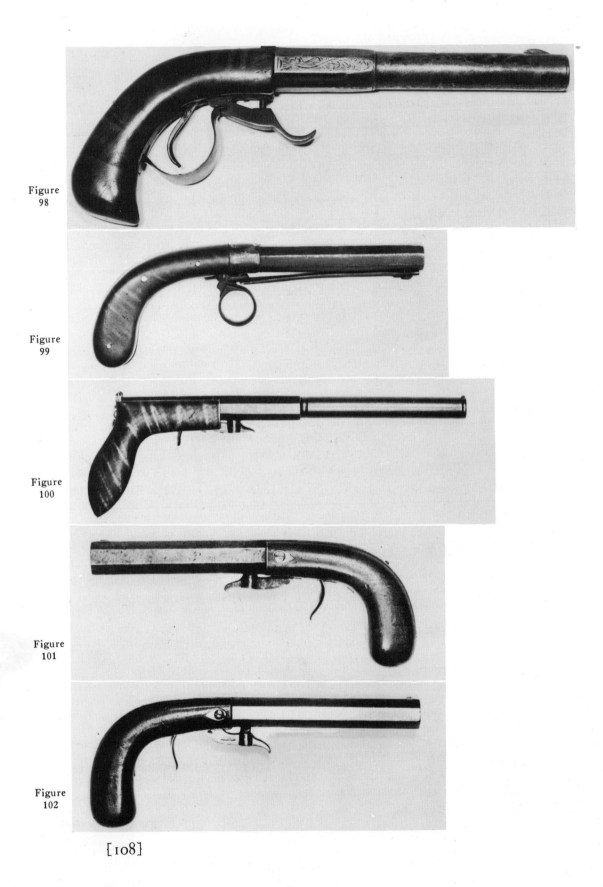

Figure
98

Figure
99

Figure
100

Figure
101

Figure
102

A. COOK. Fig. 98 .38 caliber

6½ inch, round-octagon barrel with large spread eagle on the top flat. Trigger guard also serves as the mainspring. Unusual shape of trigger and placement of guard so low on the grip sets this gun apart from any of the others. Octagon part of the barrel is engraved.

Total length, 10½ inches. *M. L. McCormack Collection*

J. R. COOPER. Fig. 99 .31 caliber

4⅛ inch, full-octagon, rifled barrel. Stamped on the left side of the rounded iron frame is the following:

J. R. COOPER
PATENT
1849

Attached to the under side of the barrel, near the muzzle, is a combination spring hammer. Swinging it to the side permits the nipple to be capped. As the ring trigger is pulled it draws the spring downward until it slips off the projection on the trigger and flies back up to detonate the cap. J. R. Cooper is listed as having worked in both American and England.

Total length, 8½ inches. *Author's Collection*

A. DAVIS, Jr. Fig. 100 .31 caliber

7⅜ inch, round-octagon, rifled barrel (138 on under side of barrel). Top strap marked:

A. DAVIS, JR.
STAFFORD
CONN.

and on either side of the name are the well-known eagle markings. Except in this instance they are not alike. The one on the right has the full detail generally known, while the one on the left follows the same shape of the other but is completely in outline, Striped curly maple grip, mounted with brass. (See Fig. 3.)

Total length, 11¼ inches Serial No. 4
Author's Collection

N. DELANY. Fig. 101 .48 caliber

4⅞ inch, full-octagon, rifled barrel. Rounded walnut grip. Iron backstrap with brass mountings on under side of grip. Right side of barrel, on top slant, stamped:

N. DELANY

Another splendid example of the early rifle barrel influence.

Total length, 9 inches *Author's Collection*

N. DELANY (unmarked). Fig. 102 .41 caliber

5½ inch, full-octagon, rifled barrel. Burnished bright metal barrel and mountings. Polished walnut grip. Identified as a Delany by close comparison with the marked specimen above.

Total length, 9¾ inches Serial No. 4
Author's Collection

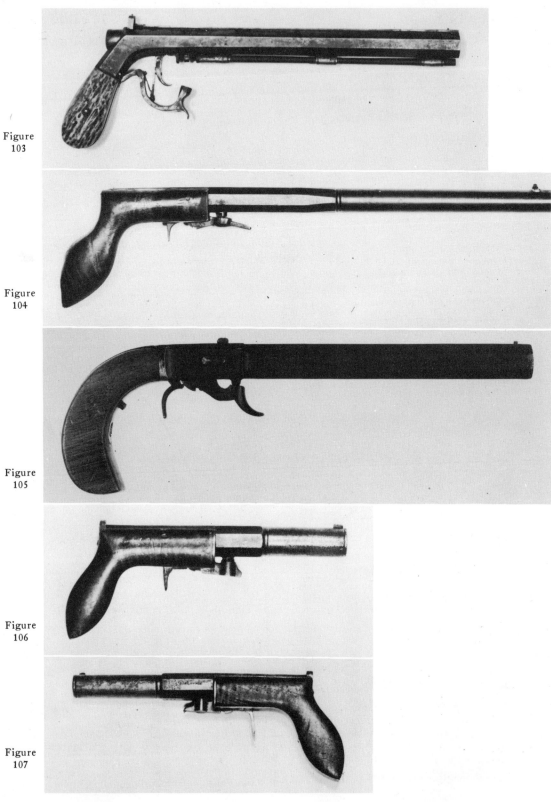

Figure
103

Figure
104

Figure
105

Figure
106

Figure
107

J. DEMERITT. Fig. 103 .27 caliber

10 inch, full-octagon, rifled barrel formed as one piece with the frame and grip. Stamped on the left side of frame, and on the right side of hammer:

J. DEMERITT
MONTPELIER
VERMONT

Breech-block unscrews to permit loading or cleaning. Trigger guard is hammer. A spring catch inside of the guard serves as a catch to hold hammer in cocked position. Set screw in trigger permits the adjusting for a feather touch in firing. Adjustable rear sight. Stag 2-piece grips.

Total length, 11½ inches. *Author's Collection*

J. H. DREW, Fig. 104 .34 caliber

10⅜ inch, round-octagon, rifled barrel, stamped on the top flat: J. H. DREW.

Silver mounted, walnut grip with metal slot for attaching extension stock. A fine old target pistol of New England styling.

Total length, 14⅞ inches. *Author's Collection*

H. ESTES. Fig. 105 .44 mm. caliber

7 inch, full-octagon barrel stamped: H. ESTES COLUMBIA, TENN.

Iron mounted birdshead grip. Flat side lock to which was originally attached a belt hook.

Total length, 11 inches. *Winchester Museum Collection*

GIBBS TIFFANY & CO. Fig. 106 .31 caliber

3 inch, round-octagon, rifled barrel (184 on under side of barrel), the top of which is stamped:

E. HUTCHINGS & CO.
AGENTS—BALTO

Top of the back strap is marked with the well-known eagle and

GIBBS TIFFANY & CO.
STURBRIDGE, MASS.

Walnut, brass mounted, grip. A typical New England Underhammer of the small pocket size.

Total length, 6½ inches. Serial No. 2
Author's Collection

GIBBS TIFFANY & CO. Fig. 107 .27 caliber

4 inch, round-octagon, rifled barrel (240 on barrel). Stamped on the top of the barrel:

E. HUTCHINGS & CO.
AGENTS—BALTO

and on the top of the engraved back strap, along with the usual eagle, is stamped:

GIBBS TIFFANY & CO.
STURBRIDGE, MASS.

Walnut grip with brass mounting. Engraved on the brass mounting in italic letters is the name D. P. EVANS.

Total length, 7¾ inches. Serial S 74
Author's Collection

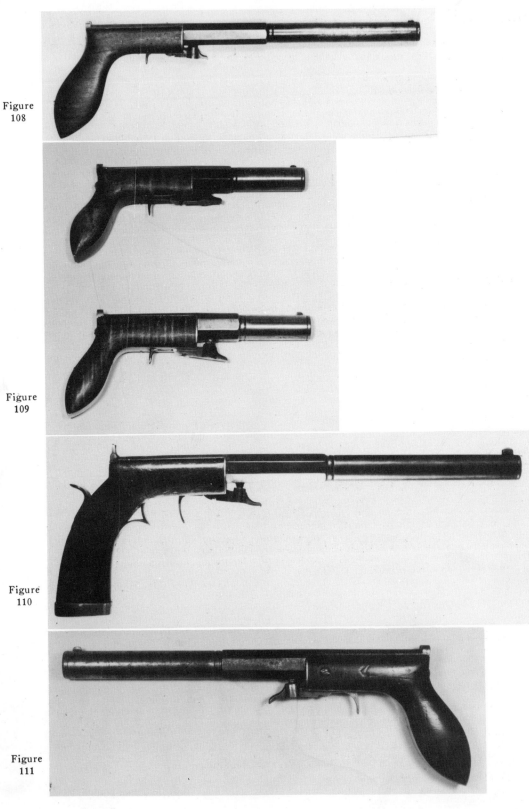

Figure
108

Figure
109

Figure
110

Figure
111

GIBBS TIFFANY & CO. Fig. 108   .34 caliber

7¾ inch, round-octagon, rifled barrel (140 on under side of barrel). Brass mounted walnut grip. Top of barrel stamped, in addition to the usual eagle:

E. HUTCHINGS & CO.
AGENTS—BALTO

GIBBS TIFFANY & CO.
STURBRIDGE, MASS.

Total length, 12¼ inches.

Serial No. 30 T

Herbert E. Green Collection

GIBBS TIFFANY & CO. Fig. 109 (a pair)   .28 caliber

4 inch, round-octagon, rifled barrel. Brass mounted curly maple grip.
An unusual pair of Underhammers with serial numbers #21 and #22. Underhammers in pairs are infrequently met with, and more so with consecutive serial numbers.

M. L. McCormack Collection

GIBBS TIFFANY & CO. Fig. 110   .34 caliber

7½ inch, round-octagon, rifled barrel (152 on under side of barrel). Smooth polished grip mounted with silver band. Stamped on top:

GIBBS TIFFANY & CO.   STURBRIDGE, MASS.

and MADE FOR ROGERS BROS. & CO., 52 MARKET ST. PHILAD.

Milwaukee Public Museum Collection .

GIBBS TIFFANY & CO. Fig. 111   .34 caliber

Another specimen by this well-known New England firm. At the risk of being repetitious it is felt that the showing of several arms by some of these well known makers may prove of interest to the readers of this study.
Total length, 10 inches.

Museum of Historical Arts

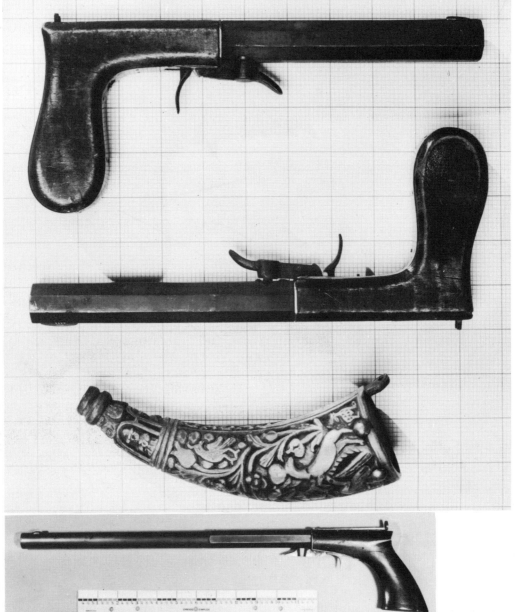

Figure
112

Figure
113

S. GOLDEN (a pair). FIG. 112

.34 caliber

6 inch, octagon, rifled barrels. The rifling is straight with no twist. Top of both barrels carry the maker's name, S. GOLDEN. On the left side flat of the barrel of one gun is stamped the word "Little". This is believed to be that of an early well-known barrel maker in Pennsylvania. Stocks are plain maple, brass mounted. An elaborately carved powder horn of Aztec or Mexican characteristics completes the set. According to an old label, dated 1862 and attached to the butt of both guns, "these guns were used by Major Robert Davenport, Kentucky Volunteer in the War with Mexico."

Total length, 10¾ inches.

Photo and description supplied by Col. L. C. Jackson

J. GRAVES. FIG. 113

.36 caliber

14⅜ inch barrel, round and octagon. Marked:

J. GRAVES
BANGOR, ME.

Saw handle grip. Blade front sight and adjustable rear peep sight.
Total length, 20 inches.

Roger C. Peterson Collection

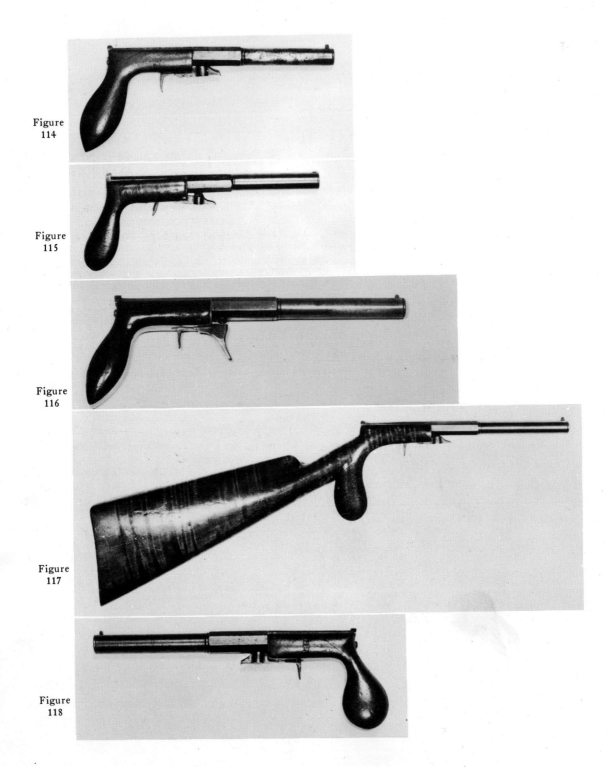

Figure
114

Figure
115

Figure
116

Figure
117

Figure
118

H. J. HALE. FIG. 114   .31 caliber

5 inch, round-octagon, rifled barrel (140 on under side of barrel). Walnut grip. Stamped on top flat of the back strap is:

H. J. HALE
WARRANTED
CAST STEEL

Total length, 9 inches.

Serial No. 920
Herbert E. Green Collection

H. J. HALE. FIG. 115   .31 caliber

5 inch round-octagon, rifled barrel (140 on under side of barrel, in front of the nipple). Engraved top strap upon which is stamped:

H. J. HALE
BRISTOL
CONNECTICUT

In addition to the familiar eagle, this gun also carries the "US" martial stamping. While there seems to be no record of any government purchase, here is a gun with the authentic marking, as found on other martial arms. Walnut, brass mounted grip. Total length, 9 inches.

Serial No. 12
Author's Collection

H. J. HALE. FIG. 116

Total length, 9 inches. Hale is another of the noted makers of Underhammer pistol, and this study is showing several of his guns. This one follows more the lines of the New England style than does his other specimens.

M. L. McCormack Collection

H. J. HALE. FIG. 117   .31 caliber

6 inch, round-octagon, rifled barrel (140 on under side of barrel). Engraved top strap on which is stamped:

H. J. HALE
WARRANTED
CAST STEEL

Integral walnut shoulder stock, with checkered pistol grip. A very unusual combination, rarely found in the Underhammers.

Total length, 21 inches.

Author's Collection

H. J. HALE. FIG. 118   .31 caliber

6 inch, round-octagon, rifled barrel (130 on under side of barrel). Stamped on top of engraved top strap:

H. J. HALE
WARRANTED
CAST STEEL

This gun has the bulbous type grip more or less peculiar to some of the arms produced by Hale. Grip is brass mounted.
Total length, 10 inches.

Serial No. 638
Author's Collection

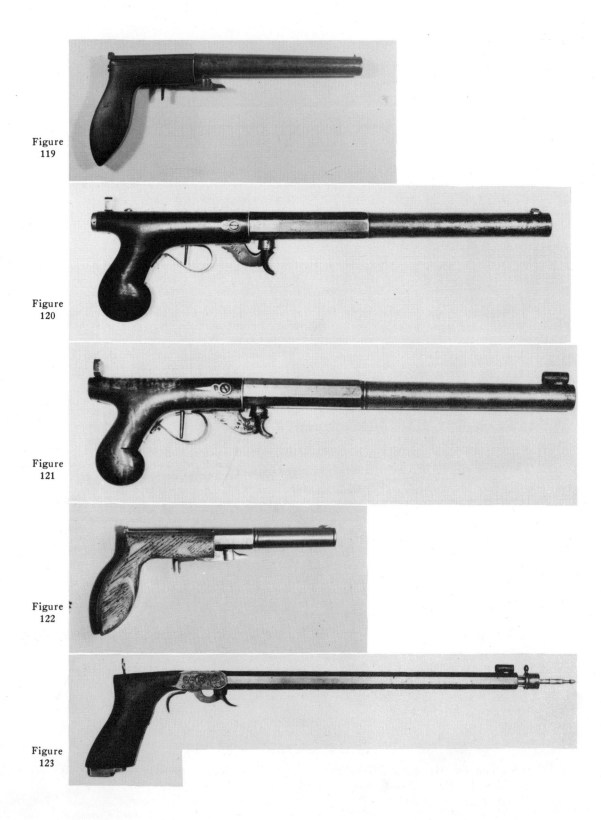

Figure
119

Figure
120

Figure
121

Figure
122

Figure
123

HALE & TULLER. FIG. 119 .44 caliber

6 inch, round-tapering barrel, stamped:

HALE & TULLER
HARTFORD
CONNECTICUT

Brass mounted walnut grip, showing the New England influence.
Total length, 9¾ inches.

Ray C. Young Collection

D. H. HILLIARD. FIG. 120 34 caliber

10½ inch, round-octagon, rifled barrel (130 on muzzle of barrel), stamped on top:

D. H. HILLIARD
CORNISH
N. H.

Barrel stamped REMINGTON. Walnut, brass mounted grip. Open front sight, adjustable rear peep sight. One of the fine Underhammer Target Pistols by this noted New Hampshire gunsmith.
Total length, 16⅛ inches.

Serial No. 98
Author's Collection

D. H. HILLIARD. FIG. 121 .34 caliber

11⅝ inch, round-octagon, rifled barrel (132 on muzzle of barrel). Stamped on the left top slant is:

D. H. HILLIARD
CORNISH
N. H.

Stamped on the underside of the barrel, in front of nipple are these figures, 2 - 3½. It has been suggested that these figure refer to the powder charge in grams. (30 to 54 grains) Engraved top strap. Hooded front sight and adjustable rear peep sight. Walnut, brass mounted, grip with iron trigger guard. Trigger must be pressed rearward to allow hammer to be cocked. A splendid example of the Target Pistols for which Hilliard was noted.
Total length, 17¼ inches.

Serial No. 167
Author's Collection

J. JENISON & CO. FIG. 122 .28 caliber

4 inch, round-octagon, rifled barrel, stamped CAST STEEL. Top strap is marked:

J. JENISON & CO.
SOUTHBRIDGE, MASS.

Oak, brass mounted, grip.
Total length, 8 inches.

Serial No. 1
Herman W. Williams, Jr. Collection

WM. JOHNSON. FIG. 123

11½ inch, octagon, rifled barrel, equipped with bullet starter with brass starter rod. Hooded front sight and rear peep sight. Engraved frame. Gun is marked:

Wm. Johnson Haverhill, Mass.

The gun is equipped for an extension stock, which unfortunately has become lost over the years. Condition of this Underhammer Target Pistol is excellent.
Total length, 17½ inches.

Mark Aziz Collection

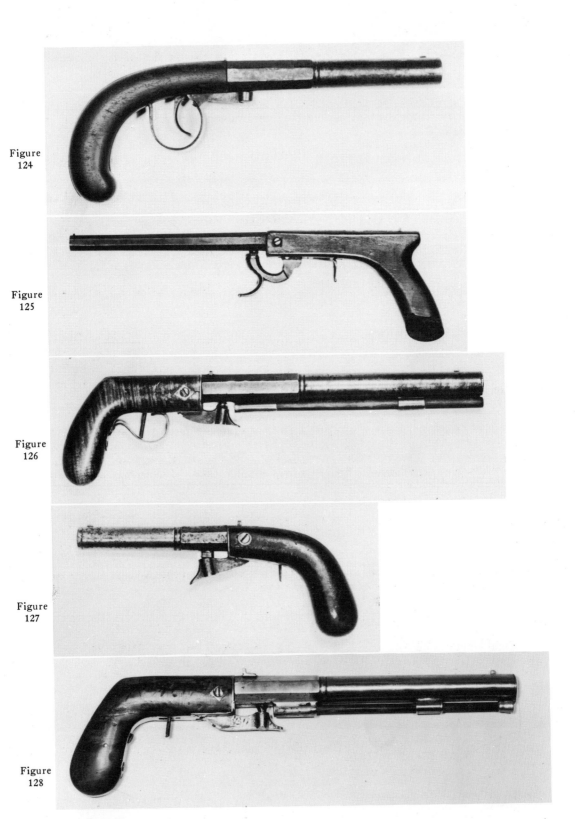

Figure
124

Figure
125

Figure
126

Figure
127

Figure
128

A. J. JONES. Fig. 124

.36 caliber

5½ inch, round-octagon, rifled barrel. Engraved on the top flat of the barrel in script letters is:

A. J. Jones

The trigger guard serves as the mainspring on this unusual double-action pistol. Iron backstrap reaches almost to the butt of the walnut grip. A Well-made gun of pleasing lines.

Total length, 9⅝ inches.

Author's Collection

KEENE. Fig. 125

.30 caliber

6 inch, full-octagon, smoothbore, tapering barrel.
Engraved top strap upon which only the following is stamped:

KEENE
N. H.

Unusual semi-circle hammer with large finger spur. Walnut grip. A very light, and rather dainty, type of Underhammer.

Total length, 11⅝ inches.

Author's Collection

N. KENDALL. Fig. 126

.41 caliber

8⅝ inch, round octagon, rifled barrel with ramrod on the underside. End of barrel stamped 89. Top of back strap stamped:

N. KENDALL
WINDSOR, VT.

Striped, curly maple grip with brass trigger plate and guard. Kendall was one of the better-known early makers, having started around 1835, after having served an apprenticeship under Asa Story.

Total length, 13⅛ inches.

Author's Collection

N. KENDALL. Fig. 127

.34 caliber

4 inch, round-octagon, rifled barrel (134 on muzzle of barrel), engraved design on the octagon part. Top of barrel stamped in two lines:

N. KENDALL
WINDSOR, VT.

Walnut grip with silver mounting around trigger. A very good representative of the small pocket pistols by Kendall.

Total length, 7½ inches.

Serial No. 12
Herbert E. Green Collection

N. KENDALL. Fig. 128

Another example of the general style followed by Kendall in making his regluar size Underhammer pistols. Kendall is perhaps more noted for his splendid target and sporting rifles of underhammer design, than for his handguns.

Total length, 12 inches.

M. L. McCormack Collection

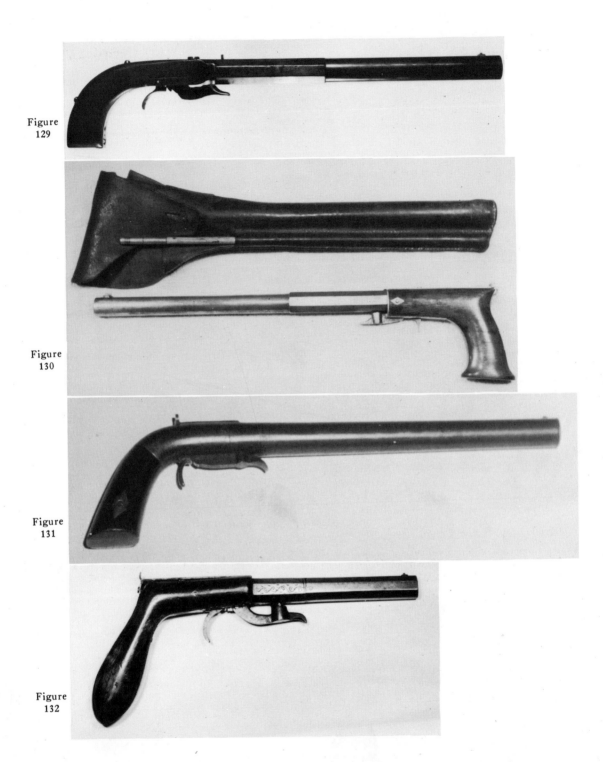

Figure
129

Figure
130

Figure
131

Figure
132

A. D. LAWS. Fig. 129 .37 caliber

11¼ inch, round-octagon barrel, the sides of which are stamped:

A. D. LAWS

Smooth flat grip.
Total length, 17¼ inches.

Milwaukee Public Museum

H. E. LEMAN. Fig. 130 .41 caliber

13⅝ inch, round-octagon, rifled barrel marked:

H. E. LEMAN

Brass trigger plate. Adjustable rear sight. Maple, saw handled, flared grip which is brass mounted. Equipped with original leather holster and ramrod, shown above the gun. Leman was a noted gun maker of Lancaster, Pa.
Total length, 19 inches.

Vincent W. Nolt Collection

LEONARD. Fig. 131 .45 caliber

10½ inch, round tapering, rifled barrel with buckhorn rear sight, and blade front sight. Rosewood grip. This is an illustration of the only-known Underhammer made by this pioneer gunsmith. Hiram Lewis Leonard (1831-1907) made most of his guns during the 1850 period while living at Houtzdale, Penna., and Central Valley, N. Y.

Dr. Harmon C. Leonard Collection

A. W. LOOMIS. Fig. 132 .32 caliber

4½ inch, tapering-octagon, engraved barrel marked:

A. W. LOOMIS
LEBANON, CT.

A variation of the typical New England style of grip, but with the customary brass mounting.
Total length, 8¾ inches.

M. L. McCormack Collection

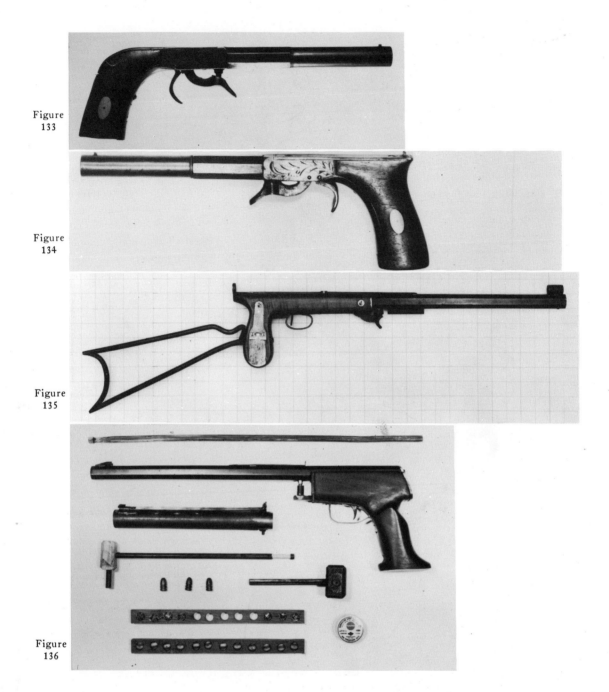

Figure
133

Figure
134

Figure
135

Figure
136

MEAD & ADRIANCE. Fig. 133   .32 caliber

5¼ inch, round-octagon, rifled barrel stamped on top:

MEAD & ADRIANCE

POCKET RIFLE   CAST STEEL   WARRANTED

Flat walnut grip with silver inlay on either side.
Total length, 10 inches.

Milwaukee Public Museum

MEAD & ADRIANCE. Fig. 134   .31 caliber

5⅛ inch, round octagon, rifled barrel. Engraved frame and top strap, upon which is stamped:

WARRANTED
CAST STEEL
POCKET RIFLE   MEAD & ADRIANCE

Walnut grip with silver oval inlay on each side. This is an Allen made Pocket Rifle, for Mead & Adriance, who were distributors and silversmiths in St. Louis, Missouri around 1835.
Total length, 10 inches.

serial No. 12
Author's Collection

H. C. MILLIKEN. Fig. 135

13½ inch, round-octagon barrel. Wooden grip with iron patchbox on right side. Hooded front sight, peep rear sight. Equipped with a skeleton extension stock of about ⅜ inch diameter. Gun marked:

H. C. MILLIKEN

Total length with stock, 32½ inches.

Mark Aziz Collection

M. I. MORGAN (unmarked). Fig. 136

.38 caliber

11½ inch, full-octagon, rifled barrel. 8½ inch round, rifled, barrel with full-ventilated rib sight. Saw-handled target type grip, brass and copper mounted.
Shown outside its case, this 1957 version with an extra barrel and accessories amply demonstrates that the art of fabricating an Underhammer pistol is not a lost art once a modern gunsmith, with a love for the old "undercock" principle sets his hand to the task of making a personal gun for shooting. Accessories include: loading blocks for patched balls, bullet starters, ramrod, patches, etc.
Etched on a diamond shape copper plate on the lid is this inscription:

Myron Irving Morgan
March 23, 1957
Portsmouth, N. H.

In addition to being a skilled gunsmith, Mr. Morgan is also a splendid shot, and has done some very impressive shooting with this gun.
Total length, 18½ inches.

Author's Collection

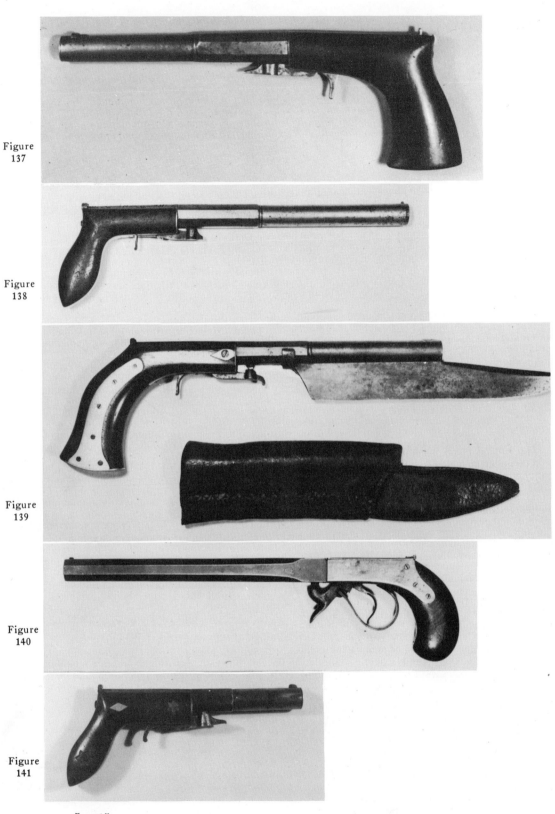

Figure
137

Figure
138

Figure
139

Figure
140

Figure
141

[126]

WM. NEAL. Fig. 137 .31 caliber

6⅜ inch, round-octagon, rifled barrel. Stamped on top:

WM. NEAL
BANGOR
ME.

A pleasingly designed Underhammer pistol by one of the noted Maine gunsmiths. Saw handle walnut grip. V-notch rear sight and open front sight.

Total length, 11⅛ inches. *Roger C. Peterson Collection*

S. OSBORN. Fig. 138 .34 caliber

7¾ inch, round-octagon, smoothbore barrel (156 on under side of barrel). Octagon part of barrel inlaid with small silver stars. Left side stamped cast steel, engraved top strap stamped with eagle and:

S. OSBORN
CANTON, CONN.

Silver mounted walnut grip, inlaid with silver diamond and bar on left side. Osborn was a partner at one time with Andrus.

Total length, 12 inches. *Serial No. 26*
Author's Collection

C. OAK & SON. Fig. 139 .34 caliber

6⅞ inch, round-octagon, rifled barrel to which is affixed a 9¾ inch blade. Top of strap and barrel is stamped:

C. OAK & SON   JACKSONVILLE   CAST STEEL

Polished walnut grip with silver mountings, including a full-butt plate of silver. Shown below the gun is the original leather scabbard. That the gun has had extensive use is indicated by the wear on the leather.

This Underhammer Cutlass Pistol is the most unique and unusual encountered in the many months of research. Some percussion rifles and shotguns carrying the stamping of C. Oak & Son are also known.

Total length, 17¼ inches. *Serial No. 19*
Author's Collection

H. PRATT. Fig. 140 .31 caliber

8½ inch, tapering-octagon, rifled barrel. Top of frame is engraved in flowing script:

H. Pratt's
Patent

Two leaf rear sight. Brass side plates. One piece curly maple grip of semi-birdshead style. Mainspring also serves as a trigger guard on this beautifully made pistol.

Total length, 13 inches. *Author's Collection*

QUINABAUG RFLE MG. CO. Fig. 141 .30 caliber

2 15/16 inch, round-octagon, rifled barrel. Top strap stamped with the spread eagle, and:

QUINABAUG RFLE MG CO.
SOUTHBRIDGE, MASS
E. HUTCHINGS
AGENT—BALTO

Brass mounted walnut grip with inlaid designs.
Total length, 6⅜ inches.

Ray C. Young Collection

[127]

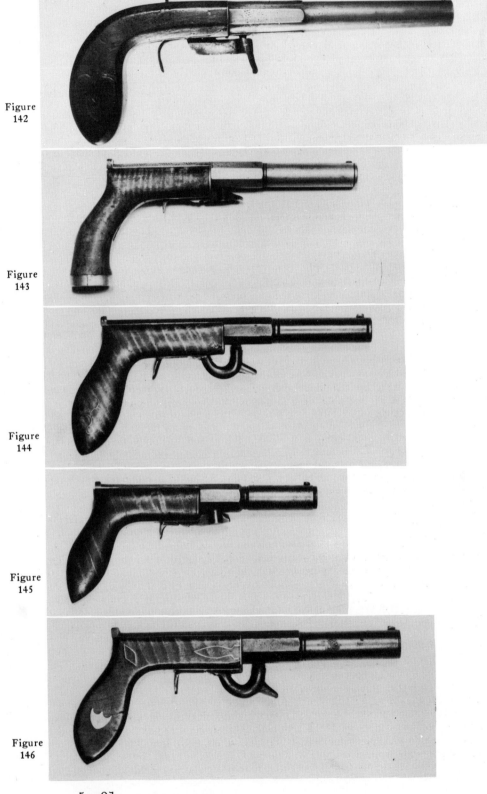

Figure
142

Figure
143

Figure
144

Figure
145

Figure
146

W. RAYMOND. Fig. 142

.36 caliber

5 inch, round-octagon barrel, fluted near the breech. Top of the barrel stamped:

W. RAYMOND

Smooth, flat grip, carved with design of heart at the lower point.
Total length, 8½ inches.

Milwaukee Public Museum

NATHᴸ RIDER & CO. Fig. 143

.31 caliber

3⅞ inch, round-octagon, rifled barrel, the left side of which is stamped: CAST STEEL. Engraved top strap stamped with eagle and:

NATHᴸ RIDER & CO.
SOUTHBRIDGE, MASS.

Silver mounted, curly maple, grip. A finely made Underhammer pocket pistol of unusual design.
Total length, 7¾ inches.

Serial No. 0
Author's Collection

A. RUGGLES. Fig. 144

.31 caliber

4 inch, round-octagon, rifled barrel (164 on under side of barrel), left side of which is stamped: CAST STEEL
Top strap is engraved, and stamped:

A. RUGGLES
STAFFORD

(CONN.)

Semi-circle type of hammer found on the earlier specimens produced by Ruggles. Curly maple grip, brass mounted, and inlaid with silver wire designs.
Total length, 8¼ inches.

Serial No. 4
Author's Collection

A. RUGGLES. Fig. 145

.31 caliber

3 inch, round-octagon, rifled barrel (130 on under side of barrel). Engraved top strap with eagle and the following stamping:

A. RUGGLES   E. HUTCHINGS & CO.
STAFFORD   AGENTS—BALT. MD.
(CONN.)

Striped curly maple grip, brass mounted. A splendid example of the unusually small pocket size Underhammer pistols.
Total length, 6½ inches.

Serial No. 2
Author's Collection

A. RUGGLES. Fig. 146

.31 caliber

4 inch, round-octagon, rifled barrel. Engraved top strap stamped:

A. RUGGLES
STAFFORD, (CONN.)

Left side of barrel stamped: CAST STEEL
This gun with the semi-circle type of hammer, instead of the usual flat type, is a splendid example of the earliest Ruggles Underhammers. Flat, brass mounted, curly maple grip with silver shield and wire inlay on each side.
Total length, 8⅜ inches.

Serial No. 1
Author's Collection

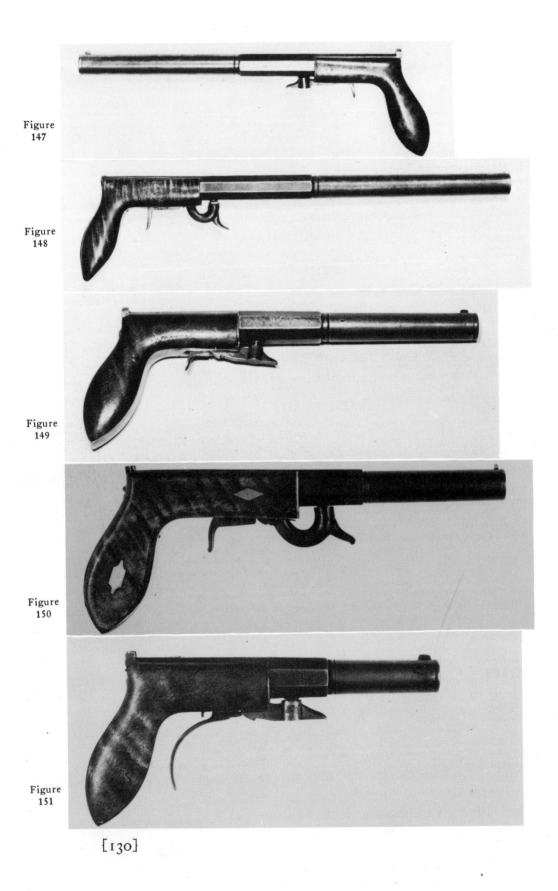

Figure
147

Figure
148

Figure
149

Figure
150

Figure
151

[130]

A. RUGGLES. Fig. 147 .31 caliber

7⅞ inch, round-octagon, rifled barrel (168 on under side of barrel.) Engraved top strap stamped:

A. RUGGLES
STAFFORD
(CONN.)

Walnut grip, brass mounted. Left side of barrel stamped:

CAST STEEL

A fine example of the larger size of New England type of Underhammer produced by Ruggles.

Total length, 11¾ inches.

Serial No. 6
Author's Collection

A. RUGGLES (unmarked). Fig. 148 .34 caliber

11⅞ inch, round-octagon, rifled barrel. Brass mounted, curly maple, grip. Hammer is of the semi-circle type found on the early pistols by Ruggles. This massive Underhammer of the familiar New England style is one of the largest of this type encountered. Such a pistol was often referred to as a "buggy rifle."

Total length, 16⅝ inches.

Author's Collection

A. RUGGLES. Fig. 149 .30 caliber

6 inch, round-octagon, rifled barrel. Another specimen by this familiar New England maker, which is included to show the variety of sizes produced by some of the better known gunsmiths.

Total length, 9¾ inches.

M. L. McCormack Collection

A. RUGGLES (unmarked). Fig. 150 .31 caliber

3½ inch, round-octagon, rifled barrel. Flat sided curly maple grip, brass mounted and inlaid with silver designs on each side.

Total length, 7⅛ inches.

Winchester Museum Collection

A. RUGGLES. Fig. 151 .32 caliber

2¾ inch round-octagon, rifled barrel marked on the side:

CAST STEEL
A. RUGGLES
STAFFORD, CONN.

and   E. HUTCHINGS & CO., BALTIMORE, MD.
AGENTS

Curly maple, brass mounted, grip.

Winchester Museum Collection

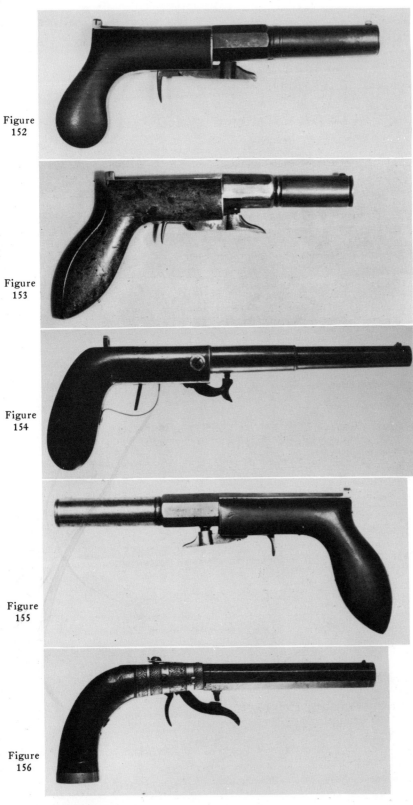

Figure
152

Figure
153

Figure
154

Figure
155

Figure
156

D. D. SACKET. FIG. 152

.34 caliber

3⅞ inch, round-octagon, rifled barrel, on the muzzle of which is stamped the figure 11. Brass top strap stamped with the familiar eagle, and:

D. D. SACKET
WESTFIELD
CAST STEEL

The small wood grip is mounted with brass. Little is known of this maker, but if one may judge by this example of his work, he was a gunsmith of considerable skill. The gun is original throughout, and the serial number is to be found on all important parts, including the mainspring.

Total length, 7¾ inches.

Serial No. 12
Author's Collection

D. D. SACKET. FIG. 153

.36 caliber

3⅛ inch round-octagon rifled barrel stamped:

CAST STEEL

Top strap marked with spread eagle, and stamped:

D. D. SACKET
WESTFIELD, MASS.

Brass mounted, burl walnut grip.
Total length, 7 inches.

Herman W. Williams, Jr. Collection

M. S. SANDERSON. FIG. 154
GEO. V. SEAVER

.35 caliber

6¾ inch, round tapering barrel (132 on the under side of barrel). Adjustable rear sight. German silver trigger guard. Top of barrel stamped:

M. S. SANDERSON
GEO. V. SEAVER

Total length, 11¾ inches.

Milwaukee Public Museum

SHAW & LEDOYT. FIG. 155

.31 caliber

3⅞ inch, round-octagon rifled barrel stamped CAST STEEL on left side (172 on under side of barrel). Top strap stamped with two identical eagles and:

SHAW & LEDOYT
STAFFORD, CONN.

The name of Shaw & Ledoyt has been stamped in heavier letters over that of A. THRESHER, a gunsmith of Stafford, Conn., the maker of the gun.

Total length, 8 inches.

Serial No. 1
Robin C. Hale Collection

H. SHEETS. FIG. 156

.31 caliber

4½ inch, octagon, rifled barrel stamped on top:

H. SHEETS

Finely engraved brass frame. Adjustable rear sight. Silver butt plate and band. A most attractive Underhammer.

Total length, 8¼ inches.

Milwaukee Public Museum

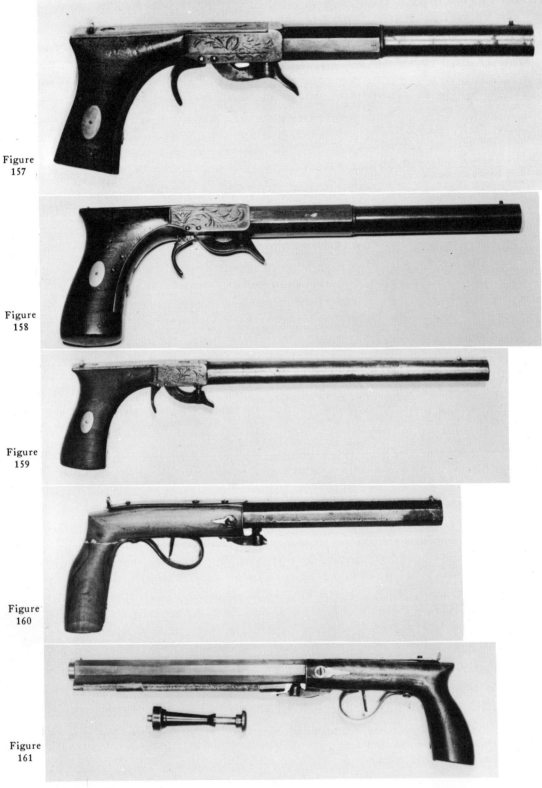

Figure
157

Figure
158

Figure
159

Figure
160

Figure
161

[134]

A. W. SPIES. FIG. 157 .31 caliber

4¾ inch, round-octagon, rifled barrel. Engraved frame and top strap, the latter of which is stamped:

A. W. SPIES MISSISSIPPI POCKET RIFLE

Walnut grip with silver oval inlay on each side. Spies was a jobber, or distributor, of Allen arms. The stamping "Mississippi Pocket Rifle" is seldom encountered on the Allen Underhammer pistols.
Total length, 9½ inches.

Serial No. 77
Author's Collection

A. W. SPIES. FIG. 158 .31 caliber

7 inch, round-octagon, rifled barrel. Engraved frame, the top of which is stamped:

A. W. SPIES   POCKET RIFLE

Total length, 11¾ inches.

M. L. McCormack Collection

A. W. SPIES. FIG. 159 .44 caliber

8¾ inch, round tapering, smoothbore barrel. Engraved frame. Stamped on top:

A. W. SPIES   POCKET RIFLE
CAST STEEL
WARRANTED

Another of the Allen made Underhammers for the firm of A. W. Spies.
Total length, 13¼ inches.

Herbert E. Green Collection

A. STORY. FIG. 160 .36 caliber

6⅝ inch, full-octagon, rifled barrel which is stamped on the top side:

A. STORY
W. WINDSOR, VT.

Adjustable rear sight. Iron trigger guard. Maple grip. Story was one of the first of the New England gunsmiths to produce Underhammer pistols. It was he who taught the noted Kendall the art of gunsmithing. Few pistols by this early maker are known.
Total length, 12¾ inches.

Author's Collection

A. STORY (unmarked). FIG. 161 .31 caliber

8⅞ inch, full-octagon, rifled barrel turned at the muzzle for a bullet starter (shown below the gun). Ramrod mounted under the barrel. Adjustable rear sight. Walnut grip, iron mounted.
This piece, though unmarked, bears enough similarity in detail, both inside and out, to place it as having been a product of Asa Story's shop.
Total length, 15½ inches.

Author's Collection

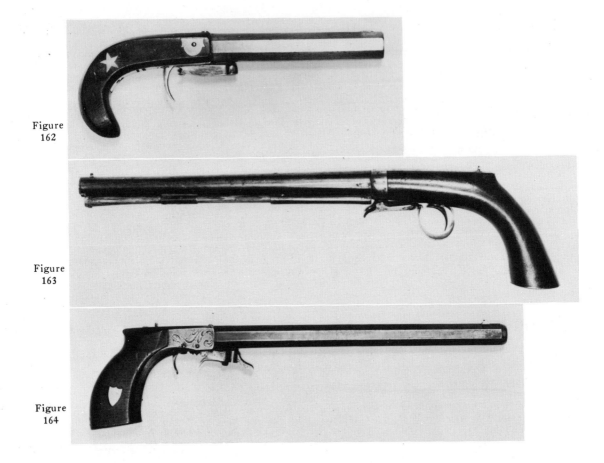

Figure
162

Figure
163

Figure
164

J. E. W. Fig. 162 .34 caliber

6 inch, full octagon, rifled barrel, the top of which is engraved in flowing script initials:

J. E. W.

Walnut, birdshead, grip with silver star on each side. The very unusual feature of this gun is that it is double-action, cocking and firing upon pulling the trigger. Total length, 10⅝ inches.

Author's Collection

B. C. WOOD. Fig. 163 .45 caliber

9½ inch, round tapering, smoothbore barrel. Engraved top strap, upon which is stamped:

B. C. WOOD
P. POST, N. Y.

Walnut grip with engraved butt plate. Trigger guard serves as the mainspring on this well designed and fabricated pistol. Total length, 15⅝ inches.

Author's Collection

A. C. WRIGHT. Fig. 164 .31 caliber

10 inch, full-octagon, rifled barrel, rounded at the muzzle. Engraved steel frame. Walnut grip with silver shield inlaid on each side, and oval inlay on butt. Top of barrel stamped:

A. C. WRIGHT

Total length, 14½ inches.

Herbert E. Green Collection

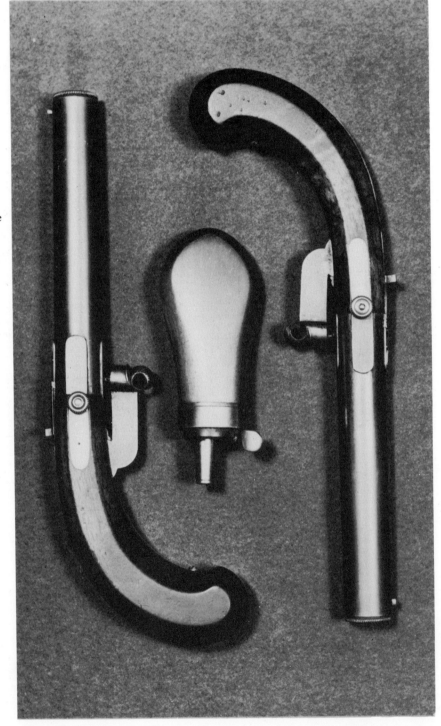

Figure
165

UNMARKED (a pair). FIG. 165   .36 caliber

4½ inch, round, rifled barrel with milled ring on muzzle. Walnut birdshead grip, with side trigger plate of silver. This distinctive, and unique, pair of guns are equipped with the most unusual firing mechanism to be found on any of the Underhammer arms. The little button on the right side of the frame is the trigger, which, when pulled backwards releases the hammer to fire the gun. A close examination of the workmanship, rifling and finish of the pistols leaves no doubt as to their American origin. It is known that the guns came from the Rochester area and, the legend surrounding them is that they were made in the shop of the noted Billinghurst. Whether by him personally, or one of his workmen, is not known. Then too it could well be that they were designed and produced by J. Miller who is known to have invented and patented some of the guns produced by Billinghurst and others. The engraving on the guns, plus the beautiful brown finish on the metal parts, bears a striking similarity to that found on some of the Billinghurst Underhammer pistols. Why these pistols were left unmarked will, no doubt, always remain a mystery. Could it be that they were an experimental pair? In any event their near original condition, and their unique mechanism place them at the top in desirability among the Underhammer Guns.

Total length, 8¼ inches.

Author's Collection

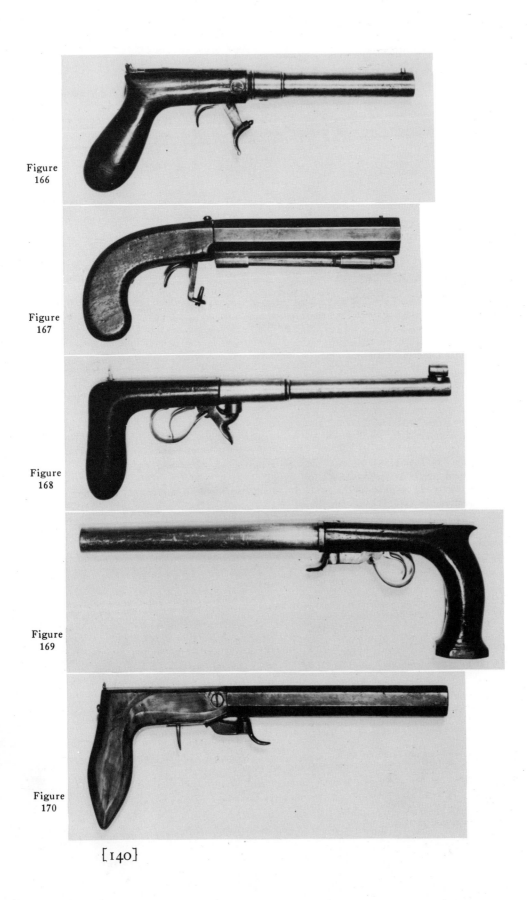

Figure
166

Figure
167

Figure
168

Figure
169

Figure
170

UNMARKED. Fig. 166 .36 caliber

5¼ inch, round-tapering, rifled barrel. Walnut grip. This gun, showing skilled workmanship, is most uncommon among Underhammer guns. Instead of using the usual percussion cap for ignition it employs the "pill-lock" form of ignition. Tiny pellets, held in place by tallow or beeswax, were crushed by the fall of the pointed hammer.
Total length, 10½ inches.

Author's Collection

UNMARKED. Fig. 167 .44 caliber

5¾ inch, full-octagon, rifled barrel. Walnut grip with iron mountings. A primitive specimen of the Underhammer which utilizes the pill-lock form of ignition rather than the regular percussion cap. Such a gun could, and did, also use the unusual cap with the fulminate on the outside, described in a previous chapter. As will be observed from the illustration the hammer of this interesting piece moves in an almost vertical manner.
Total length, 10 inches.

Author's Collection

UNMARKED. Fig. 168 .34 caliber

8 inch, round-tapering, rifled barrel. Hooded front sight, peep rear sight. Walnut, right angle grip, with brass top and back strap.
This gun employs the simple mechanism of the mainspring also serving as a trigger guard. A well made target Underhammer.
Total length, 12¾ inches.

Author's Collection

UNMARKED. Fig. 169 .50 caliber

8¼ inch, round, smoothbore barrel. Walnut grip with octagon-shaped butt. The mainspring on this rather massive piece serves a dual purpose—that of trigger guard.
Total length, 14⅛ inches.

Author's Collection

UNMARKED. Fig. 170 .36 caliber

7 inch, full-octagon, rifled barrel. Brass mounted grip of an unusual wood. Shows the New England influence in style. A very good example of a primitive Underhammer pistol—built for service rather than show.
Total length, 11½ inches.

Author's Collection

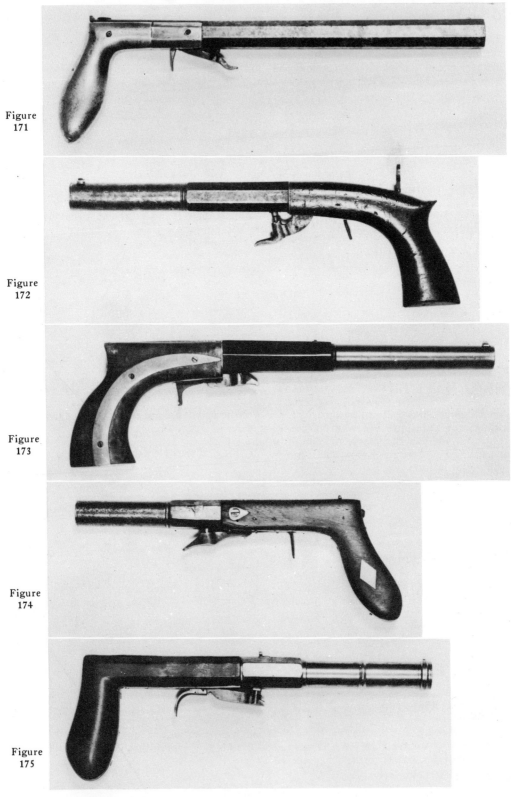

Figure
171

Figure
172

Figure
173

Figure
174

Figure
175

ALL-METAL (unmarked). FIG. 171 .31 caliber

9 inch, full-octagon, rifled barrel. Adjustable rear sight. German silver all-metal grip of New England style. Underhammers made entirely of metal are seldom encountered, and this one, weighing nearly three pounds, is a splendid example.
Total length, 13¾ inches.

Author's Collection

UNMARKED. FIG. 172 .31 caliber

6⅜ inch round-octagon, rifled barrel. Walnut grip of rather unusual design. Adjustable peep sight mounted on top strap. Another well built pistol of unknown origin.
Total length, 11¼ inches.

Author's Collection

UNMARKED. FIG. 173 .31 caliber

8¾ inch, round-octagon, rifled barrel. Brass mounted walnut grip, with cap-box in the butt.
Even though this gun is unmarked it is a well designed and made pistol, and one reason why even guns by unknown makers can be so interesting.
Total length, 13¾ inches.

Author's Collection

UNMARKED. FIG. 174 .44 caliber

4¼ inch round-octagon, rifled barrel. Brass mounted, walnut grip with silver diamond inlaid on either side. Top strap and part of barrel engraved.
Total length, 9½ inches.

Author's Collection

UNMARKED. FIG. 175 .38 caliber

5⅝ inch, round-octagon, rifled, cannon-shaped barrel. Brass mounted walnut grip of near right angle design.
Total length, 11 inches.

Author's Collection

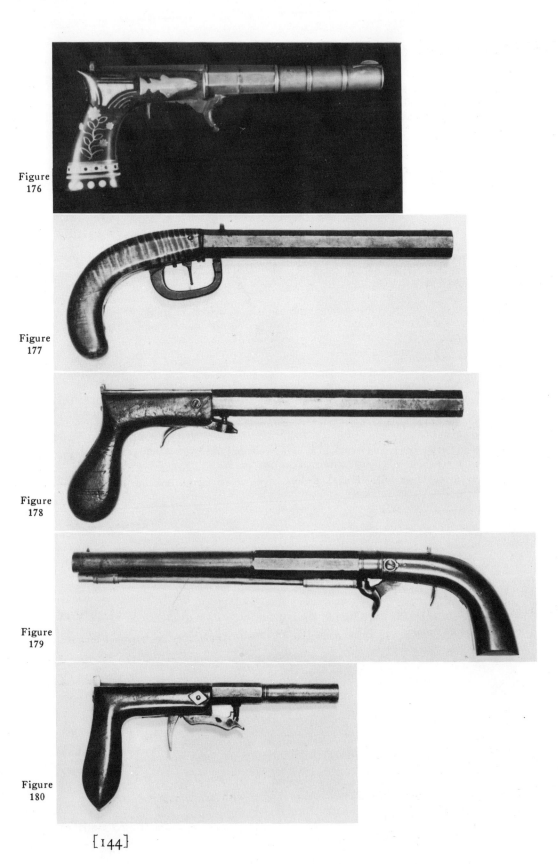

Figure
176

Figure
177

Figure
178

Figure
179

Figure
180

UNMARKED. FIG. 176

.40 caliber

5¼ inch, round-octagon barrel completely overlaid, or sheathed in silver, which is engraved with simple designs. Top strap is inlaid with silver and tortoise shell. The walnut grip is inlaid with ivory and silver wire. Flower designs and fish are engraved sheet silver. The hammer is designed as a fish with eyes on each side of the cup; the spur represents the tail. The fish design was a symbol of early Christianity, knowingly or not it has been used by the early gunsmiths to decorate their guns, perhaps as a charm to keep the evil spirits away from the gun and its owner. This gun is one of the most ornate specimens known and a real treasure for its owner.
Total length, 10 inches.

Dr. Norborne R. Clarke Collection

UNMARKED. FIG. 177

.31 caliber

8½ inch, full octagon, rifled barrel, the muzzle of which is stamped with designs similar to those found on some of the early rifles. Curly maple stock. Trigger guard is the hammer on this plain, but primitive, Underhammer.
Total length, 13¼ inches.

Author's Collection

UNMARKED. FIG. 178

.36 caliber

8½ inch, full-octagon, rifled barrel. Bulbous type walnut grip. Another of the primitives fabricated by an unknown gunsmith.
Total length, 13⅝ inches.

Author's Collection

UNMARKED. FIG. 179

.34 caliber

10⅝ inch, round-octagon, smoothbore barrel. Plain maple grip with iron backstrap and brass under plate.
Total length, 15¼ inches.

Author's Collection

UNMARKED. FIG. 180

.31 caliber

4 inch, round-octagon, rifled barrel. Walnut grip with brass trigger plate.
Total length, 8 inches.

Robin C. Hale Collection

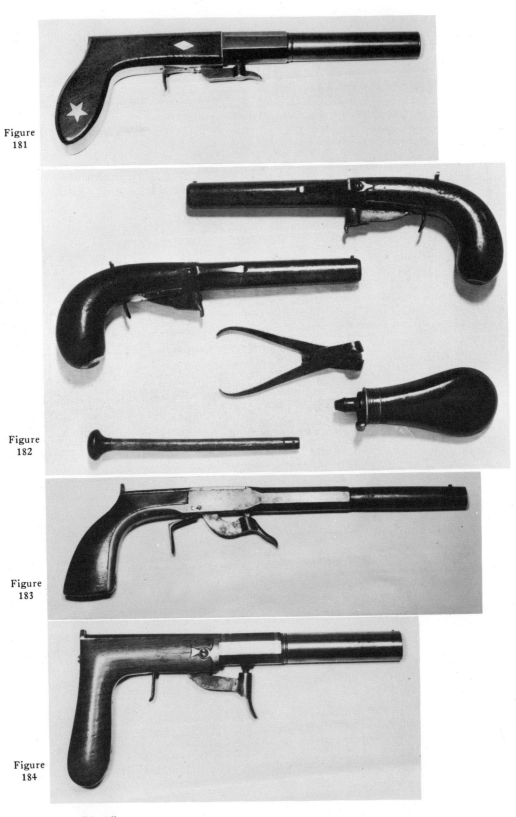

Figure
181

Figure
182

Figure
183

Figure
184

UNMARKED. Fig. 181 .32 caliber

5¾ inch, round-octagon barrel. Brass mounted walnut grip with silver star and diamond inlay on each side. A well-made pistol following the familar New England styling.
Total length, 10 inches.

M. L. McCormack Collection

UNMARKED (a pair). Fig. 182 .48 caliber

4¾ inch, round, tapering barrel. Wooden grips with iron mountings. A rather unusual set in that both guns are equipped with a belt hook. One gun has it attached, to the rounded frame, on the right side and the other gun has it on the left side. Though not cased the set includes: bullet mould, powder flask and ramrod for seating the bullet.
Total length, 9⅛ inches.

Cecil A. Brown Collection

UNMARKED. Fig. 183 .32 caliber

8½ inch, round-octagon barrel. Resembling the type produced by E. Allen, but differing enough in details to exclude the possibility of his manufacture.
Total length, 16½ inches.

M. L. McCormack Collection

UNMARKED. Fig. 184 .32 caliber

4¾ inch, round-octagon barrel. Right angle walnut grip. An unusual piece showing excellent workmanship. Hammer has an almost vertical finger spur.
Total length, 9 inches.

M. L. McCormack Collection

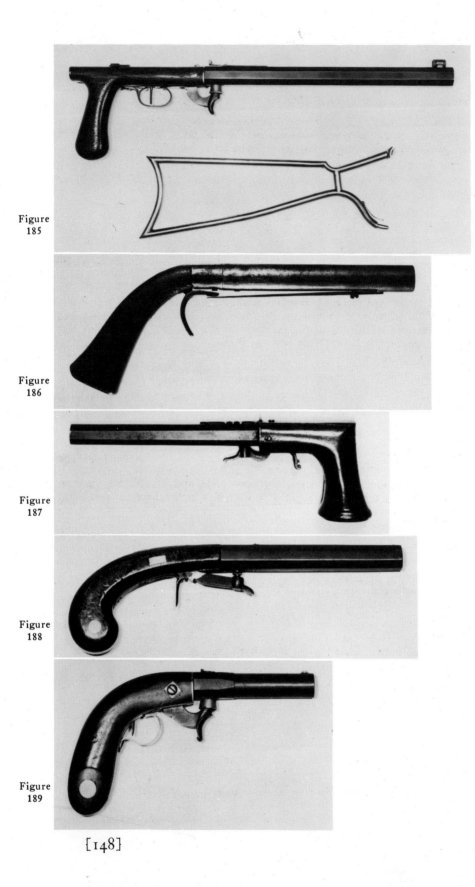

Figure
185

Figure
186

Figure
187

Figure
188

Figure
189

UNMARKED. Fig. 185   .34 caliber

12¼ inch, octagon, rifled barrel with hooded front sight and two rear sights, one an open elevating and one a folding leaf, peep type. Walnut grip with brass trigger plate. Trigger is stamped with date 1870.

This mint condition pistol with its metal skeleton extension stock was found in Vermont, wrapped in grease soaked newspapers bearing the date 1872. As will be observed, the gun shows the influence of the Hilliard style.
Total length of pistol, 19 inches.

Author's Collection

UNMARKED. Fig. 186   .47 caliber

5⅝ inch, round, smoothbore barrel, which may be unscrewed for loading. The "spring-hammer" is affixed to the under side of the barrel, near the muzzle. Pulling the trigger puts a tension on the spring, which when it slips off the trigger spur snaps back to detonate the percussion cap. The rounded, flaring, grip is made of black walnut and carries the initials D S cut into the butt.
Total length, 8¾ inches.

Milwaukee Public Museum Collection

UNMARKED. Fig. 187   .41 caliber

7¼ inch, full-octagon, smoothbore barrel. Top strap ends in an arrow design pointing towards the muzzle of the gun. Walnut grip having a rather unusual flared butt. A well-built piece of unknown origin.
Total length, 11¾ inches.

Author's Collection

UNMARKED. Fig. 188   .36 caliber

5 inch, full-octagon barrel. Silver inlays in wooden grip, of birdshead styling.
Total length, 9¾ inches.

M. L. McCormack Collection

UNMARKED. Fig. 189   .32 caliber

3¼ inch, round-octagon barrel. Silver mounted wooden grip with ivory inlay.
Total length, 6¾ inches.

M. L. McCormack Collection

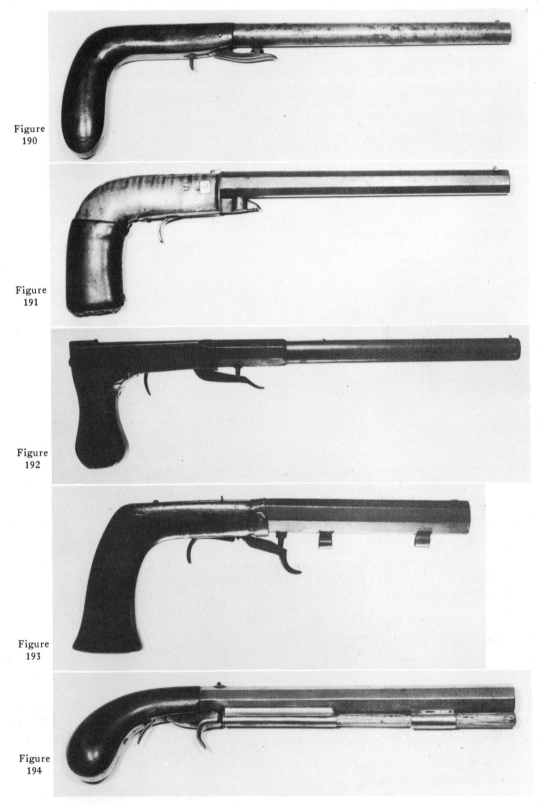

Figure
190

Figure
191

Figure
192

Figure
193

Figure
194

[150]

UNMARKED. FIG. 190

.30 caliber

8½ inch, round barrel with right angle walnut grip.
Total length, 13½ inches.

M. L. McCormack Collection

UNMARKED. FIG. 191

.32 caliber

8½ inch, full-octagon barrel. Curly maple grip with rawhide laced cover.
Total length, 13 inches.

M. L. McCormack Collection

UNMARKED. FIG. 192

.45 caliber

10 inch, round-octagon barrel. Right angle wooden grip.
Total length, 14¾ inches.

Milwaukee Public Museum Collection

UNMARKED. FIG. 193

.32 caliber

5½ inch, full-octagon, rifled barrel. Smooth flat polished grip with flaring butt, which is covered with a silver plate. Originally equipped with a ramrod.
Total length, 11 inches.

Milwaukee Public Museum Collection

UNMARKED. FIG. 194

.54 caliber

9¾ inch, full-octagon barrel with hickory ramrod on underside. Brass mounted, walnut, grip.
Total length, 13¾ inches.

M. L. McCormack Collection

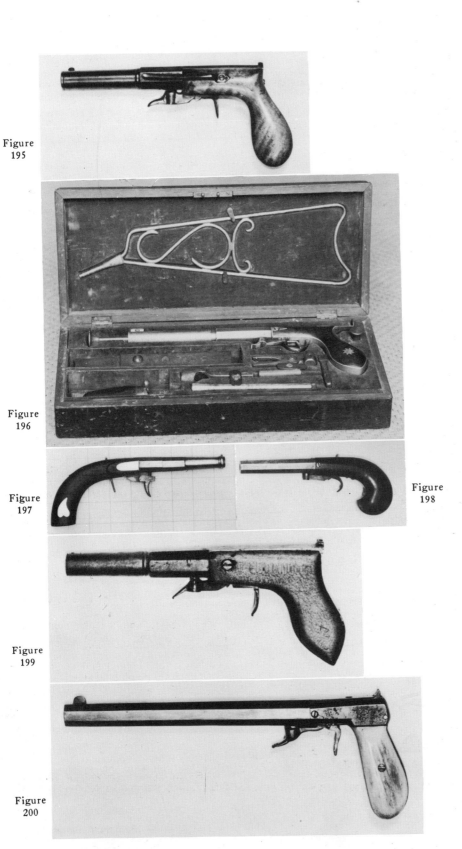

Figure
195

Figure
196

Figure
197

Figure
198

Figure
199

Figure
200

UNMARKED. Fig. 195 .36 caliber

4 inch, round-octagon, rifled barrel. Top strap and octagon part of barrel stamped with designs. Brass mounted curly maple grip of bag shape design. Belt hook on left side of stock.

Total length, 7½ inches.

Serial No. 475
Author's Collection

UNKNOWN. Fig. 196

A nicely appointed cased set, including many accessories and an all-metal extension stock. The whereabouts of this cased set is not known, thus a more complete description is lacking.

Photo supplied by Ray C. Young

UNMARKED. Fig. 197

4½ inch, round-octagon, engraved barrel. Silver inlays set in side of wood grip. The barrel on this piece is known as the cannon shape.

Total length, 8½ inches.

Mark Aziz Collection

UNMARKED. Fig. 198 .31 caliber

4⅜ inch, octagon, rifled barrel with rear sight on topstrap. Curly maple grip of birdshead design.

Total length, 8¾ inches.

Col. L. C. Jackson Collection

UNMARKED. Fig. 199 .28 caliber

4⅝ inch, round-octagon and tapering, rifled barrel. Maple, brass mounted, flat type grip. A good example of a primitive Underhammer, showing the New England influence.

Total length, 9 inches.

Author's Collection

UNMARKED. Fig. 200 .38 caliber

8 inch, full-octagon, smoothbore barrel. Stag grips. This piece is illustrated only to show what some contemporary gunsmith could, and did, do in the fabricating of a shootable underhammer. It is totally unmarked.

Total length, 11¼ inches.

Author's Collection

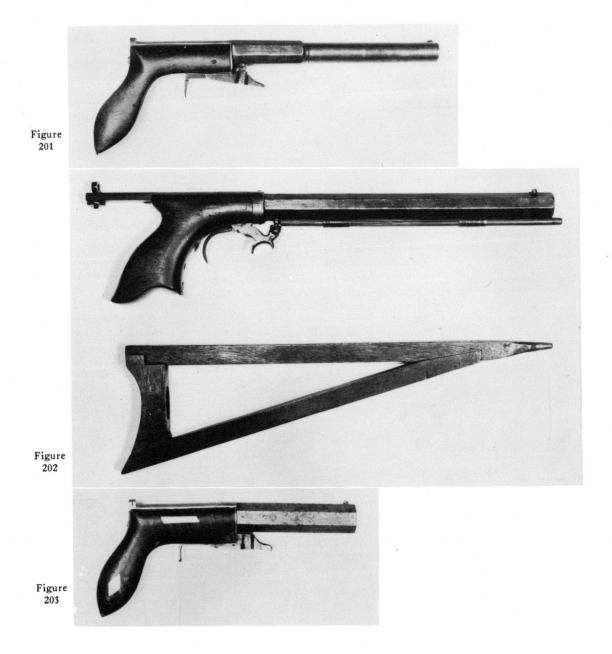

Figure
201

Figure
202

Figure
203

UNKNOWN. FIG. 201 .28 caliber

6 inch, round octagon, rifled barrel stamped on the left side: CAST STEEL (192 on under side of barrel). Walnut, brass mounted grip of the typical New England style. Top of top strap engraved with a leaf design.

Total length, 10 inches.

Serial No. 13
Author's Collection

UNMARKED. FIG. 202 .31 caliber

10½ inch, full-octagon, rifled barrel. Extra long backstrap for target peep sight. Walnut grip of the Billinghurst design. This Underhammer target pistol is equipped with an extension stock of unusual construction. Built with square, instead of rounded pieces the skeleton stock is held together by means of wooden pegs. A hole through the top bar of the stock provides a sheath to house an extra ramrod. A very splendid American Underhammer by an unknown maker.

Total length without extension stock, 17 inches.

Author's Collection

UNKNOWN. FIG. 203 .38 caliber

3½ inch, full-octagon, rifled barrel. Stamped on the top flat of the barrel, just ahead of the backstrap is the familiar eagle of the New England pieces, of which this is a splendid example. The eagle is also stamped on the backstrap. Walnut, brass mounted, grip with German silver inlays.

Total length, 7½ inches.

Serial No. 2
Author's Collection

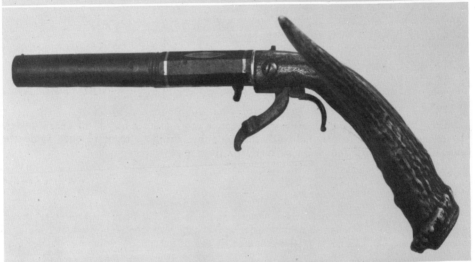

Figure
204

Figure
205

Figure
206

UNMARKED (a pair). FIG. 204 .36 caliber

4¼ inch, round-octagon, rifled barrel. Notched rear sight. Engraved bright steel frame with side plate screw entering from left side. One pistol stamped 66 on side of grip strap; other pistol stamped O. Inside of sideplate and frame of one marked XVIII (an interesting point of similarity to the unmarked "Anderson" pistols). This with the distinctive type of screw plate in the grips, and other features, leads to the thought that these guns may have been produced by the maker of the guns designated as Anderson, a maker as yet unidentified. Truly it is a most attractive pair of Under-hammers.

Total length, 8 inches.

J & I Boffin Collection

UNMARKED. FIG. 205

6 inch, round-octagon barrel, which is stamped only: CAST STEEL. Silver bands and two silver inlays on the barrel.

Unusual feature of the gun is the grip which is made from a section of deer's antler. It appears to be quite original with the gun, thus bringing to mind once again the rugged individuality found on so many of these guns.

Total length, 11 inches.

Jack Ross Collection

UNMARKED. FIG. 206 .35 caliber

3 inch, round-octagon barrel marked only:

CAST STEEL   POCKET RIFLE

A dandy example of the small, pocket type, of Underhammer pistol.

Total length, 7 inches.

Winchester Museum Collection

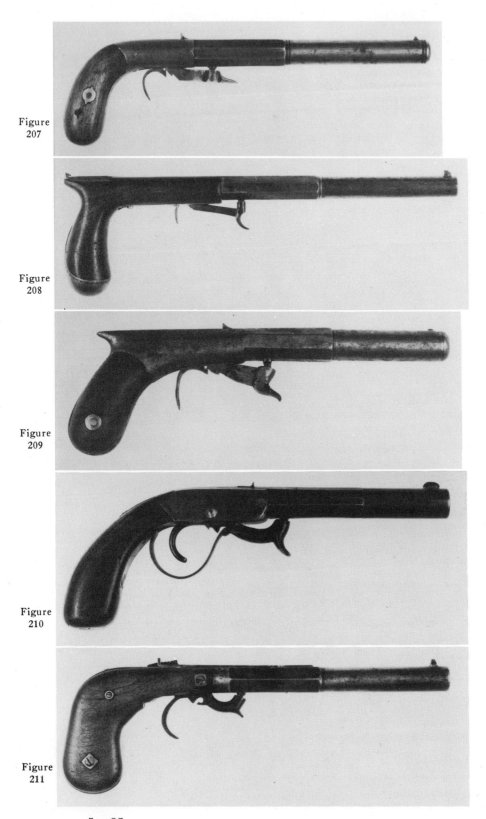

Figure
207

Figure
208

Figure
209

Figure
210

Figure
211

UNMARKED. FIG. 207   .38 caliber

6⅜ inch, round-octagon barrel. Rounded frame with elevating rear sight. Here again is found the unusual screw plates with projections, not commonly found on Under-hammer pistols, except the Anderson, Blunt & Syms and European pepperbox types. Total length, 10⅛ inches.

Winchester Museum Collection

UNMARKED. FIG. 208   .35 caliber

7½ inch, round-octagon barrel. Saw handle walnut grip with iron butt cap. Total length, 12½ inches.

Winchester Museum Collection

UNMARKED. FIG. 209   .36 caliber

4¼ inch, round-octagon barrel. Rounded all-metal frame. 2-piece walnut grip. Another of the interesting pieces bearing a similarity to the Blunt & Syms and Anderson pistols. Total length, 7¾ inches.

Winchester Museum Collection

UNMARKED. FIG. 210   .34 caliber

3¾ inch, round-octagon barrel. Trigger guard also serves as the mainspring for the gun. Total length, 7¾ inches.

Winchester Museum Collection

UNMARKED. FIG. 211   .36 caliber

6 inch, round-octagon barrel. Top strap with elevating rear sight. Massive wooden grip of unusual design. Total length, 9¾ inches.

Winchester Museum Collection

[159]

Figure
212

Figure
213

Figure
214

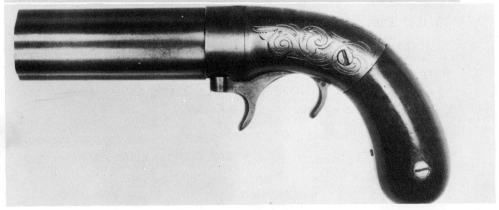

Figure
215

Section 3 — Multi-shot Underhammer Pistols

UNKNOWN. Figs. 212 and 213

Illustrating how the underhammer principle was adapted to multishot arms, these two beautfully made pistols of American make are here shown together.

On the upper one the hammer works through the slot in the trigger guard, while on the lower specimen the trigger guard also serves as the mainspring.

Barrels are manually revolved to bring the nipple into alignment for firing. The owners of these two fine specimens are unknown to the author, thus a more complete description is lacking.

JARVIS. Fig. 214

4¼ inch, octagon, superposed barrels which are reversible and locked by a thumb lever on the left side. Engraved brass ribs extend along each side, one holding the ramrod. Stock is of beautiful dark, naturally striped, maple. Butt plate and side inlays are of nicely chased silver.

On one barrel flat is marked in script: Present to W. H. Harrison President of US, and on the other side: Jarvis (?) The Gunsmith in Heidelberg Township, Pa. Unfortunately the gunsmith's name, being near the nipple, has become somewhat roughened from the cap fouling, and is not as clear as all the other lettering. The pistol can be accurately dated as of 1840.

Data and photo supplied by James E. Serven
William M. Locke Collection

BACON & CO. Fig. 215   .31 caliber

3¼ inch, round, ribbed cylinder containing 6 chambers. The barrel group is revolved by drawing back the hammer, by means of its trigger like projection. Stamped on the cylinder is the following:

BACON & CO.   NORWICH, CT.   CAST STEEL

Engraved steel frame with two piece walnut grips.
Total length, 7⅝ inches.

Miles W. Standish Collection

Figure
216

UNMARKED. Fig. 216   .28 caliber

3½ inch, round, fluted cylinder with six smoothbore chambers, which are numbered one to six on the muzzle. The cylinder rotates as the hammer is cocked. Brass mounted, curly maple grip. The style and shape of the grip, peculiar to and typical of those of New England manufacture, plus the workmanship all tend to confirm the origin of this rarity as being strictly American. Comparison with the rare Darling first model pepperbox shows a distinct similarity of the dished fluting on the cylinder, nipple arrangement, bores, and even in the revolving mechanism. Indeed rumor has it that an individual named Goddard did assemble a few guns from some Darling parts, after production had been discontinued on the first model. Whether this is correct is not known, however the similarity is quite well established. Certainly this unmarked primitive pepperbox ranks high in desirability among collectors.

Total length, 8½ inches.   Serial No. 6
                                                      Author's Collection

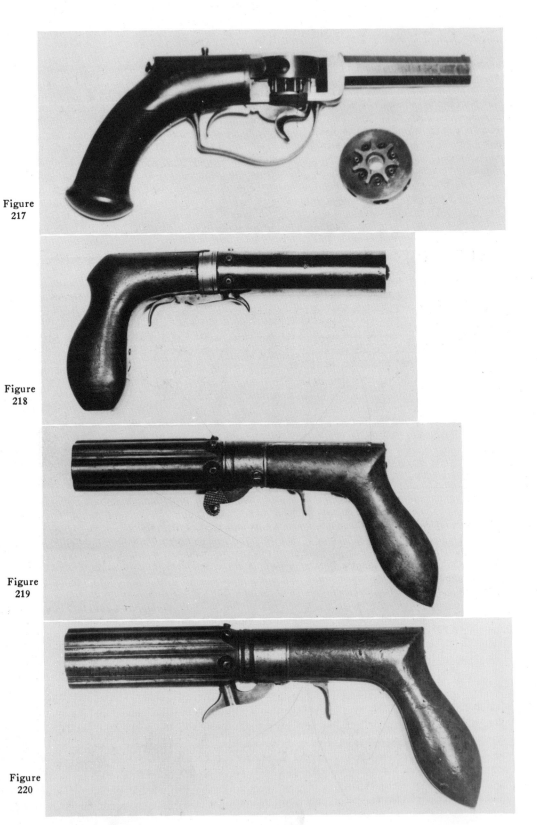

Figure
217

Figure
218

Figure
219

Figure
220

[164]

WILKINSON TURRET PISTOL. FIG. 217

This interesting Wilkinson Turret pistol is one of only three known specimens out of a total of nine fabricated. The gun seems to have been made on an English patent communicated from Cochran to Moses Poole in 1837. The cylinder is removed for loading by lifting the top strap that holds it in position. The elongated under hammer reaches over the rear chambers to fire the charge directly in line with the breech of the barrel. In many respects this gun is quite similar to the Cochran, after which it apparently was patterned.

Henry M. Stewart, Jr. Collection

E. B. WHITE. FIG. 218   .27 caliber

3⅞ inch, round, cylinder barrel containing six, smoothbore, chambers. Cylinder is rotated by hand, against the pressure of an inside spring. Brass top strap stamped:

E. B. WHITE

Walnut grip with brass mounting, save for one small silver mounting on top rear slant. A beautiful example of an early American multi-shot Underhammer.
Total length, 7½ inches.

Samuel E. Smith Collection

UNMARKED. FIG. 219   .31 caliber

3½ inch, round, fluted cylinder with six, smoothbore, chambers. Cylinder rotates as hammer is cocked. Brass mounted curly maple grip.
The style and shape of the grip, peculiar to and typical of those of New England manufacture, plus the workmanship all tend to confirm this piece as of American origin. Certainly no comparable piece of foreign manufacture has put in its appearance during the many months of this study. A most desirable multi-shot Underhammer pistol.
Total length, 8½ inches.

Samuel E. Smith Collection

UNMARKED. FIG. 220

A mate to the two just described. As on the specimen with serial #6, the chambers on this gun are numbered from 1 to 6 on the muzzle. The fluted barrel group is very similar to that found on the first model Darling Pepperboxes, and, which incidentally are to be found on the patent drawings of the Darling. Serial number is marked in various places on the gun.
Total length, 8½ inches.

Serial No. 2
Miles W. Standish Collection

Figure
221

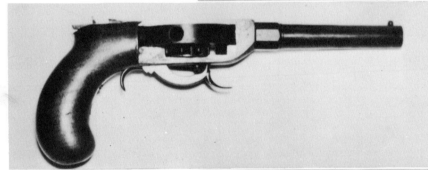

Figure
222

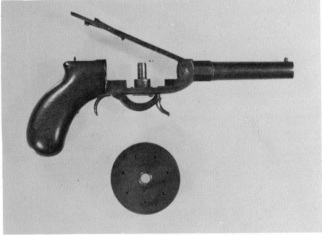

COCHRAN ALL-METAL TURRET PISTOL. FIG. 221   .36 caliber

4¾ inch, round-octagon tapering barrel. Seven shot horizontal cylinder. Weight 2½ pounds. Engraved German silver grips. John W. Cochran of New York secured a patent in 1837 for this odd arm, which is often referred to as the Cochran "Monitor" Pistol. It was manufactured by C. B. Allen of Springfield, Mass. (1836-1841) Total length, 10¾ inches.   Serial No. 74

Photo from James E. Serven

COCHRAN. FIG. 222

The "Monitor," as this turret pistol was often called, was made with two types of grip, all-metal and wood. Both are illustrated in this study. One of the easily recognized multi-shot revolving arms, it is a most desirable rarity and, an unusually valued member of the Underhammer family.

Henry M. Stewart, Jr. Collection

[167]

UNMARKED. FIG. 223   .44 caliber

7½ inch, round-octagon, rifled barrel. Horizontal, manually operated, cylinder is 6-shot. In operation the gun is quite simple, resembling as it does the Cochran Turret Pistol. The decoration on it is reminiscent of the punched design to be found around the muzzle of some Kentucky rifles. Mountings are of brass, and the gun has a weight of 4 lbs. 20 ozs.

Total length, 15 inches.

Osborne Klavestad Collection

M. CERWENKA. Fig. 224 .42 caliber

3¼ inch barrels. The cylinder of this massive European Underhammer Pepperbox is composed of 16 barrels, eight in the periphery and eight in the inner concentric circle. On one of the barrels is engraved the following:

M. CERWENKA

Barrels are individually numbered from 1 to 16. Weight of this rare collector's arm is 4 lbs. 6 ozs., truly the heavyweight of Underhammer pepperboxes.
Total length, 8 inches.

Miles W. Standish Collection

[169]

Figure
225

Figure
226

Figure
227

BLUNT & SYMS. Fig. 225 .28 caliber

3¼ inch cylinder composed of six chambers. Rounded, engraved frame. Iron backstrap with walnut grips. This ring-trigger, double-action, Underhammer pepperbox is quite typical of those produced by Blunt & Syms. While this firm is known to have imported many such guns for resale in this country, they are also believed to have produced some guns themselves.

Total length, 7¼ inches.

Miles W. Standish Collection

DESSAGNE A ST. ETTIENNE. Fig. 226 .43 caliber

3⅛ inch, round barrels of Damascus pattern. Revolving cylinder is composed of a 6-barrel group, in which the barrels are bored through and set into the standing breech. The tiny 2¼-inch dagger may be reversed and concealed in the hollow cylinder pin. Engraved round frame and backstrap, the latter engraved in flowing script:

Perfectionne par Dessagne a St. Ettienne

This double-action gun is a fine example of a French Underhammer pepperbox of the Mariette type.

Total length without dagger, 8 inches.

Serial No. 498
Author's Collection

UNMARKED. Fig. 227 .36 caliber

4¾ inch, round, fluted cylinder containing five chambers. The mainspring forms the trigger guard on this interesting arm of American origin. Unusual feature of this gun is that it employs a link between the hammer and the mainspring.

Total length, 9¾ inches.

Miles W. Standish Collection

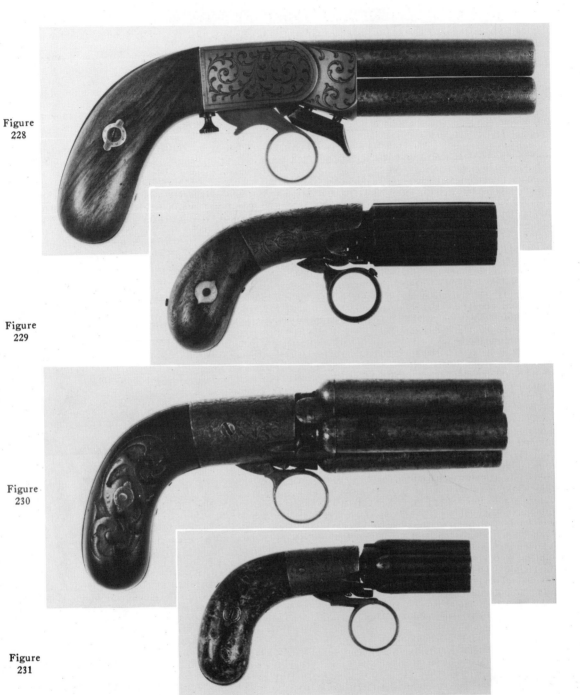

Figure
228

Figure
229

Figure
230

Figure
231

J. HERMAND. Fɪɢ. 228   .48 caliber

3¼ inch, over and under Damascus barrels with Belgian proofmarks. Double action with ring trigger. The underhammer is designed to hit both nipples simultaneously. The lower strap is marked:

J. HERMAND

Engraved frame, with polished wooden grips.
Total length, 9 inches.

Winchester Museum Collection

UNMARKED. Fɪɢ. 229   .28 caliber

2 inch, 5 shot barrel group. Ring trigger. Engraved frame with 2-piece walnut grips. Another beautiful specimen of a foreign made Underhammer pepperbox.
Total length, 5 inches.

Winchester Museum Collection

UNMARKED. Fɪɢ. 230   .48 caliber

2¾ inch barrel group of 4 shot. Barrels unscrew to load. Engraved steel frame. Two-piece carved wooden grips. Double action with ring trigger.
Total length, 7 inches.

Winchester Museum Collection

UNKNOWN of Belgian origin. Fɪɢ. 231   5mm. caliber

1½ inch cylinder composed of a 4-barrel group. Damascus barrels. Engraved frame with unusual wooden grips. Double action with a ring trigger. A beautiful specimen of a very near miniature Underhammer pepperbox of Belgian origin.
Total length, 5 inches.

Winchester Museum Collection

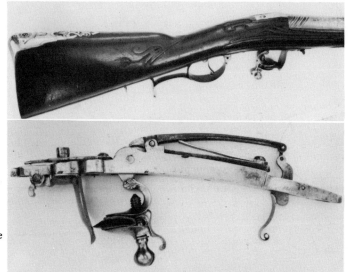

Figure
232

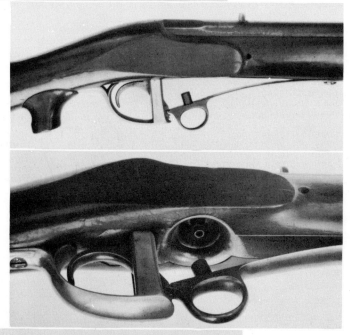

Figure
233

Figure
234

GERMAN UNDERHAMMER FLINTLOCK. FIG. 232   .685 caliber

42 inch round, rifled barrel. Rifling is 7 grooves and *straight*. Being a shotgun, the straight grooves are to accommodate a certain size of small shot in a concentrated pattern, to improve the resulting pattern. It was not made for ball. Metal work is highly decorative and the stock is carved to simple, yet effective designs.

One of the earliest, if not the first, known arm to employ the unique principle of an underhammer. Truly a remarkable example of gunsmith ingenuity.

W. Keith Neal Collection

HAWKER PATTERN MUSKET. FIG. 233   .775 caliber

39 inch round, smoothbore barrel. The underhammer action consists of a mainspring, the head of which forms the hammer. The ring at the top is for putting the thumb into to cock the gun. The stock is equipped with a detachable pistol grip. For detonating, the gun is primed with a Westley Richards Patent Mushroom Primer.

This musket is the patent of Henry Wilkinson of London. Improvements made by Col. Peter Hawker involved the use of the mushroom primer, and the pistol grip to the stock.

W. Keith Neal Collection

BELGIAN MILITARY RIFLED MUSKET   .752 caliber
(Model of 1858). FIG. 234.

36 inch, round-octagon, rifled barrel, marked GB, the official mark (Gouvernement Belge) together with other proof and inspection marks. Of the gun the owner writes:

"The lock is a complete unit combining hammer, mainspring and self priming magazine. This takes the form of a tape primer working along a horizontal groove in the base of which is a serrated wheel, which is connected with a link to the base of the hammer. Each time the hammer is cocked the strip of primers is moved up. A sharp cutting edge on the face of the hammer cuts off the primer from the strip immediately before striking. The entire unit can be detached by hand by removing one screw and drawing out a lateral bolt. The lock unit is of brass and precision made."

W. Keith Neal Collection

[175]

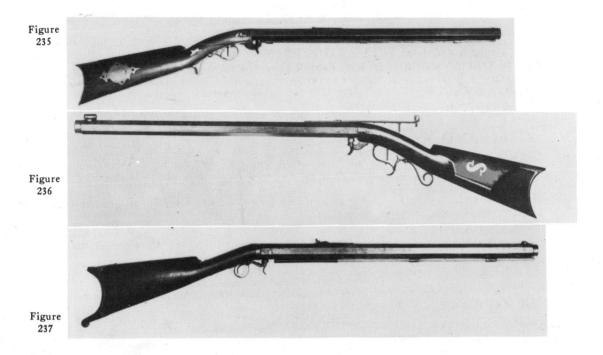

Figure
235

Figure
236

Figure
237

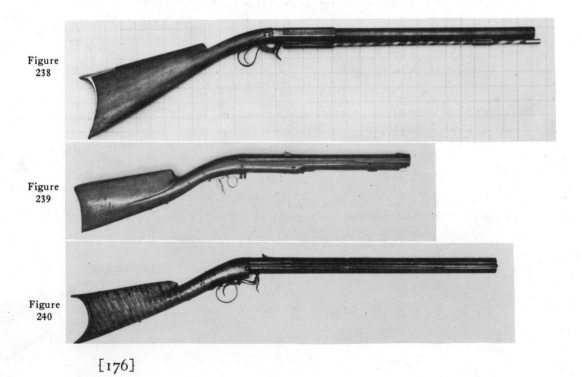

Figure
238

Figure
239

Figure
240

KENDALL-LAWRENCE. FIG. 235 .38 caliber

23¾ inch, full-octagon, rifled barrel, the top of which is stamped:

N. KENDALL
R. S. LAWRENCE
WINDSOR, VT.

and, on the under slant: P & S REMINGTON
Silver mounted, walnut stock with patch box on the right side, and cheek piece on the left side. This is a nice example of the finely designed rifles by these noted makers. Adjustable rear sight.
Total length, 41 inches.   *Author's Collection*

D. H. HILLIARD. FIG. 236 .45 caliber

24 inch, octagon, rifled barrel turned at the muzzle for bullet starter. Hooded front sight and peep rear sight. Walnut stock with cheek piece on left side and brass patch box on right side.
A splendid example of an Underhammer target rifle by one of the really fine gunsmiths of his time.
Total length, 39¾ inches.   Serial No. 1481
                                                                                 Ray Mitchell Collection

T. HEATON. FIG. 237 .38 caliber

26¼ inch, full-octagon, rifled barrel turned for bullet starter. Stamped on the right side under slant:

T. HEATON

and, on the left under slant:

REMINGTON CAST STEEL

Adjustable rear sight. Walnut iron mounted stock with Schutzen type butt plate. Trigger guard serves as the mainspring on this heavy target rifle.
Total length, 43 inches.   *Author's Collection*

J. D. PILLSBURY. FIG. 238

18 inch, round-octagon barrel marked:

J. D. PILLSBURY

Brass butt plate. Trigger guard serves as the mainspring. Striped hickory ramrod.
Total length, 31½ inches.
                                                                                 Mark Aziz Collection

SWISS. FIG. 239 .60 caliber

17 inch octagon barrel. Hammer is in the nature of a flat spring on the under side of the stock. Trigger operates through a slot in the spring. Ring on hammer is for cocking. Full stock with cheek piece on left side. Weight 5½ pounds.
Total length, 33¼ inches.   *Golden State Arms Collection*

UNMARKED. FIG. 240 .34 caliber

19¾ inch, full-octagon barrel, rifled. Curly maple stock with brass butt plate. Mainspring also serves as a trigger guard.
An early unmarked primitive underhammer rifle, utilizing a previously used rifle barrel.
Total length, 34½ inches.   *Author's Collection*

[177]

Figure
241

Figure
242

Figure
243

[178]

BILLINGHURST. Fig. 241
.48 caliber

25½ inch, octagon, rifled barrel, turned at the muzzle for bullet starter. Telescope sight on top was made by L. N. Mogg. Checkered walnut grip with engraved butt plate. One of the fine rifles made by this noted maker of Rochester, N. Y.

Total length, 41½ inches.

John K. Lounsbury Collection

UNMARKED. Fig. 242
.50 caliber

32¾ inch, full-octagon, rifled barrel with ramrod on the underside. Tiger maple stock with inlays of ivory and silver. Though the rifle stock appears to be of the detachable type it is all of one piece with the pistol grip. The right side of the stock is identical with the left side, even to the patch-box. In addition there is a cap-box on the under side of the stock, about midway between the butt of the stock and its junction with the pistol grip.

Total length, 49¼ inch.

Jack A. Smith, Collection

BILLINGHURST. Fig. 243
.34 caliber

25 inch, rifled barrel, encased in lead for off hand shooting. Pistol grip type of stock. Telescope sight on this splendid rifle was made by Wm. Malcolm, one of the most noted of the early scope makers. It was he who established, in 1855, the first rifle telescope making business in this country.

Total length, 41 inches.

John K. Lounsbury Collection

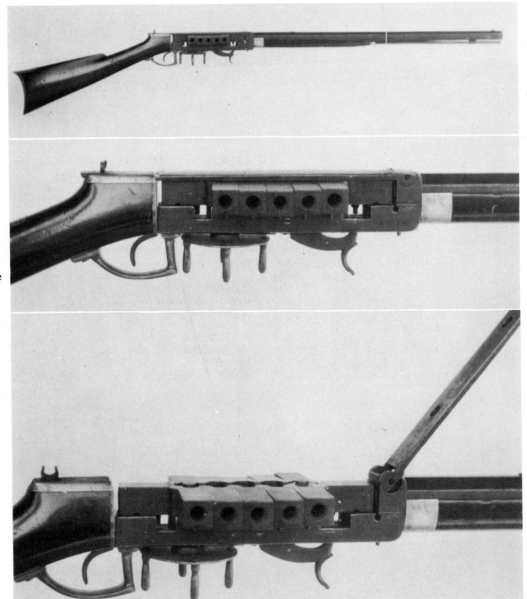

Figure
244

24½ inch, octagon, rifled barrel. Based on the patent (#603) of E. A. Bennett and P. F. Haviland, dated Feb. 15, 1838, this 12-shot repeating rifle was produced in the gunshop of N. Kendall, Windsor, Vt. It is the only known specimen of this scarce arm. The action is described by its owner as follows:

"The chambers consists of rectangular blocks with their breech ends formed like elements of a link belt. This belt passes around a pair of four-lobed gears, the rearmost of which is turned manually by four spindles mounted on a disc. This disc rotates in a horizontal plane between the under hammer and the trigger guard. The disc is most conveniently turned by twisting opposite spindles with thumb and fore-finger. The chamber aligned with the barrel is locked in position by a pin inserted from beneath. A button under the breech releases this pin while the next chamber is being moved around. The top strap over the action is made just like that on a Cochran gun."

The stock is cherry wood with silver or silver-plated brass trim. Top of the barrel is stamped: N. KENDALL WINDSOR VT. and the strap over the cylinder is marked with a spread eagle holding a ribbon in its beak. The ribbon bears the words, BENNETT'S PATENT.

Total length, 46 inches.

Serial No. 6
Col. B. R. Lewis Collection

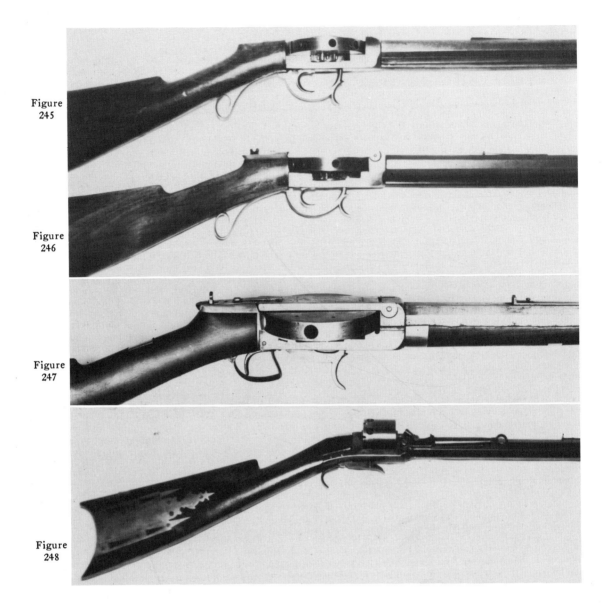

Figure
245

Figure
246

Figure
247

Figure
248

COCHRAN. FIGS. 245 & 246

Illustrated here are the first and second patents of the Cochran Turret rifle. Top specimen, bearing serial number 1, is the first patent on which the top strap does not lift for the removal of the cylinder. Lower gun is of the improved model, bearing serial number 162, on which the cylinder is removed for loading by release of the top strap. John Webster Cochran was the inventor of these unusual revolving arms in which the chambers in the horizontal cylinder radiate out like the spokes in a wheel. These scarce, American, Underhammer, revolving rifles were made in the plant of C. B. Allen at Springfield, Mass.

Henry M. Stewart, Jr. Collection

COCHRAN. FIG. 247   .46 caliber

29 inch, rifled barrel. Round, turret-like cylinder of horizontal design contains seven chambers. Release of a catch ahead of the rear sight permits the raising of the top strap for the removal of the cylinder for loading. These repeating Underhammers were known as the "COCHRAN'S MANY CHAMBER & NON RECOIL RIFLE." For the most part they were made by the firm of C. B. Allen, Springfield, Mass. Walnut stock with German silver butt plate and trim. The specimen illustrated here is known as the third model.

Total length, 49½ inches.   Serial No. 207
                                                                Mark Aziz Collection

JACQUITH REVOLVING RIFLE. FIG. 248

A unique 8-shot rifle on which the cylinder is placed above, instead of below, the barrel. It was produced under a patent secured on July 12, 1838 (#832) by Elijah Jacquith. As will be observed from the photo, there is a loading lever on the side of the barrel just ahead of the cylinder. This is not shown on the specimen illustrated in the chapter on Long Arms. Few rifles based on the Jacquith patent are believed to be in existence, hence they are choice items for the collectors of multi-shot rifles. Top of barrel marked: E. JACQUITH BRATTLEBORO PATENT.

Serial No. 9
Henry M. Stewart, Jr. Collection

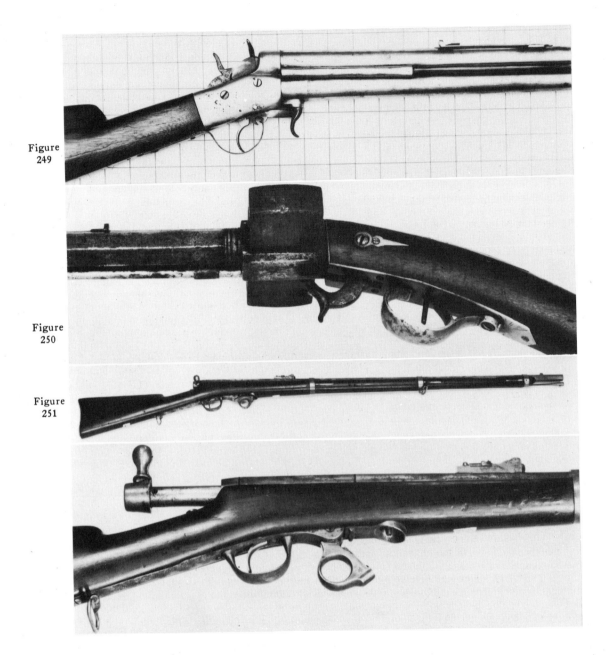

Figure
249

Figure
250

Figure
251

BOWN. FIG. 249

top barrel, .41 caliber
lower barrel, 20 gauge

Over-and-under barrels with a cleaning rod attached to the right side. Top barrel employs a rolling block action and uses a .41 center fire rimmed cartridge. A mainspring trigger guard is used on the underhammer for the lower, shotgun barrel. Frame, tang and butt plate are of brass. The name BOWN is stamped on the gun in a distinctive rectangle design. In addition to the name, the word Standard is also to be found. The name of a former owner, C. Weis, is likewise found on the gun.

Mark Aziz Collection

N. KENDALL. FIG. 250

.44 caliber

20 inch, octagon, rifled barrel, stamped on top:

N. KENDALL
WINDSOR, VT.
PATENTED

This unusual repeating arm is often referred to as a "harmonica rifle," due to the nature of the rectangular breech-block, which contains five chambers. The chambers may be brought into alignment with the bore of the barrel by bringing the underhammer to half cock, and depressing the spring catch on top of the frame. Kendall was one of the pioneer makers of Underhammer Arms, and this is his most novel arm.

Total length, 39 inches.

Paul C. Janke Collection

GREENE BREECH-LOADING PERCUSSION RIFLE. FIG. 251.

.54 caliber

35 inch, round, oval bore, rifled barrel. Dull oil finished walnut stock with trap well in butt to hold cleaning brush. Marked on breech tang:

GREENE'S PATENT
NOV. 17, 1857

An invention of Lt. Col. J. D. Greene, U. S. Army, the guns were manufactured at the A. Waters Armory, Millbury, Mass. Nine hundred of the rifles were purchased by the government during the Civil War.

Total length, 52¾ inches.

Photos courtesy of Thomas E. Holt
Joe Desserich Collection

Figure
252

Figure
253

Figure
254

[186]

NORWEGIAN RIFLE. Fig. 252 .50 caliber

W. W. Greener in his book, THE GUN, (1884) describes the action of this piece as follows: "The hollow breech-block is pivoted upon a strong pin, and worked by a side-lever which works upon an eccentric affixed to it. By depressing the lever the breech-block is withdrawn from the barrel and raised, as shown in the illustration (top) and the cock situated beneath the barrel must be depressed to full cock. The charge is placed in the breech-block, and the cap placed on the nipple, which when returned to its proper position for firing is in a vertical position, projecting from underneath the barrel."

A similar piece but with slight variations was called the Model of 1842.

Harry E. Lewis Collection

NORWEGIAN BREECH-LOADING RIFLE. Fig. 253 .48 caliber

30 inch, round, rifled barrel. A side lever, when simultaneously raised and pulled back, raises the breech block to permit the loading of a paper cartridge. In this action it is not unlike the Hall breech-loading flintlock martial rifle of this country. What appears to be a guard around the under hammer is in reality the mainspring which operates the hammer. The rear guard circles the trigger. This Model of 1860 incorporates some new features of the earlier Model 1842 illustrated above. The gun shown here is the issue of 1864.

Total length, approximately 50½ inches.

John K. Lounsbury Collection

DANISH. Fig. 254 .69 caliber

35 inch, octagon-round, rifled barrel. Ring hammer within an unusually large trigger guard. Trigger is a notched spring engaging the hammer. Buttplate and ferrules are of brass. Gun is marked with Danish crown and date, 1841.

Total length, 52 inches.

Golden State Arms Collection

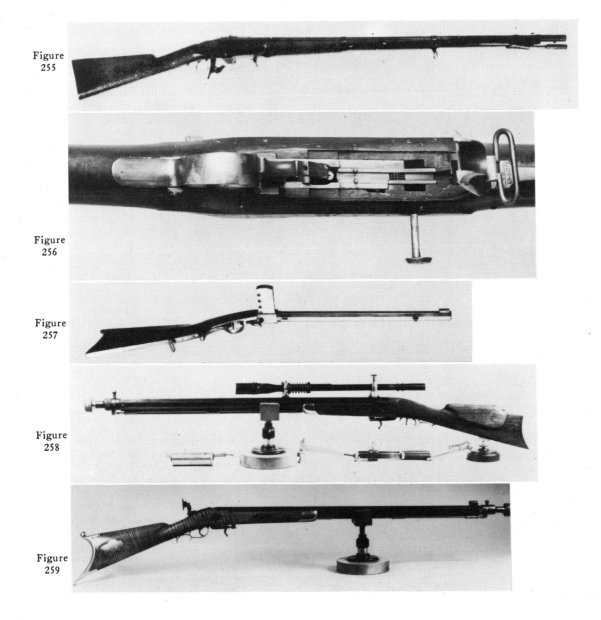

Figure
255

Figure
256

Figure
257

Figure
258

Figure
259

BARON HEURTELOUP MUSKET. FIGS. 255 and 256 .74 caliber

36 inch, round-octagon barrel, the left side of which is marked 1868 and stamped with proof marks. Holding the gun upside down, an iron strap on the left side of the frame is pulled, permitting the brass plate to be swung upward. Percussion caps in the form of a continuous role is placed in a groove and the brass plate replaced. The movement of the hammer due to cocking, actuates a milled wheel which draws the fulminate loaded strip backward so as to place a fresh section opposite the nipple each time the hammer is cocked. (see Figure 34 page 47).

Total length, 52 inches.

Milwaukee Public Museum Collection

N. KENDALL. FIG. 257 .43 caliber

21⅛ inch octagon, rifled barrel, stamped on top:

N. KENDALL
WINDSOR, VT.
PATENTED

A full view of another of the Kendall "harmonica" Underhammer rifles. It is similar in all details to the preceding one.

Serial No. 108
Milwaukee Public Museum Collection

WOODY. FIG. 258 .32 caliber

30 inch, octagon, rifled barrel which is equipped with a false muzzle and bullet starter. This rifle, with a set trigger, an innovation not usually found on Underhammer arms, was fabricated in its entirety by Al H. Woody of Cheyenne, Wyo. It is graphic proof that the "understriker" principle has its devotees even in this day and age. Mr. Woody describes the gun as follows: "I wanted to try the .32 Pope bullets using the muzzle loading Schuetzen method combined with the muzzle loading method, instead of using a cartridge as used by the old time Schuetzen method. I bought a .32 caliber Ackley rifled liner a turn in 18 inches. I used an extra heavy old octagon barrel, bored and reamed it out and sweat the liner in. The octagon barrel was cut to 30 inches long, the Ackley liner was 32 inches long and 2 inches was cut off the liner and used in making the false muzzle. The gun complete weighs 17 pounds. It is stocked with wild cherry and has cheek pieces on both sides of the stock. The trigger guard, butt plate, fore-end cap, and ramrod ferrules are all German silver. It has a ten power Urnertel target scope. I have made all my locks and set triggers, have made back action, front action, mule-eared, flintlock, and an understriker lock of my own design, which I like the best of all."

Al H. Woody Collection

WOODY. FIG. 259 .38 caliber

This rifle, built with a regular type trigger, is another of the fine Underhammer rifles designed and built by Al H. Woody, a machinist by trade, a talented gunsmith by avocation.

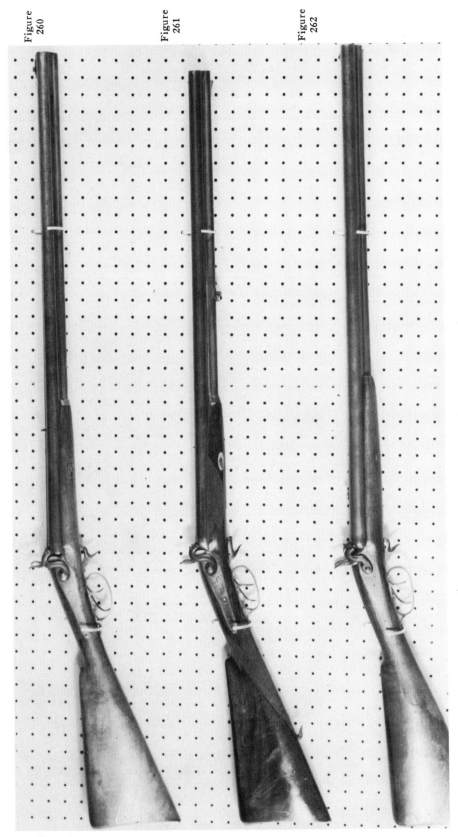

SLOTTERBEK. Fig. 260

shotgun .70 caliber
rifle .375 caliber

29¼ inch barrels. Marked on the top:

CHAS. SLOTTERBEK'S PATENT
MAY 18, 1868   SAN FRANCISCO

Total length, 45½ inches.

VILLEGIA & SLOTTERBEK. Fig. 261

shotgun .75 caliber
rifle .375 caliber

27 inch barrels. Marked on top:

VILLEGIA & SLOTTERBEK MAKERS
SAN FRANCISCO

SLOTTERBEK. Fig. 262

shotgun .75 caliber
rifle .375 caliber

28¼ inch barrels. Marked on the top:

CHAS. SLOTTERBEK'S PATENT
MADE BY HENRY SLOTTERBEK, LOS ANGELOS

(The town spelling is as it appears on the gun.)

James E. Serven Collection

Figure
263

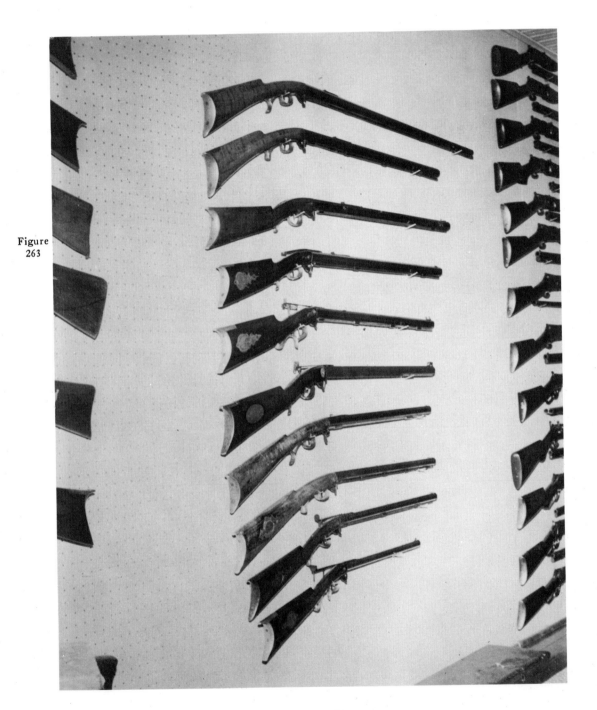

A splendid group of Vermont made Underhammer rifles. Fig. 263

From top to bottom:

Nicanor Kendall
Nicanor Kendall
N. Woodbury & Co.
A. Parker
M. S. Sanderson
Turner Lull & Co.
J. D. White
Robbins, Kendall & Lawrence
A. Story
S. S. Baird

Eldon J. Owens Collection

Figure
264

Six Underhammer guns of New Hampshire manufacture. FIG. 264

From top to bottom:

John Brown
J. Eaton
H. B. Harrington
D. H. Hilliard
D. H. Hilliard
D. H. Hilliard

Eldon J. Owens Collection

Figure
265

Figure
266

Figure
267

Figure
268

Figure
269

10

DAY CANE GUN. Fig. 265 .52 caliber

18¼ inch, round, tapering, smoothbore barrel. Top round frame stamped:

DAY'S
PATENT
JR.   and British proofmarks.

Rifle shaped stock is of brier wood and the entire gun is finished to simulate the appearance of a wooden walking stick, which it also does in general design. A composition cap covers the barrel's muzzle when the gun is used as a cane. John Day, of Barnstaple, Devon, England patented his cane gun (#4861) in 1823. The guns were popular for nearly forty years.
Total length 35½ inches.

Serial No. 7
Author's Collection

CANE GUN. Fig. 266 .53 caliber

30 inch, round-tapering barrel. Detachable wooden extension stock.
Total length with stock, 40 inches.

Golden State Arms Collection

UNMARKED CANE GUN (of English origin). Fig. 267 .20 gauge

21 inch, round tapering barrel with British proofmarks. 11½ inch, detachable, burl stock with engraved German silver butt plate. An interesting specimen of a typical Poacher's Walking Cane Shotgun.
Total length 32½ inches.

Photo courtesy of J & I Boffin

BROWN'S PATENT CANE GUN. Fig. 268 .48 caliber

2½ inch, round, rifled barrel stamped with British proofmarks. Rounded frame engraved on the top strap: "BROWN'S PATENT." Walnut grip is equipped with a metal plate on the back side for attaching the extension stock. Cane barrel is 28½ inches in length. It is equipped with a polished knob for the breech, and a ramrod which fits into the muzzle end of the barrel, thus completely disguising its real purpose. A combination bullet mould and barrel wrench completes the set, which is in excellent condition.
Total length of pistol, 8 inches.

Author's Collection

CASE WILLARD. Fig. 269 .38 caliber

29½ inch, round-octagon barrel which screws into a regular Underhammer pistol. Top marked:

CASE WILLARD   NEW HARTFORD, CONN.

An early gunsmith's version of a cane gun.
Total length, 33½ inches.

Winchester Museum Collection

DAY CANE GUN (unmarked). Fig. 270 .53 caliber

28½ inch, round-tapering barrel. Hook handle which has a hole for attaching the extension stock, shown below the gun. Another of the interesting cane guns made by John Day of England.
Total length, 34½ inches.

Winchester Museum Collection

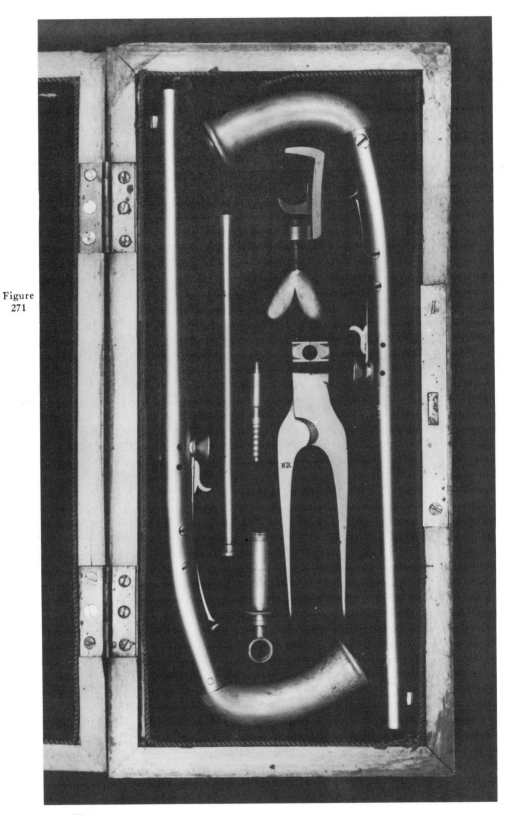

Figure
271

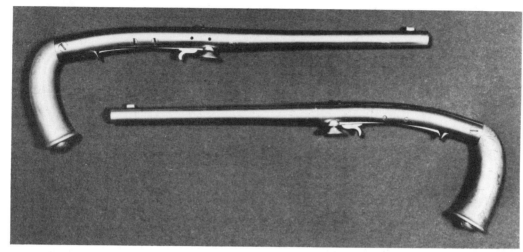

Figure
272

H. ANSCHUTZ & SOHNE. FIG. 271-272   .44 caliber

6¾ inch, round-tapering, rifled barrel. All-metal brass grip engraved on the left side (same on both pistols) in flowing script:

H. Anschutz & Sohne in Suhl

Folding trigger, which is hinged at the front, drops down into position as the hammer is cocked. A sliding safety on the hammer when in forward position prevents it from detonating the cap. Another unique feature on the guns is the grips. A large straight screw in the butt, when removed reveals that the handles also served as a flask for powder or ball. This unusual and distinctive pair of all-metal guns is cased in the original wood veneer case with ramrod, bullet mould, powder measure, worm screw and barrel vice.

Total length, 12½ inches.

Author's Collection

[199]

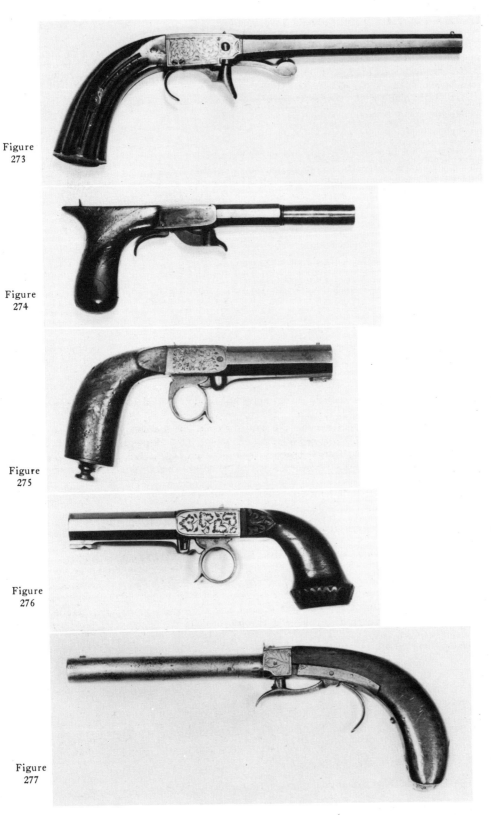

Figure
273

Figure
274

Figure
275

Figure
276

Figure
277

UNMARKED (of European origin). FIG. 273 .21 caliber

6¾ inch, tapering-octagon, smoothbore barrel. Fluted walnut grips. Highly engraved frame and buttplate. Breech-loading. Lever on underside of the barrel is swung to the right turning a drum which permits the powder and ball to be loaded through a small hole on the right side of the frame.

This beautifully made pistol is believed to be of French or Belgian origin.

Total length, 12½ inches.

Author's Collection

UNMARKED (of British origin). FIG. 274 .34 caliber

4¼ inch, round-octagon, rifled barrel. Both barrel and frame are case hardened. British proofmarks appear on the left side of both barrel and frame. Walnut saw handle grip with brass top strap.

Total length, 9 inches.

Author's Collection

UNKNOWN (of European origin). FIG. 275 .44 caliber

2¾ inch, octagon, rifled barrel. Engraved frame, stamped on the left side in oval:

BREVETE
SGDG

and, on the right side is to be found the initials CR surmounted by a crown. A five pointed star is below the letters, all within an oval. The number 91 or 16, depending upon the way it is viewed, appears on the top of the frame. The long spring hammer under the barrel is swung to the right to permit capping the nipple. As the ring trigger is pressed backwards it pulls the hammer spring down until at a certain point it slides off the trigger projection and falls to detonate the cap. In principle it is very similar to the American Cooper. The projection on the bottom of the grip is a combination ramrod and powder measure, which screws into the grip. A trigger is concealed in the backside of the ring trigger. Just what purpose it serves is not clear, as the ring trigger itself appears to function as a release agent for the hammer. Grip is of walnut.

Total length, 7 inches.

Norman E. Sharp Collection

UNKNOWN (of European origin). FIG. 276 .44 caliber

2¾ inch, full-octagon, rifled barrel. Beautifully engraved floral design on both sides and top of the frame. The figure 44 is stamped on the under side of the barrel and on the under side of the frame just ahead of the ring trigger. The figure 5 is stamped on the right side of the trigger. No other marks are to be found. The dark wood grips are carved to floral pattern. This gun employs a combination spring and hammer, which when drawn downward by the ring trigger slips off the trigger and flies upward to detonate the cap.

Total length, 7¼ inches.

Author's Collection

A. W. SPIES. FIG. 277 .34 caliber

5¼ inch, round, rifled barrel. British proofmarks on both barrel and frame. Walnut grip with German silver and brass mountings. Silver top strap engraved: A. W. SPIES, NEW YORK. Silver shield set in back curve of the grip. Cap box in the butt of grip. An interesting English-made Underhammer carrying as it does the name of the well-known American dealer.

Total length, 10 inches.

Author's Collection

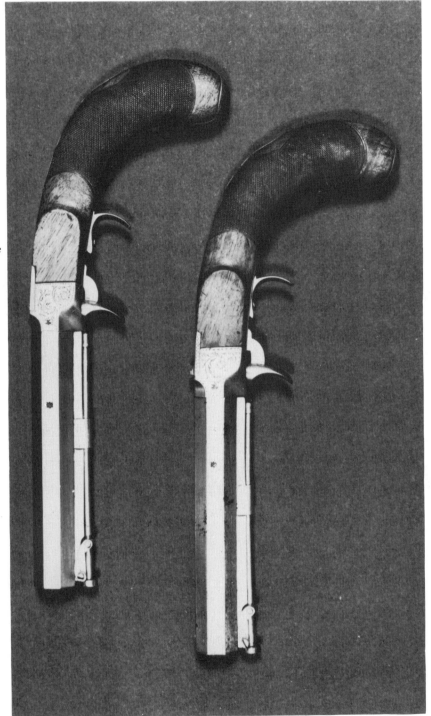

Figure
278

J. BARLOW (a pair). FIG. 278   .41 caliber

5 inch, octagon, rifled barrel with swivel ramrod on the under side. Left side of barrel and frame, is stamped with the well-known British proofmark. Engraved brass frame, with German silver top strap upon which is engraved in Old English letters:

J. Barlow   Lichfield

Checkered walnut grip with engraved silver mounted cap box in the butt, and an oblong, pointed, escutcheon on the back curve. Uniform throughout, the pistols are splendid examples of fine English gunsmithing, this plus the swivel ramrods, a feature seldom found on Underhammers, make this a most intriguing pair of guns.

Total length, 10¼ inches.

Author's Collection

Figure
279

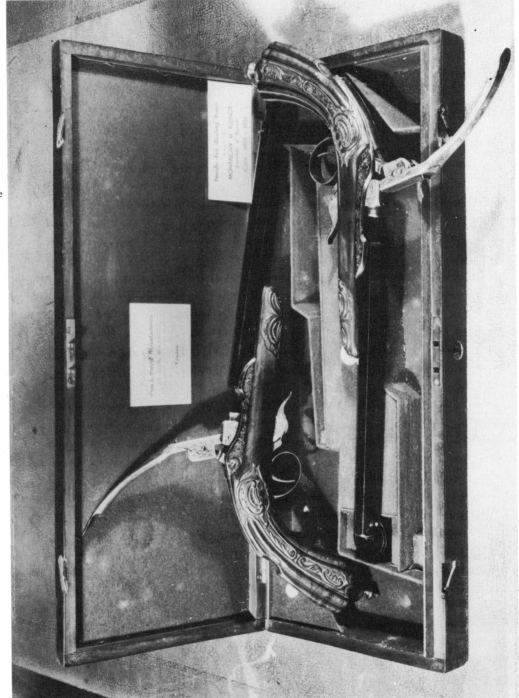

MONTAIGNY et FUSNOT. Fig. 279

These Needle-Fire Underhammer pistols are pictured to show the elaborate ornamentation employed by some of the Continental gunsmiths. The levers on the back
of the grips, when raised upward, open the breech and cock the hammer at the same
time. The guns are cased in a green felt lined case, 8 by 20¼ inches in size. Accessories included a powder flask and an ebony grease box. Casing was done by the
London firm of Wilkinson & Son, and the entire set is near original condition.

Paul Gruenberg Collection

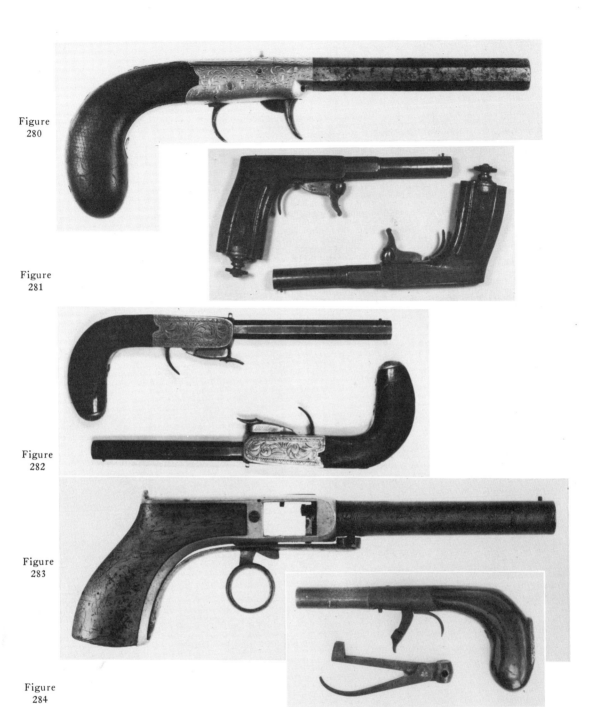

Figure
280

Figure
281

Figure
282

Figure
283

Figure
284

BENTLEY. FIG. 280   .45 caliber

5 inch, full-octagon barrel. Engraved round frame marked:

BENTLEY LONDON PATENTEE

Checkered rounded grip. This attractive pistol shows the influence of some of the English side-hammer single-shot pistols of that era.
Total length, 10½ inches.

Winchester Museum Collection

UNMARKED (of French origin) FIG. 281 a pair.   .45 caliber

Round-octagon barrels. Engraved frame. Fluted, walnut grips with carved design on each side. Ramrod screws into butt of each gun.
A splendid pair of the small pocket-type Underhammers of French make.

Museum of Historical Arms Collection

UNMARKED (of French origin) FIG. 282 a pair.   .36 caliber

5½ inch, octagon barrels. Engraved frames. Checkered walnut grips with cap-box in butt. A finely made pair of French Underhammers of the period around 1860.
Total length, 11½ inches.

Museum of Historical Arms Collection

UNMARKED (of Belgian origin). FIG. 283   .48 caliber

5 inch, round-twist barrel. Brass frame. Revolving barrel puts underhammer in engagement at same time it puts nipple in position for cap. Underhammer then becomes double action. A very odd and unusual Underhammer.
Total length, 11 inches.

Winchester Museum Collection

BROWN'S PATENT CANE GUN. FIG. 284   .48 caliber

A larger illustration of the Brown pistol which was pictured, and described, with all accessories on the Cane Gun Plate, Fig. 268.

Author's Collection

[207]

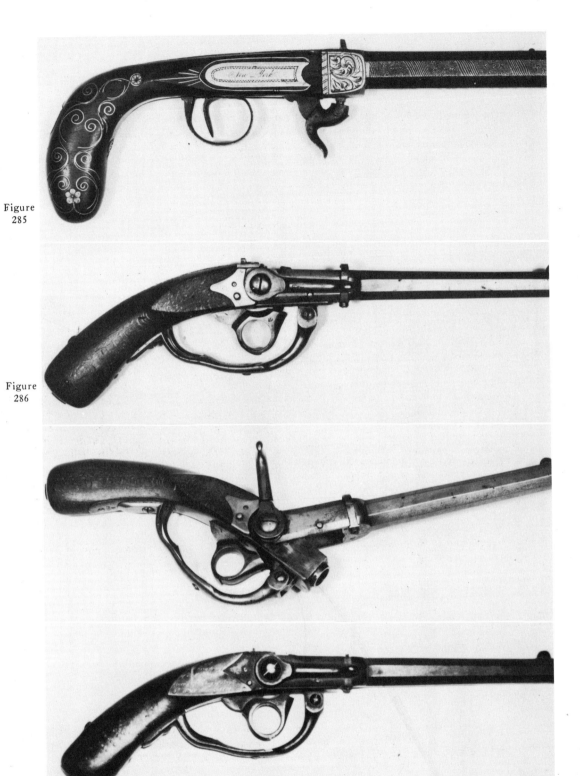

Figure
285

Figure
286

Figure
287

UNKNOWN. Fig. 285 .36 caliber

3½ inch, octagon, rifled barrel of highly embossed Damascus design. Top of the barrel is stamped with the single word LONDON. Top-strap and breech are fully engraved with foliage motifs. Left side of the breech bears the well-known (ELG over a star) Belgium proofmark. The walnut grip is attractively inlayed with fine silver wire and flower designs. Set in the back side of the grip is a silver escutcheon. Silver plates in the fore part of the grip are engraved in flowing script: "New York" (right side) and "W.K." (left side).

Total length, 9½ inches.

Author's Collection

DANISH BREECH-LOADING PISTOL. Fig. 286 .65 caliber

8½ inch, full-octagon, tapered, rifled barrel with an unusual type of concave rifling of six land and grooves. This massive Model 1841 Danish Dagroon martial pistol employs a very unusual mechanism. When the side lever is simultaneously pulled up and back, it pushes the barrel forward, allowing it to be raised up. This permits loading of the breech chamber in the frame. Once loaded the lever is turned back to its original position, thus effectively sealing the breech. The trigger is a flat-type spring, the front end of which is fastened to the trigger guard. When the ring hammer is pulled downward a notch on it engages a notch on the trigger, holding it in a cocked position. Pressure on the trigger releases the hammer to fire the gun. On the left side of the frame is stamped the Danish proofmark, a script R and C followed by the numeral VIII, and the whole surmounted by a crown. The initials stand for King Christian VIII, who was King of Denmark at the time gun was fabricated. The gun bears the date 1842 (year of production) in addition to M-1841 (Model 1841). Serial number is to be found on all major parts. In addition each screw head bears the numeral 20.

Total length, 18½ inches.

Serial No. B-255
Author's Collection

DANISH DRAGOON PISTOL. Fig. 287

A similar gun to the one above, differing only in minor details. It will be noted that this one has a lanyard ring in the butt of the grip. A brass plate mounted on the right side of the grip, just back of the frame, contains the following inscription: (translated from the Danish)

"In memory of his Majesty King Frederich VII by Overo (officer) Kloppenborg of 3rd Dagroons Reg - d 28 March 1848."

Total length, 18½ inches.

Henry M. Stewart, Jr. Collection

[209]

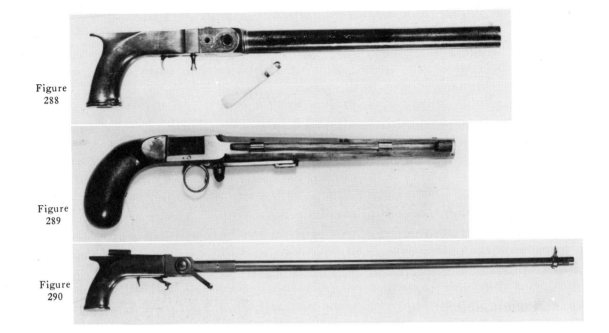

Figure
288

Figure
289

Figure
290

UNMARKED. Fig. 288

An unusual small-bore, percussion pistol-rifle, target arm. The side lever turns chambered breech-drum and permits the loading of a small ball and light powder charge. Hooded rear sight. The gun, which shows excellent workmanship, has most of the original blue-brown finish.

Data and photo supplied by James E. Serven

UNMARKED. Fig. 289 .65 caliber

9 inch, round-octagon, smoothbore barrel which tapers gracefully towards the muzzle. Spanish proofmarks on top of the barrel with letters SALA under crown. Burled walnut grip. Hammer is swung to left to permit capping of the nipple. Firing is achieved by pulling the ring trigger, which pulls hammer downward until it slips off of trigger spur and detonates the cap. Another quite similar method to the American Cooper pistol.

Total length, 14 inches.

Author's Collection

UNMARKED. Fig. 290 .40 caliber

12 inch, heavy, round, rifled barrel. The breech-drum, holding loading chamber, turns to load at the side instead of at bottom. A detachable key is used to turn the drum to load, and then to the capping position, where a detonating pill is used.

Data and photo supplied by James E. Serven

Addenda

Through the kindness of the publishers it is a real privilege to include this addenda containing material unknown or not available at the time the main body of the book was compiled. That it is not in its proper sequence, insofar as chapters or subject matter is concerned, will be, we believe, offset by the interest it adds to the story of UNDERHAMMER GUNS, a story which will undoubtedly continue to unfold more and more long after this work is in print.

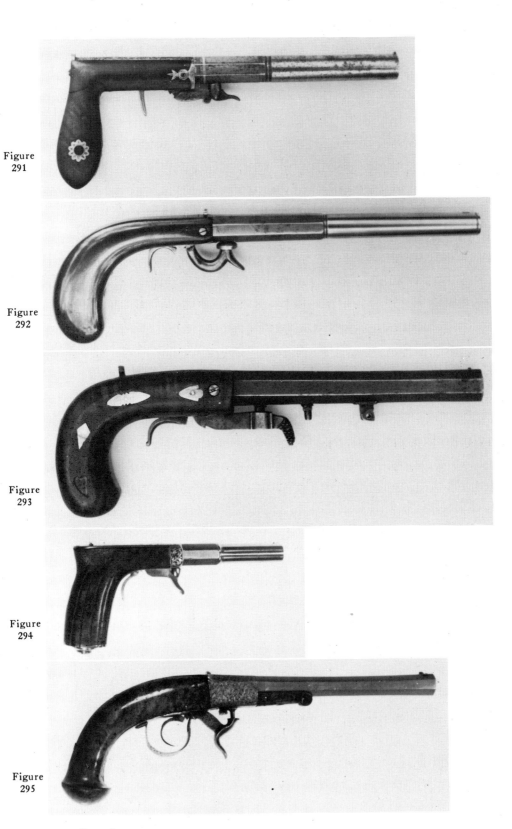

Figure
291

Figure
292

Figure
293

Figure
294

Figure
295

[214]

UNMARKED (AMERICAN). FIG. 291 .31 caliber

6 inch, round-octagon, rifled barrel stamped on top CAST STEEL. Two silver and one gold band encircles the octagon-part of the barrel. Engraved top strap. Walnut, right-angle grip with german silver inlay and escutcheons on each side. A most decorative hammer sets this gun apart from the ordinary type underhammer of its period. Total length 10 inches. *Author's Collection*

UNMARKED (AMERICAN). FIG. 292 .36 caliber

8 inch round-octagon, rifled, barrel. Polished walnut grip. Brass guard around the nipple, as is found on same of the early American target Underhammers produced by Hilliard and others. Shotgun-type hammer with spur. Total length 12¾ inches. *Author's Collection*

UNMARKED (AMERICAN). FIG. 293 .36 caliber

5¼ inch full-octagon, rifled, barrel. Walnut grip with ten inlays of pearl and german silver, four on each side, one on the butt of grip and the other on the back curve of the grip. Three inlays are missing. The unusual feature of this gun is the two nipples, which permit the loading of two charges in the single barrel, one in front of the other. It is most unfortunate that the front hammer, or bar, has been lost, because it would have been most interesting to see how the gun originally functioned. Examination seems to indicate that the rear hammer served the dual purpose, perhaps striking a projection on the front hammer with enough force to detonate the cap without coming in contact with the cap on its own nipple. The front hammer, or bar, is believed then to have been folded back to permit the firing of the rear charge. A most ingenious mechanism on an Underhammer, to say the least. Total length 9 inches. *Bernard Braverman Collection*

FRENCH UNDERHAMMER. FIG. 294 .41 caliber

3¾ inch round-octagon, rifled, barrel. Engraved frame and top strap upon which appears the following wording in two oval panels:

BREVET D'INVENTION
C. R. (monogram)
SANS GAR DU GOUVT

and

PORTEE
100 METRES
GARANTIE

Fluted walnut grip with decorative metal butt plate. A splendid example of an European Underhammer. Total length 8 inches. *Author's Collection*

GYOREEN. FIG. 295 .31 caliber

6⅜ inch octagon, rifled, barrel. Engraved frame, hammer, trigger guard and back strap. Engraved on the top flat of the barrel is the following:

HAJNY GYOREEN

Burled walnut grip and forestock. Butt of grip flares to right, as on some of the fine target pistols from Austria. Indeed, the former owner of this pistol was using it for some present-day target shooting. Total length 13¼ inches. *Author's Collection*

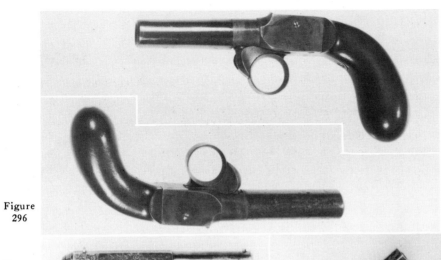

Figure
296

Figure
297

Figure
298

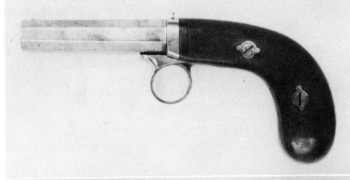

Figure
299

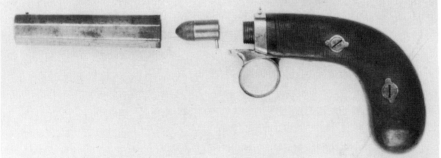

Figure
300

[216]

UNKNOWN (A PAIR) OF EUROPEAN ORIGIN. Fig. 296

.41 caliber

2¼ inch round, rifled, barrel which unscrews to load. Round bulbous-type grip of very dark wood. Ring trigger with hammer of the Mariette-type, a system which releases the hammer at a given point on the rearward pull of the ring trigger. This pair of Underhammers, though plain and totally unmarked except for No. 1 on one gun and No. 2 on the other, are believed to be of either French or Belgian origin. In condition they are strictly fine, with blued barrels and case-hardened frames and hammers.

Total length 6¼ inches.

Author's Collection

DELVIGNE BREECH-LOADING. Figs. 297 and 298   .36 caliber

3½ inch round-octagon, rifled, barrel which tips down for loading, and for capping. Beautifully engraved barrel, frame and release lever. Left side of the frame engraved,

INVENTION DELVIGNE

and right side engraved,

FALISE ET TRAPMAN A LIEGE

Relief carved grips. To release the barrel a long lever which lays close to the back of the grip is rotated to the right. To cock the gun the projection at the bottom center of the grip is pushed forward. Trigger is on the face of the grip. This scarce arm was invented by Col. G. Delvigne of Paris, France. The Colonel was a noted French army officer and Ordnance designer from 1826 to 1842. It was he who designed the hollow base cylindroconoidal bullet adopted for use in the Thouveniu's rifle. The manufacturers, Falise & Trapman of Liege, Belgium were noted arms makers of the 1850's. Arms produced by them were exhibited at the noted International Exhibition, London in 1851. This Underhammer, in excellent condition, is a fine example of their workmanship. Certainly it is a most unusual member of the Underhammer family.

Total length 4⅝ inches.

Serial No. 14.
Author's Collection

BELGIAN Pin-Fire. Figs. 299 and 300   12 mm. caliber

3¼ inch octagon, smoothbore barrel which unscrews to load. Right side of frame stamped with the familiar "ELG*" proofmark. Ring trigger with Mariette-type hammer. Checkered walnut, 2-piece grip with screw escutcheons. A splendid example of a seldom-found cartridge Underhammer.

Total length 7 inches.

Author's Collection

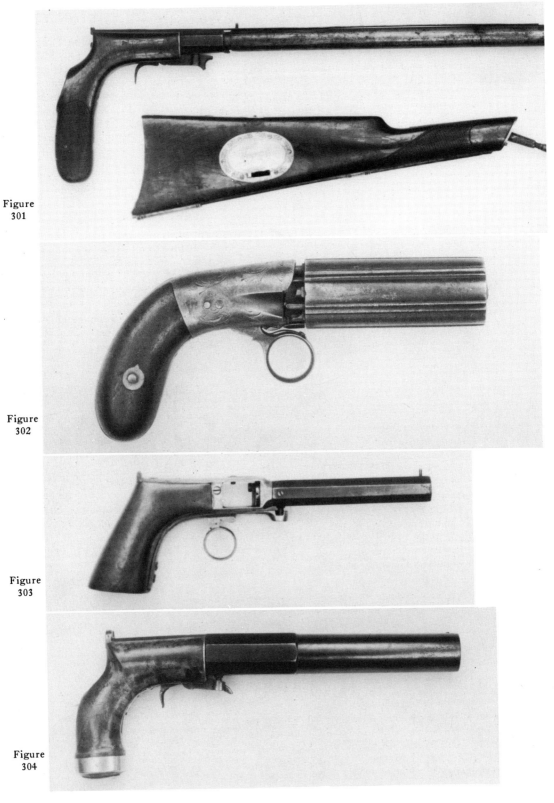

Figure
301

Figure
302

Figure
303

Figure
304

[218]

UNMARKED. FIG. 301

.26 caliber

14 inch round-octagon, rifled, barrel. Around the barrel is an unusual sleeve, the purpose of which seems to be to move the front sight further out for sighting when the extension stock is used. Walnut, engraved-silver, mounted grip. Checkered extension stock is of walnut, with an engraved silver butt plate and patchbox. Ramrod is attached to the under side of the extension stock. A rather unusual and well-made Underhammer.

Total length 19½ inches.

Harry Berry Collection

UNMARKED PEPPERBOX. Fig. 302

.28 caliber

3⅜ inch round, ribbed cylinder containing six smoothbore chambers. Engraved rounded frame with V-shaped groove in the right side for capping the nipples. Walnut grips. Ring trigger revolves the cylinder and trips the hammer. This pepperbox closely resembles the Blunt & Syms illustrated elsewhere. The only markings are R.C. 3 found on one of the dividers between the nipples, and on the left side of the metal frame under the wood grip. Whether they are the initials of one of the workmen who made the piece is not known. A James Rock Cooper of England is known to have patented, and produced a percussion pepperbox. Thus there exists the possibility that the gun was produced in his shop.

Total length 7½ inches.

Author's Collection

UNMARKED. FIG. 303

.50 caliber

4⅝ inch octagon, smoothbore barrel. Walnut grip. Operating in the same manner as the pistol shown in Fig. 283 this gun differs in some points. It has an octagon barrel and an iron frame. The hammer is much heavier. As the barrel is turned counter clockwise, a lever, which acts as an eccentric on the breech end, pushes the hammer downward to engage the ring trigger. The gun then works as a double action when the barrel is returned to its proper position. A spring in the top strap holds the barrel in alignment. No markings are to be found on this unusual arm.

Total length 10 inches.

Author's Collection

E. CHAMBERLAIN & CO. FIG. 304

.41 caliber

7⅜ inch round-octagon, rifled barrel stamped CAST STEEL on the left side. Top strap stamped with two of the familiar New England eagles, and

E. CHAMBERLAIN & CO.
SOUTHBRIDGE, MASS.

Silver-mounted burled walnut grip. This massive pistol weighing 2¾ pounds is the only specimen encountered marked with Chamberlain's name. A definite similarity between it and a smaller piece by Nathl. Rider & Co. will be noted. Whether or not there was any connection between the two makers is not known, though it is highly probable.

Total length 11⅜ inches.

Author's Collection

Figure
305

Figure
306

D. S. EBERSOL. FIG. 305 .48 caliber

3¼ inch octagon-sexadecimal, rifled barrel, stamped on top CAST STEEL. The name D. S. Ebersol is stamped three times to form a triangle, with a six pointed asterisk-like mark in the center. Top strap and underside of the hammer is also stamped with the maker's name. Walnut grip, the fore end of which is held to the frame by means of a pin. An unusual primitive Underhammer of rather massive construction.

Total length 8 inches. Serial No. 5.
Author's Collection

UNMARKED PILL-LOCK. FIG. 306 .34 caliber

3¾ inch round-octagon, rifled barrel. The full stock of maple is fastened at the fore end by means of a pin. The hammer, shown in cocked position, also serves as a trigger guard. Tiny pellets held in place in the touch-hole by beeswax or tallow served as the detonating agent for this most unusual pill-lock pistol. Displaying the familiar lines of the noted Kentucky-type pistols, this full-stocked Underhammer is only the second one to come to light in this study, the other being the full-stocked J. Chase in Fig. 96. Even its tiny ramrod is striped "à la Kentucky." It is entirely fitting that this fine old, and highly desirable, American Underhammer should ring down the curtain on this study of the unique guns "with the hammer under the barrel."

Total length 7¾ inches.

Author's Collection

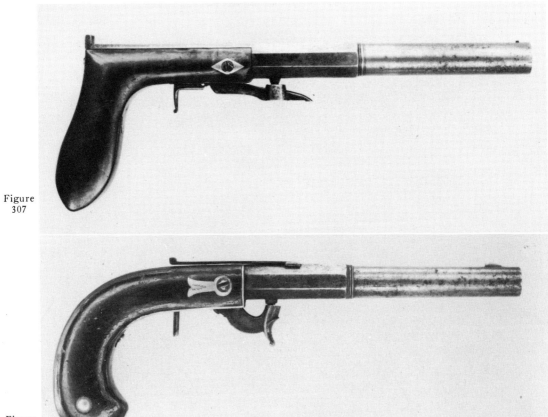

Figure
307

Figure
308

SMITH. Fig. 307 .28 caliber

6-inch, round-octagon, smoothbore, barrel. Stamped on the top flat of the octagon section:

M. SMITH
CAST STEEL

Trigger plate and escutcheons are of brass. Polished walnut grips. A splendidly preserved piece by a little-known maker.
Total length 10-inches.

Author's Collection

LULL. Fig. 308 .31 caliber

6-inch, round-octagon, rifled barrel (160 on muzzle of barrel). Top flat of the octagon part of the barrel is stamped:

M. D. & A. G. LULL
WOODSTOCK, VT.

The gun is equipped with an elevating rear sight. Birdshead grip of walnut with escutcheons and trigger plate of silver. The Lulls are known to have made Underhammer rifles but this is the first pistol bearing their name to come to light in the course of this research.
Total length 10¼-inches.

Serial No. 66
Author's Collection

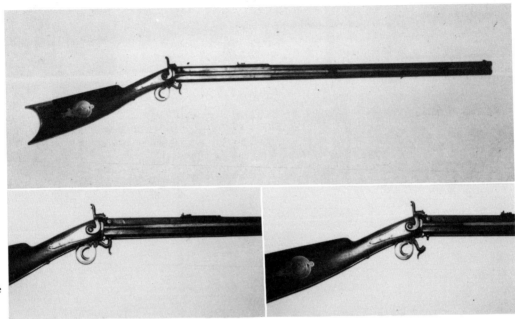

Figure
309

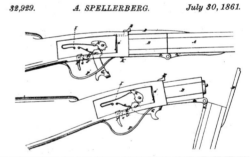

32,929.   *A. SPELLERBERG.*   *July 30, 1861.*

ANTON SPELLERBERG.

No. 32,929 .... **July 30, 1861.**

Upon the upper side of the movable part of the barrel, is attached a bar which engages with a sliding catch, by which means the barrel is held in position for discharging.   The hammer is placed underneath the lock and projects downwards.

CLAIM:—The combination of the barrel A, stationary breech B, projecting bar D, and spring catch E, with a lock of substantially the construction described and a downwardly projecting hammer G, the whole arranged and operating in the manner and for the purpose explained.

Figure
310

34-inch barrels of the banister-turned type, round-octagon. Top barrel is rifled while the bottom barrel is a smoothbore; both are of the same caliber. The trigger guard, made of spring steel, serves both as a trigger guard and as the mainspring for the underhammer which fires the lower barrel. Stamped into the top flat of the barrel, near the breech, is:

J. HARDING COVINGTON, PA.

Etched in script just ahead of the stamping are the initials "J. H." Lock plate bears the name of MOORE. The walnut stock has a deep brass bound crescent at the butt. A round patchbox is set into the stock, well forward of the butt plate. The gun is in excellent shooting condition, and is a splendid example of a combination over-and-under gun employing both top hammer and under hammer.

Albert M. Sullivan Collection

SPELLERBERG BREECH-LOADING RIFLE. Fig. 310

Patent data on the Anton Spellerberg rifle taken from "Digest of Patents Relating to Breech-Loading and Magazine Small Arms." by V. D. Stockbridge, 1874. 22⅛-inch full-octagon, rifled barrel which tips down for loading. Stamped on the top of the barrel is:

A. SPELLERBERG

and on the left upper flat of the breech:

PATENT JULY 30, 1861

The hammer operated through a slot in the trigger guard. The woodwork is nicely finished and the gun well preserved.
Total length 42-inches.

Joe Race Collection

SPELLERBERG. FIG. 311

Enlarged, breech view of the Spellerberg Underhammer breech-loading rifle with
the barrel tipped down to permit loading in the chamber, which projects rearward
approximately two inches. The gun was designed to use either loose powder and ball
or combustible-type ammunition.

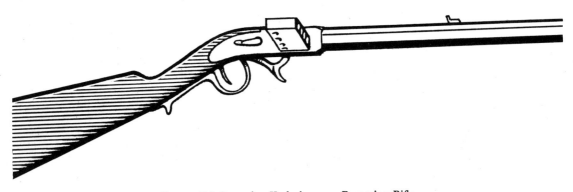

FIGURE 312. Browning Underhammer Repeating Rifle.

[226]

JONATHAN BROWNING

It may come as a surprise to many to know that Jonathan Browning, father of the world renowned John M. Browning, was one of the earliest makers of Underhammer guns in the Middle West.

When he located in Kanesville, Iowa around 1848 he already had a background of some eighteen years of gunsmithing in Kentucky and Illinois. However it was in this new location that he perfected and produced the slide-action repeating Underhammer rifle illustrated here. It and his other productions were announced in the following advertisement which appeared in the Kanesville, Iowa *Frontier Guardian,* under the date of September 19, 1849:

GUNSMITHING

The subscriber is prepared to manufacture, to order, improve Firearms, viz: revolving rifles and pistols; also slide guns, from 5 to 25 shooters. All on an improved plan, and he thinks not equalled this far East. (Farther west they might be.) The emigrating and sporting community are invited to call and examine Browning's improved firearms before purchasing elsewhere. Shop eight miles south of Kanesville on Musquito Creek, half a mile south of TRADING POINT.

JONATHAN BROWNING

Browning's stay in Kanesville was rather short, for in 1851 he and his family moved to Ogden, Utah where the firm of Browning was to become world famous as designers of arms.

The Browning Underhammer rifle is described in *A History of Browning Guns,* published in 1942 by the J. M. & M. S. Browning Co., of Ogden, Utah, as follows:

One of the new guns he developed was a "slide" repeater which had features of considerable ingenuity and merit, notably a five-shot magazine consisting of a rectangular bar of iron with holes to accommodate the hand loads, the bar sliding through an aperture at the breech from right to left and being manually operated. This gave it the advantage of being loaded so that the magazine could be put into the gun and moved quickly into firing position for five comparatively fast shots.

It was possible also for the shooter to carry several extra loaded magazines which could be readily slipped into the gun as required. The proximity of the forefinger to the hammer, which could be cocked without taking the gun down from the shoulder, also added to the speed with which the gun could be fired as compared with the ordinary muzzle-loader.

Loss of pressure was prevented and velocity increased by making a positive gas-tight connection between the slide-magazine and the barrel. It was accomplished by means of a lever located on the right-hand side of the gun, and operated by the thumb which forced the slide against the barrel as each load moved into line with the bore. This gun was a great improvement over guns of that day and age, and to this designer goes the credit for the craftsmanship necessary to forge by hand such an arm with the few crude tools available in a frontier country.

Through the wonderful assistance of LaDow Johnston; J. E. Evans, editor of MUZZLE BLASTS; Edward Ellis; H. Lloyd Resor; Walter Grote; William Moslander; Eddie Null, and others, all prominent in Muzzle-Loading Shooting, it is a rare privilege to include in this book a birdseye view of the Underhammer Target Rifles in present-day shooting matches. It is a most fitting and proper closing for the book. My sincere thanks to each of them for taking the time to make it possible.

. . . The Author

General Observations on Muzzle-Loading Rifles as Shot Today

By LaDow Johnston*

Muzzle-loading rifles were and are now entirely hand made with no two exactly alike, and are encountered in three general types characterized by the rifling, the patch, and the bullet. They are: the picket, the round ball, and the slug rifle. Most are not understrikers but have the conventional bar lock found on the traditional Kentucky rifle. All types of cap-lock rifles and pistols, except the flintlock have been made on the understriker principle.

The least used and perhaps the least known is the picket bullet rifle. Its bullet is shaped about like the old fashioned European bee hive. It is also referred to as a sugar loaf bullet. Perhaps it is best described as resembling an old-fashioned chocolate drop. It is most difficult to load without upset because of the small area of the bullet which bears on the rifling. The barrel from which it is shot may have grooves as deep as .140. The twist of the rifling seems to have varied with the theory of each individual maker. Billinghurst seemed to prefer one turn in 27 inches while Edwin Wesson preferred one turn in 72 inches. Wesson also made rifles with a gain twist.

The bullet for the picket bullet rifle is encased in a lubricated cloth patch, generally bed ticking of about .015 in thickness. The picket bullet is not eligible to compete in matches against round ball bullets, and it will not successfully compete against the slug bullet. It is not used in modern-day muzzle-loading competition.

The round-ball rifle is best characterized by the traditional Kentucky or Pennsylvania rifle. Its bullet is what the term connotes, a round ball of soft pure lead. An original Kentucky rifle is flintlock ignited and if there is an objective standard by which it may be classified perhaps it can be

---

*LaDow Johnston, or "Doc" as he is known among his friends, is a member of Bugbee, Johnston & Conkle, prominent law firm of Toledo, Ohio. His hobby is Muzzle-Loading Target Rifles, and he is an outstanding authority on them, and their use. Doc is co-author of the book, "HOW" published by the National Muzzle-Loading Rifle Association, of which he is a Board member. He is likewise a member of the North-South Muzzle-Loading Committee of the National Rifle Association, sometime member of the N.R.A. Gun Collectors Committee and Range Officer of the Muzzle-Loading Shoot at Camp Perry, 1953 to date. Doc also delights to shoot the old black powder rifles, principally the scope-equipped slug guns, which he says, due to the scope, present no astigmatical optical problems. And, he gives a good account of himself on the firing line.

In addition to building Kentucky-type rifles for his own use he also produces fine silver mounted powder horns, one of which is pictured on the cover of the *American Rifleman* for May, 1957. His collecting interests include Pennsylvania Rifles and Pistols, Muzzle-Loading Target Rifles and Engraved Powder Horns.

Not content with one hobby LaDow Johnston is a recognized authority on Prehistoric American Artifacts, particularly of Birdstones, a prehistoric ceremonial form made by the Indians of the Great Lakes area. He is a collector of these interesting and unusual artifacts, and has authored many articles on them. Currently he is Vice-President of the Toledo Zoological Society.

[230]

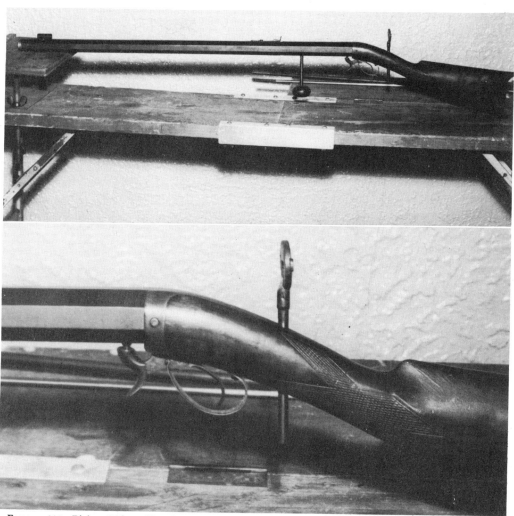

FIGURE 313. Picket Rifle, offhand or bench style. The gun was made by Peter Reinhard of Loudonville, Ashland County, Ohio. Though not dated, it is believed to have been made around the Civil War period. The 36-inch "cast steel" barrel was made by Remington. It measures 1 1/8 of an inch across the flats, one turn in 36 inches, and the caliber is .40. False muzzle is 1 1/4 of an inch in length. Rifling grooves are .013 deep. Figured walnut stock with a modified Schuetzen butt plate. Original hooded front sight, open rear and adjustable rear peep for windage and elevation. Palm rest is original with the gun. Breech affixes to barrel by a drift pin. The rear sight appears to be one of Reinhard's own make.

said, the typical Kentucky or round-ball rifle has an octagonal barrel 40 inches to 44 inches long. It is about 7/8 of an inch across the flats. It has a full-length curly-maple stock with brass furniture. Oft times it is relief carved or silver inlaid. The rifling of the barrel is composed of, generally, eight lands and grooves of about equal width. The calibers range from approximately .40 to .55 with some being smaller and some larger. The grooves vary in depth from about .006 to .014. The rifling turns rather slowly, the most frequent turn and the one generally preferred today, as then, by shooters is one turn in 48 inches. Slower turns up to one in 72 inches are occasionally found. The ball is round of pure softest lead encased in cotton fabric, usually bed ticking or pocket drill lubricated with saliva for target shotting, or with sperm or bear oil for hunting.

The slug gun, in its various manifestations was developed about the time or a bit later than the picket type by a group of New York state and New England gunsmiths immediately prior to and following the Civil War. Its ignition was by percussion cap and in its later phase by pistol

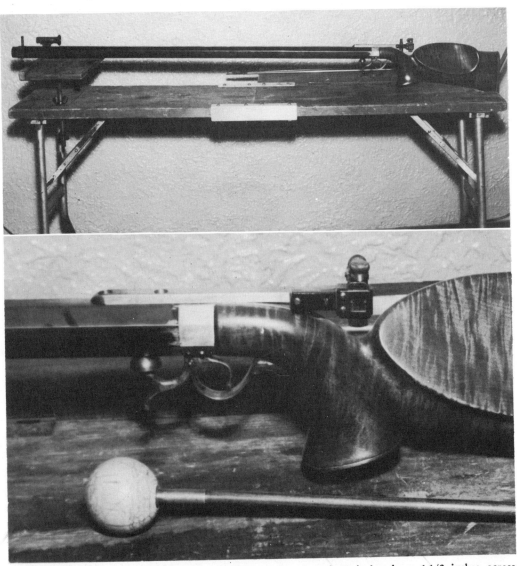

FIGURE 314. Round Ball Target Rifle. Weight 30 lbs., barrel 44 inches long, 1 1/2 inches across flats, false muzzle 2 inches long. Caliber .485, one turn in 48 inches. Grooves .007 deep. Charge is 110 grains FFg black powder, with ball patched in pocket drill .013 thick. Redfield Olympic front and Redfield rear peep adapted especially for this rifle. The gun is shown mounted on a portable shooting bench with adjustable muzzle rest. Barrel by Weichold of Cincinnati; action by Ed Ellis, Detroit; and stock by LaDow Johnston, Toledo. The gun is new and has not been shot in competition, but experimental test firing has produced a 3X possible at 50 yards.

primers. It was made with the side lock or the understriker action. Some of the famous makers and shooters of an earlier day were Billinghurst, Brockway, Warner, Ferris, Perry, and Reinhard; and in its late stages the celebrated Harry Pope. The slug gun was infrequently light enough to be shot offhand but its general use was at the bench rest seeking extreme accuracy. Old and newly made slug guns weigh up to 50 pounds or so; the average, if such can be said, being about 35 pounds. The barrels are usually octagon about 30 inches long including the false muzzle, which facilitated loading and which was removed when the piece was shot. It was on this gun, and the picket rifle, that the early makers developed and used the telescopic sight. Tolerances in slug guns, bullet and bore considered, are so close that a paper patched bullet cannot be forced down the bore if it has not been thoroughly cleaned of the fouling from the previous shot. The slug gun is an instrument of precision, and for successful operation must be regarded and treated as such. Slug guns are usually of large caliber, generally .45 to .50. Bullets are of two types: the solid soft lead, and the swaged composite or two-piece bullet. Any bullet used in a slug rifle must be swaged. The composite bullet is cast in two pieces, the base of rifle bearing surface being softest lead and the nose being of hard lead alloy. The length of the bullet is about three times its diameter. The shape of a slug gun bullet is approximately that of a modern jacketed bullet. It is encased in pure rag-content linen paper about .003 thick which has been soaked in sperm oil. It is the most accurate of all muzzle-loading arms and will shoot as well as most modern rifles using fixed ammunition. The bullets for all muzzle-loading rifles are cast in a mould especially made for the particular rifle.

Walter Grote of Canton, Ohio, perhaps the foremost slug gun collector and certainly one of the better slug gun shooters, possesses many of the original notes and records of Brockway and of Warner. Grote has this to say: "The twist of the rifling of a slug gun depends on its calibre. Warner's rule, which was also used by Brockway, was a 16 inch twist for .40 calibre, and 18 inch twist for .45 calibre, and a 20 inch twist for .50 calibre, etc. In later years all the makers favored a faster twist, say one turn in thirty calibres; and they also used tempered bullets. Warner's favorite temper was one part tin to twenty-four parts soft lead. Brockway used one part tin to twenty soft lead and both had good results." Grote remarks, based upon his own extensive shooting experience, that he has never seen a gun above a .45 calibre shoot a tempered, one piece bullet, successfully.

The process of casting bullets for slug guns is laborious and slow because of the necessity of engaging in several swaging processes. All bullets are weighed and those varying two grains, plus or minus, are used to warm the piece in practice, not for match competition. A solid lead bullet of .45 caliber weighs 510 grains, while its composite counterpart of lead base and hard lead alloy nose weighs 500 grains. If the shooter can cast, swage and weigh 10 slug bullets an hour, he does well. Black powder only is used, the

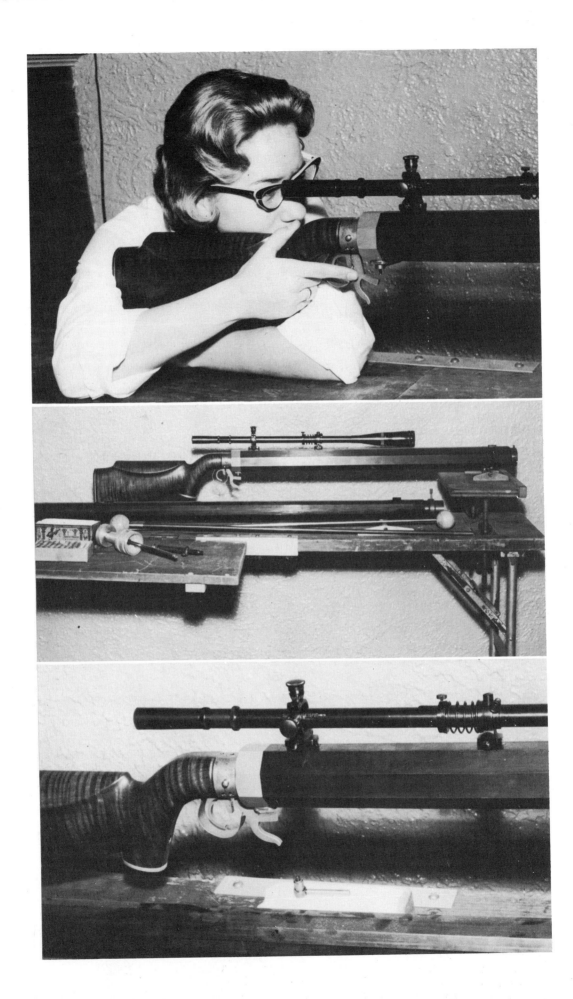

FIGURE 315. Susan Johnston, beautiful and charming daughter of Mr. and Mr. LaDow Johnston of Toledo. She is shown posing with her father's Resor Slug Gun, with which she is no stranger. Miss Johnston has been shooting the gun for the past four years, and has shot many possibles with it. However, she does prefer the Weichold round ball and has many medals won at Friendship, to attest to her excellent marksmanship with a similar Underhammer owned by Clark Frazier, National Champion.

Three pictures herein depicted are of the Slug Gun by Lloyd Resor, Union City, Indiana. The gun was made in 1954 and has a primer ignition, by primer adapter of Resor's own design, being a half threaded screw. Equipped with a Lyman Super Spot 20X scope. Accessories include: cleaning and loading ramrods, ivory butts, bullet starter, powder measure, bullets and cleaning patches in boxes, and portable shooting bench. The octagon barrel is 2 1/2 inches across the flats and is 28 inches in length. The false muzzle, not shown, is 2 1/2 inches long. Bore is .45 caliber with one turn in 20 inches. Composite bullet weighs 500 grains and is loaded with a .003 pure linen paper patch soaked in sperm oil. A solid lead bullet weighs 510 grains. FFg black powder charge for the gun is 95 grains. Weight of the gun is 40 lbs. and it will shoot constant 5X possibles at 100 yards. An extra barrel for the same action is made of the new Timken barrel steel, 44 inches in length and 2 1/8 of an inch across the flats. Caliber is .50 with one turn in 48 inches. It is a round ball barrel by Resor. Close up view shows the action and primer attachment.

FIGURE 316. H. Lloyd Resor, nationally-known maker of Cap-Lock Rifles, takes careful aim with one of his Underhammer Slug Rifles during a Bench Rest Position Event at the Muzzle-Loading Matches at Camp Perry, August 8-9, 1959. Rifles in the background were also made by him.
Photo by Paul Gunnell, Staff Photographer of "The American Rifleman"

loads varying with the particular gun of any given caliber. The average load is from 95 to 135 grains usually of granulation.

A general summary of scores needed to win highly contested muzzle-loading matches at the tournament level are approximately:

PICKET:
These rifles are not shot in competition.

ROUND BALL:
Offhand at 25 yards on a 50 yard target, a possible.
Offhand at 50 yards on a 100 yard target, 48 to 50.
Bench rest at 50 yards, a possible, X's to break ties.
Bench rest at 100 yards: 47 to 49 with an occasional possible. *(Muzzle Blasts* magazine for January, 1960 pictures the shooter, Mr. Mort Geiger, his Weichold bench rifle and his target. His score is an unheard of 5-X possible. This is probably the best score ever made at 100 yards with a round ball.)
Bench rest at 200 yards: 43 to 46 with an occasional 48.

SLUG GUN:
Possibles at any range shot, with X's or string measure to break ties. Slug guns will successfully compete with modern rifles in accuracy. At long range of 100, 200, 300 and 600 yards, Walter Grote of Canton, Ohio at Camp Perry in 1955 had all X counts at 100, 200 and 300 yards. He tied with a 7 V possible at 600 yards. Pat Patton of Canton, Ohio also shot a 7 V possible, which necessitated a string measure to break the tie. Grote had a string measure of 28¾ inches, Patton 29 inches

for each of their 10 shots at 600 yards. Each shot a Horace Warner rifle of about 1870 vintage.

At the 1957 National Shoot of the National Muzzle-Loading Rifle Association at Friendship, Indiana, Edward Ellis of Detroit, Michigan, shooting at 100 and 200 yards with a new rifle he had made only a month before shot some events with any iron sights and some events with scope, and dropped only 5 X's in 30 record shots. His best effort for any of his perfect scores was a 10 shot group at 100 yards, all X centers, with a .49 caliber bullet—all in one hole, which could be covered with a dime and no paper tear showed beyond the dime.

An elaborate treatise of the rifle types, and bullets, here discussed in generalities, can be found in Ned Roberts' *The Muzzle-Loading Cap Lock Rifle,* or in Walter Cline's *The Muzzle-Loading Rifle, Then and Now.*

NOTE: The following article by LaDow Johnston originally appeared in the January, 1958 issue of *Muzzle Blasts,* official magazine of the National Muzzle-Loading Rifle Association. It is presented here through the kindness and special permission of Mr. Joseph E. Evans, Editor.

Casual Reflections on Ed Ellis of Detroit, Michigan

by LaDow Johnston

The chief engineer of one of Toledo's large nationally-known corporations, when away from his corporate duties is a "mountain man" replete with proper accessories which include a smoke-tanned buckskin outfit; beaded moccasins, Shoshone pattern; a tomahawk; a coonskin cap; a bear claw necklace to which is appended a peace medal; a bowie knife; a hunting bag; a hunk of "eatin' tobaccy," and a long flint rifle of his own make. The lock is one which, in all respects, he has made himself. Clint Boothby after having made that lock for his rifle, bought a fine Purdy, detached lock, in flint, circa 1800-1810, which he caused to be studied metalurgically. The metalurgist gave him the report of his findings and of the steel analysis and the heat treatment of the working parts of the Purdy lock, saying in effect that it was the equal of anything that could be made today. Clint Boothby, as a result thereof and upon his own experience, after due reflection, made a pronouncement, which to muzzle-loading addicts in the Ohio-Michigan area, assumed the proportions of an Empirical law or even an Axiom. The pronouncement is: "There has not been a practical invention in the field of firearm ignition since the development of the flintlock!"

A young man of Detroit, Michigan, Ed Ellis by name, is a curious fellow possessed of a know-how and the ability to properly work and

FIGURE 317. Underhammer Slug Rifle designed and built by Ed Ellis of Detroit, Michigan, in the amazing time of less than six weeks. Below the gun are shown two of the targets with which he won the 1957 National Slug Gun Championship at Friendship, Indiana.

Five shots in the right-hand target a 50-4X. Left-hand target has a perfect 50-5X. The match was for a ten shot total. Result, 100-9X.

process ferrous metals. Despite the Empirical law pronounced by Boothby, and its effect on muzzle loaders in the Ohio-Michigan area, and the Ellis and others have for Boothby, Ellis overtly sought to disprove or certainly cause Boothby to modify or amend his pronouncement. Ellis had an idea that, Forsyth, in his invention of the cap lock form of ignition about 1810 or so, performed an act of marked benefit to shooters of muzzle-loading arms. Therein lies Ellis' disagreement with Boothby's pronouncement. Admittedly, Boothby could be prejudiced as his shooting activity is almost wholly confined to flinters. The disagreement between these two men seems to have taken on an air of philosophical or perhaps objective competition. At any rate Ellis says the cap lock is practical, Boothby denies it and considers the cap lock, not to mention fixed ammunition, an instrument of the devil.

Ed Ellis is a young man, now age 28. He is a tool and die maker. He is a graduate of Detroit Southwest High School. His home has always been Detroit. Among his many friends are two men who are muzzle-gun addicts, Ed Ballotts and Ernie Swaine. Each may help the other when a gun making project is at hand. All are capable workers with ferrous metals and each is a credible shooter of muzzle-loading arms.

A few years ago Ellis decided the old-time squirrel rifle he was shooting left things to be desired, so determined to make, lock stock and barrel, a cap-ignited, round-ball rifle. After it was completed, he entered a shooting match at Wyandot Muzzle-Loaders Club in Detroit. It was then that Boothby decided his Empirical law might have to be modified, because Ed Ellis, using the cap lock rifle he had made, and being possessed of abilities to properly operate it, posted a better score than Boothby, Ballotts or Swaine, the latter two men being interested in the argument but must be considered passive bystanders, at least in part.

During the last couple of years someone exposed Ellis to the intricacies and accuracies of slug-gun shooting. It may have been Bill Carr, that old-time shooter of every kind and type of muzzle-loading arm. Ellis soon began a period of observation and theoretical study of slug guns and of making inquiries about design, operation and the like. He decided to construct a slug gun. Walt Grote made some suggestions, which, coupled with Ellis' other observations and information, set the pattern. Ellis had a billet of C-1144 stress proof steel bored in anticipation of his slug gun project. About a year after he had the steel, he decided to make up the rifle. This was about July 15, 1957. Ellis hoped to have it finished, tested and ready to shoot at Camp Perry on August 24 and 25. If not by that date, certainly for the 1957 National at Friendship the Labor Day week-end. Examina-

FIGURE. 318. At the left Ed Ellis is pictured in his gun room with the Slug Gun Championship trophy, and the gun with which he won the match—(Match No. 29).

100 yards ......5 shots......Score, 50-5X
100 yards ......5 shots......Score, 50-5X

Right photo is two other targets shot by Mr. Ellis and his Slug Gun.

tion of the barrel steel was discouraging because the hole was off center. Time to make this new rifle ready for the shoots in the fall was short. Ed Ballotts and Ernie Swaine, to aid the timely completion of the rifle, had lapped the hole to true it to center consuming two days in the process. After they had trued the hole, Ellis rifled the barrel.

The barrel, shooting length, is 28⅜ inches. The false muzzle attached adds two inches. The bore is .4975, eight lands and grooves. The grooves are .0057 deep and .108 wide. The lands are .085 wide. The rifling is conventional in design with one turn in eighteen inches.

While Ballotts and Swaine were lapping the hole to true it, Ellis worked on his swage, mould and action. Thereafter he rifled the barrel and had the rifle ready for a test firing August 18, 1957.

The action is an understriker greatly resembling the Billinghurst actions of old. He has modified it somewhat in minor detail. The trigger guard is constructed of 70/85 cold rolled carbon spring steel, heat treated, serving double duty as guard and main spring. The trigger is adjusted for tension by setting a screw. The piece is percussion cap ignited.

The bullet is a composite-type, swaged; overall length 1.461 of an inch. Its diameter at the base is .4975, thus being of .4975 calibre. The base is pure lead .693 long. The nose is alloy, one part tin to 10 parts lead and is .768 long. The bullet has a flat nose 3/16 of an inch across. After swaging, the bullet is .477 at the seam of about .010 taper on either side.

On August 18 experimental test firings were made to determine powder quantity and patch thickness. The bullet used on the 18th was a couple thousandths smaller than the measurements above given, resulting in groups which Ellis deemed unsatisfactory. He immediately increased the size of the bullet to the dimensions given, and on August 23 the rifle was ready for another try. Ernie Swaine spent an afternoon experimenting with it on that day, shooting some satisfactory tight groups.

The rifle is equipped with a 20X Unertl spotting scope, with a Lyman 17A front and a Redfield micrometric rear sight with Merit iris attachment.

Loading technique is about traditional for slug guns. Snap a few caps to remove the moisture and oil. Wipe clean with requisite number of patches. One hundred and five grains of King's FFg black powder is poured into breech through a plastic tube. A paper, cross patch of .003 pure linen, paper cut with the grain and unglazed, is soaked in sperm oil. Immediately before use, patches are placed between blotters to remove excess sperm oil. The cross patch is placed in the slots on the false muzzle; the bullet is seated in to the false muzzle with the fingers; the bullet starter is seated on the false muzzle then revolved a few times to be certain the bullet is centered. The starter is struck a sharp blow to force the bullet through the first five inches of the choked barrel. The ramrod then seats the bullet on the powder. Ellis hooks a finger of each hand on the ramrod butt using as much pressure as his fingers will permit without discomfort in seating the bullet firmly on the powder.

Ellis had hoped to complete the rifle to enable him to compete in the long-range slug events at Camp Perry on August 24 and 25, at 300, 400, 500 and 600 yards. He didn't make it. He did, however on August 25 have the opportunity to shoot it, thereby objectively verifying Swaine's conclusion gained as a result of the test firing on the 23rd. The rifle performed for Ellis as Swaine had reported it would perform. Ellis fired it a couple more times in late afternoons, just prior to the 1957 Nationals.

He arrived at Friendship Friday morning with some apprehension, nonetheless, although his last five-shot group was 3X possible. At Friendship he first fired a practice target at 100 yards scoring a 3X possible. Then he commenced his record target at 100 yards in Match 29. He chose to commence firing for record in a relay which began about 11 a.m.

Friday, at the 1957 Nationals is known as the day of the "Great Mirage," at least it is so known to those using scopes. All Friday morning and well into the middle of the afternoon a pronounced and vigorous mirage was running and boiling from approximately 7 o'clock to 1 o'clock across the target. Ample testimony to the pesky conditions are testified to by Marv Manny, who until his last shot in the 100 yard scope Match No. 29, had a possible working with 9X's. His 10th shot went out with the mirage for a 10. The writer experienced the same mirage trouble at the same time. Paul Traucht, who the week before had won the long-range slug-gun championship, as he also did in 1956, at Camp Perry at 300, 400, 500 and 600 yards, dropped points with the mirage. Ernie Swaine was having his troubles with it. All of which makes Ellis' score of 10X possible, the more remarkable because he was shooting Match No. 29 during the noonday when the mirage was at its diabolical worst. Then too, this was the first competitive match fired with his new rifle. How better can one initiate a rifle in competition? When Ellis came up with a 10X possible at 100 yards with his new rifle, the score was made while the thermometer was 104 degrees in the shade and a mirage was running. Each of Ellis' five-shot targets had just one hole in it, solidly within the X ring in the general position of 1 o'clock. And each hole of five shots each, calibre .4975 could be covered adequately by a thin dime, although one target did show some paper tear a bit beyond the circumference of the dime. In the 1957 Nationals, Ed Ellis did not lose a point in the entire aggregate of his competitive effort, nor did he shoot at the 1957 Nationals, with this rifle, anything less than a possible. He did drop a few X counters in the aggregate; that is, he dropped 3 of the 25 possible X counts.

That dainty gentleman from Akron, Mr. Skonk Porter, and that arch competitor of Canton, Mr. Walt Grote, each of whom is a seasoned slug gun shooter, and incidentally very capable, and former National champions in their own right, were undividely of the opinion that Ed Ellis had shot, with his new rifle, lock, stock and barrel of his own make, perhaps best score in aggregate competition ever shot with any muzzle gun in a National match.

The writer had departed Friendship the morning of Labor Day so did not know how the slug matches had ended. A day or two later in Toledo, he asked Clark Frazier for the information. Frazier replied: "Ed Ellis won the slug gun championship, score 250-22X. How about that?"

Photos illustrate his rifle and his 10X possible. He's happy and he's proud of his rifle. Then too, he seems to have given direct and positive evidence that Boothby's Empirical Law or Axiom, whatever it is, may not be as true as its declarant would lead one to believe.

I suppose a great many of us wonder how soon Ellis can make a new club rifle on a commercial basis, that is, for sale. The answer is he can't do it. Rifles and shooting are his fun and recreation, a side line for his own entertainment. Unfortunately he has not time available for commercial gunsmithing.

We wonder, too, if all guns should not be made running against a time limit or deadline, especially so if they would all do as well as this slug gun, Number 1, by Ed Ellis of Detroit, Michigan.

In a letter to the author of this book, dated Dec. 14, 1959, Mr. Edward Ellis gave this unsolicited opinion of the Underhammer principle as applied to target rifles. "I have built 6 understriker rifles. The lightest, 16 lbs., the heaviest, 42 lbs. The understriker action is the fastest, simplest, and surest type of ignition for a M.L. arm. It is the only action I would advise for a target arm."

Incidentally Mr. Ellis, shooting a rifle of his own make won three of the Camp Perry Muzzle-Loading Matches on August 8-9, 1959. They were:

Match No. 22 100 yards 10 shots . . . . .score 99-8X
Match No. 23 200 yards 10 shots . . . . .score 99-5X
Match No. 24 100 yards 5 shots .score 50-3X

What could be a better testimony to the effectiveness of these interesting guns with the hammer on the under side of the barrel?

Echoes from the Firing Line

Most Slug Guns are Underhammer. In 1954 at Camp Perry shooting 100, 200, 300 and 600 yards Walt Grote of Canton, Ohio, had possibles in all events. At 600 yards he had 7V-50 and tied with Patton, also shooting a Warner (but the latter was a side lock). To break the tie a string measure was resorted to. Pat had 29 inches for 10 shots; Walt had a 28¾ inches.

Muzzle Blasts is the Official Magazine of the National Muzzle-Loading Rifle Association. It is published monthly by the Association at 12 East Franklin Street, Shelbyville, Indiana. It is the only magazine of its kind devoted entirely to the shooting of the old black powder muzzle-loaders.

Present day makers of Underhammer Target Rifles include such notables as H. Lloyd Resor, Union City, Ind.; Edward Ellis, Detroit, Mich.; Bob Morris, Hagerstown, Ind.; Jack Weichold, Cincinnati, Ohio; and Dave Taylor, Little Hocking, Ohio.

The American Rifleman is the Official Journal of the National Rifle Association of America, a nonprofit organization supported by the membership fees of public-spirited citizens. Its purposes are to educate and train citizens of good repute in the safe and efficient handling of firearms, to foster a knowledge of small arms and the ability to use them among members of law enforcement agencies and the armed services and all other citizens who would be subject to service in the event of war, to promote social welfare and public safety, law and order, and the national defense. Membership in N.R.A. is available to any reputable citizen of the United States.

Published monthly at 1600 Rhode Island Ave., N.W., Washington 6, D.C. it contains interesting and informative articles on arms for the shooter, hunter and collector.

Most unusual gun made by H. Lloyd Resor of Union City, Ind., is a massive 100 lb. 69 caliber, cross-patch Underhammer Slug Gun. It was made for William Moslander of Talent, Oregon. The rifle shoots a composite bullet weighing four to the pound, backed up by 275 grains of Fg Dupont powder.

Resor's primer attachment is a simple interrupted thread, one turn in and out. The 1½ pistol primer, which is detonated by a firing pin, is completely sealed in when the primer is locked in shooting position.

FIGURE 319. Resor Underhammer Slug Rifle made for Eddie J. Null of Oakland, California, and with which he shot the target shown below the gun. Weight of gun, 45 lbs.

Shooting the .457 caliber rifle from a double bench rest in the California Muzzle-Loading Matches at Fresno, Mr. Null had a string measure of 6 5/8 of an inch at 200 yards to win the event and the Resor Silver Pitcher string measure trophy illustrated with the rifle.

It is said that the Resor big .69 caliber rifle will put 5 to 7 shots in about 1 inch at 200 yards, and that it is a lot of fun to shoot and has plenty of recoil, straight back.

The Gun Report is a monthly magazine "Dedicated to the Interests of Gun Enthusiasts Everywhere." It is a magazine devoted primarily to collector arms and cartridges, and as such, is full of much valuable information on these subjects. It is published at Aledo, Ill.

A grease wad mix: beeswax 80%, tallow 20%, plus one-half cup of sperm oil to 10 lbs. of mix.

Suggested wiping method: first run a nylon bristle brush (dipped in water) down to bullet seat then back about 8 inches, then down and out. Follow this with a wet patch, both sides, then a dry patch in and out, then once with a lightly oiled patch. Then load as usual.

In the event you are wondering about the cost of a fine shooting Underhammer Target Rifle, here is one authority's estimate, less some 200 hours of time-consuming labor of stock, inlaying and engraving. The following is just for the parts alone:

Wood (fancy)	$ 35.00
Barrel by Ellis, $75 by Dave Taylor	50.00
Furniture in German silver including patch box	30.00
Trigger by Buchele	15.00
Action—Cap-Lock, fine English	20.00
Action—Flintlock, fine English	50.00
Rammer and jags	4.50
Mould	10.00
SIGHTS:	
Lyman 17 front	3.75
Stence open rear	10.00
Lyman or Redfield adapted peep rear and tang	20.00
	$228.25

Values are for the best components available; cost can be reduced by sacrificing quality.

Guns is a magazine planned principally to appeal to the hunter, shooter and the adventurer, but it does frequently have articles of real interest to the devotees of the old firearms and those who like to shoot the guns of other days.

Favorite gun of Joseph E. Evans is an Underhammer Bench Rifle which he designed and built himself. With it he has won several matches and would still be on the firing line except that being Editor of *Muzzle Blasts* seems to require most of his time.

FIGURE 320. Eddie J. Null of Oakland, California, proudly displays his target, shot with his .457 Resor Underhammer Slug Gun, which won first place in the California State Muzzle-Loading Rifle Matches at Fresno, California. Distance 200 yards, score 100-7X.

FIGURE 321. Target shot by William Moslander, Talent, Oregon, at the California Muzzle-Loading Matches at Fresno, April 16, 1955. Distance 200 yards, The ten shot group was made with a Resor .50 caliber Underhammer Slug Rifle. The result, a 3 3/4 of an inch string measure.

Index

Since the Pictorial Section of the book is arranged alphabetically as to makers, where known, it is felt that an Index covering that section is not necessary. Hence the following Index covers only the fore part of the book—up to Chapter X.